OPERATION BITE BACK

OPERATION BITE BACK

Rod Coronado's War to
Save American Wilderness

Dean Kuipers

B L O O M S B U R Y

New York   Berlin   London

Lyrics from "This is the A.L.F." copyright by Conflict. Reprinted by permission.

Published by Bloomsbury USA, New York

All papers used by Bloomsbury USA are natural, recyclable products made
from wood grown in well-managed forests. The manufacturing processes
conform to the environmental regulations of the country of origin.

LIBRARY OF CONGRESS CATALOGING-IN-PUBLICATION DATA HAS BEEN APPLIED FOR.

Kuipers, Dean.
    Operation Bite Back : Rod Coronado's war to save American wilderness / Dean
Kuipers.—1st U.S. ed.
        p. cm.
    ISBN 1-59691-458-0 (alk. paper)
    1. Coronado, Rod, 1966–   2. Animal rights activists—United States—Biography.
3. Environmentalists—United States—Biography.   4. Ecoterrorism—United
States.   5. Animal rights movement—United States.   I. Title.
    HV4716.C67K85 2009
    179'.3092—dc22
    [B]
                                                          2009006600

First U.S. Edition 2009

1 3 5 7 9 10 8 6 4 2

Designed by Sara E. Stemen
Typeset by Westchester Book Group
Printed in the United States of America by Quebecor World Fairfield

To my brothers, Brett and Joel,
for keeping the wilderness alive in me

And for Rod

Rod Coronado going into federal court in Tucson for a bail hearing in October 1994. (Max Aguilera-Hellweg)

CONTENTS

A NOTE ABOUT NAMES IN THIS BOOK

Many of the people I've contacted for this book have asked that their names not be used—some because activists who share their beliefs, and acted on them, are going to prison with terrorism sentences; others because they fear being victims of what they consider terrorist attacks. Most of the time, I've respected this request, the exception being if the person in question is already well identified in multiple press or court documents and so already part of the public record. Notes and interviews provided to me in the course of researching this book sometimes go well beyond what is publicly known, though, and in those cases I've used pseudonyms and identified them as such.

For at least two characters in this book, however, even a pseudonym would leave the person in question open to easy identification, especially by other activists. Not being in the business of dangling unidentified coconspirators, I've completely rearranged these characters' identities, changing living situations, names, physical descriptions, etc. Be assured, these are still real persons, now living real lives having nothing to do with Operation Bite Back. This is a work of nonfiction, and, other than obscuring these few key facts, everything in here is true to the best of my knowledge.

—DK

On Nonviolence

We now no longer camp as for a night, but have settled down on earth and forgotten heaven.

—*Henry David Thoreau*

ROD CORONADO AND I met face-to-face for the first time at Figtree's Café in Venice Beach, on April 29, 1992. That night, the Rodney King riots would break out and burn for six days, killing fifty-three people and leaving great corridors of L.A. in ashes. But you couldn't tell that from the still, acid-washed blue of the sky earlier in the day, when Rod turned up with his air of bright calm. He had bicycled over from the Santa Monica offices of the Sea Shepherd Conservation Society, an oceangoing marine mammal protection group, where he was working. He wore jeans and a black T-shirt.

For a second, we hesitated to sit outside. Rod was a "person of interest" to the FBI, but it was unclear whether he was in any trouble. I had ascertained there was no warrant for his arrest, so we knew that much, but his status worried him, and it was one of the primary subjects of our discussion.

"They're not looking for me here," he reasoned, so we sat outside and he threw bread crumbs to the birds while the beach and its denizens baked. Roller skaters whirred past. The burnt-brown homeless convened under the palms, wearing heavy coats against the white-hot Pacific sun. Police coasted by on bicycles.

If they had been looking for Rod, he wouldn't have been hard to spot. People noticed him. His eyes were bright and alert. He was chatty but could turn on a heavy silence unique to his Native American blood like flipping a switch. At twenty-five years old, he was sinewy and strong, five foot eleven and in ideal trim at about 140 pounds. He was built like a runner, and he came from a people who engaged in sacred running, the indigenous Yaqui, from the Sonoran Desert of Mexico and Arizona. Though he had grown up an American kid in the suburbs of San Jose, California, his ancestors on both his mother's and his father's side were Yaqui. His skin was a dark, burnished brown, and his black hair lay tight to his skull in short curls. He was intense, coiled, but there was also something comic about his face; his big ears stood out from his head, and even when he was upset or scared, he seemed always on the verge of a sly grin. This face put people at ease.

I knew Rod as one of the most notorious eco-radicals on the planet, after an incredibly brazen act in Iceland in 1986 in which he and another member of Sea Shepherd had sunk two modern whaling boats in Reykjavik harbor. He had come to talk to me, however, as the spokesman for the Animal Liberation Front (ALF), an adumbral network of radical activists who engaged in high-dollar sabotage and freed animals from university laboratories and roadside animal shows and farms. He admitted to being a "former" ALFer, having smashed up some fur shops in Vancouver in the late eighties. But he had since withdrawn from direct action—he claimed—to take on a purely supporting role.

He and I had been talking for months by phone about Operation Bite Back, a series of Animal Liberation Front arsons attacking mink farms and mink researchers in Oregon, Washington, Utah, and Michigan—one of the most infamous campaigns ever attributed to American environmental activists. Rod was supporting it in the press. He'd founded an aboveground group called the Coalition Against Fur Farms (CAFF) and was speaking out in public in defense of the arsons.

The law was clearly homing in on him. At Figtree's, he produced a federal affidavit someone had faxed him. It was in support of a search-and-seizure warrant issued for the Maryland home of a volunteer for People for the Ethical Treatment of Animals (PETA) where agents of the Federal Bureau of Investigation had gone looking for materials related to Rod. The raid had just happened, and we didn't know what the feds had found there, but the document itself had Rod worried. The FBI agent quoted on it stated, "The ANIMAL LIBERATION FRONT (ALF), in particular, RODNEY ADAM CORONADO . . . was responsible for the destruction of animal research facilities at Washington State University on August 12–13, 1991" [emphasis in the original].

Well, that was news to me. Law enforcement officers routinely exaggerate on search warrant documents, but if Rod were really hot, why didn't the authorities pick him up? He wasn't exactly hiding. He was working out in the relative open of the Sea Shepherd offices, doing interviews, taking calls. If an agent had called Sea Shepherd, he probably would have picked up the phone. This troubled him. What were they waiting for?

"I knew we [CAFF] were gonna put our heads on the chopping block," he said. "But *I'm* not the one out there breaking into buildings or releasing animals and burning things down. I consider it to be such a minute risk to actually defend those people who *are* doing that. Those people create this wave; it's our responsibility to follow through with it."

And it wasn't just the law that was circling him. He'd begun to get death threats—a trickle at first, then a steady stream. He wanted to make sure I knew about that, in case. Farmers, law enforcement, and many others considered him a terrorist for even supporting these arsons. The scent of blood had been in the air for a few years, and Rod was feeling downhearted about his chances of survival. Someone had tried to kill his friends Judi Bari and Darryl Cherney, forest activists who'd been car-bombed in 1990. They'd been accused of being eco-terrorists, too.

Terrorism would always be a subtext of my relationship with

Rod—it was the label his opponents used, as casual as you like, a very dirty word, and he wanted nothing to do with it. That day in Venice, he was already commonly referred to as an "eco-terrorist," by Iceland's Ministry of Justice and the fur industry, by the medical research lobby and product-testing companies and agribusiness and even the FBI, which, in a 1989 report, called the Animal Liberation Front a "terrorist organization."

We treated it like a joke, right? *Terrorist*, ha ha. That's because, until the passage of the Animal Enterprise Protection Act in late 1992, and even for a decade after that, what Rod was doing was not prosecuted as terrorism. Sinking empty whaling boats was not terrorism. Spiking trees was not terrorism. Even burning barns was not terrorism. Not legally. At that point in time, terrorism was defined under federal law as being an act of violence against a person—not property—designed to influence government or private action. It was about visiting physical hurt on people.

"[Edward] Abbey properly said that terrorism targets people and that sabotage, or eco-tage, targets property," said Dave Foreman in an interview for this book. Foreman was one of the cofounders in 1981 of Earth First!, a radical movement well known for endorsing sabotage. "I think that 'terrorism' has been used so carelessly, it doesn't have any meaning anymore. It's just absurd. You disagree with somebody and they're a terrorist," he said.

Rod saw his tactical destruction of property as an escalation of the nonviolent sit-ins, boycotts, strikes, and marches employed by the Reverend Dr. Martin Luther King Jr. and King's hero, Mahatma Gandhi.

"As a spokesperson for the ALF and as a representative of CAFF, we consider nonviolent actions to include the destruction of property that is used for the destruction of life," he said that day. "We don't see anything that you can do to an inanimate, human-made object to be violent, as long as there isn't a loss of life. It seems to be the most effective tactic that grassroots activists can take."

It was so easy, however, to make him look violent. If someone succeeded in hurting him, it would resonate in the minds of the public that he was bloodied, that his movement must be bloody, that this was a violent, terroristic campaign. That would be a hard image to shake. Rod was not afraid to die, but he was deadly afraid of being misunderstood.

We drank coffee and ate light. The *LA Weekly* picked up the tab. When Rod left on his bicycle, he pedaled straight into the underground, a fugitive. For the next two and a half years, there was no way to contact him. He would just show up at my apartment when he wanted to talk.

During these years, before terrorism charges had any teeth, the radical movement was a reporter's dream: their commitment drove them to outrageous, often hilarious actions, and the public—who mostly assumed they were nonviolent hippies—treated them as more of a nuisance than a threat.

In 1991, for example, a truckload of us were hammering over a washboard desert road on the Nevada Test Site, the bomb-pocked expanse of dusty sage about sixty-five miles northwest of Las Vegas where the U.S. Department of Energy tests the nuclear arsenal, when an elderly rancher hailed us from a pickup going the other way. We stopped, and he asked if we'd seen his cows and if the windmill was pulling water in the tank. We told him we had and it was. A squinty smile crept over his face, and he leaned out his window a little, eyeballing all five or six of us individually.

"Are ya protesters?" he asked conspiratorially.

The driver, a great big man with an antinuclear group called Nevada Desert Experience, did not hesitate. "Yes, sir," he said, "I guess we are. Everybody except him." Meaning me.

The group had been training with Greenpeace and some Shoshone elders to stop an underground nuclear test. The method was to trespass onto the test site, which was a two-day hike, and sit on top of the bomb with a good radio close to the final countdown, then call in and force the cancellation of the test. I was on assignment, and we'd been hiking out there for about four days before being picked up.

"Well, I think yer fulla shit and you're probably gonna get yourself killed," the man said. "But that's your right to do that, I guess. Free country."

We talked a bit more. The rancher said he wasn't worried about his cows getting irradiated, because the government had assured him it was safe.

"A bomb moved the house clean off the foundation one time," he added, as an example of how the government did him. "They come and put it back, though. Yeah, they put it back."

He thanked us for letting him know about the cows.

Another action camp, another flapping two-man tent. Tears of laughter pouring out of our eyes as a lanky, rawboned fellow, a former white-water kayaking champion, told me on tape how he got the nicknames Sergeant Sphincter and Captain Kaka. Around 1990 or so, he used his climbing skills to rope a clever plywood platform above a new logging road being cut into the pristine Walbran rain forest on Canada's Vancouver Island. Probably not more than a handful of people in North America even knew the road was happening, but there he was, strung to just the right trees to halt construction. It was at a pinch point on a ridge where the road couldn't go anywhere else.

The Sarge had decided to occupy his platform buck naked, even in the chill of the coastal fogs, but when the Mounties came with a cherry picker to get him down, he resorted to desperate measures, smearing himself with his own feces. Hence the nicknames. They parked the cherry picker for a few days and thought about that. When a female officer arrived on scene, he masturbated in order to drive her away. That bizarre whiff of sexual violence pissed everybody off, and finally a climber was brought in to get up in that rigging and cut him down. The climber was a logger from Montana, and he and the Sarge were jawing away at each other as they maneuvered in the air. The funniest bit was, as the last rope was being released, which would have sent the platform to the ground, Sarge produced a knife and slashed the line himself, grabbing a free end and sailing away into the bush.

"I swung out of there like Tarzan, naked, covered in shit, swung way out wide of the road, and landed in a slash pile. I was totally unhurt!" Sarge howled. He scrambled down a steep embankment, more like a cliff, and got away. He ran nude through the forest for days and survived on what he found there. They never did catch him.

I was up on Vancouver Island later doing some reporting and talked to a cop who recounted this story with almost the same details, and by the time he was done telling it, we, too, were both in tears. How could you help it? These people were funny.

Today, none of this is funny anymore.

"I don't want to be mentioned in your book," stormed one of Rod's former friends, interviewed under condition of anonymity. A friend, it should be noted, who never participated in Operation Bite Back but was scared anyway. "Why is [Rod] talking about this? He should know better. And right now? If you put your name out there right now, they're going to fuck with you. This isn't a safe time. Because of these terrorism charges, they're treating it like Abu Ghraib."

No more small talk about the cows. Today, even minor eco-radical action can get you decades in prison. Operation Bite Back made Rod a hero to a generation of activists, but the government's scorched-earth response made him a legend too risky to believe in.

"I'm going to give you my truth about the guy: he's dangerous.

He never realized fully the impact he was having on other people's lives, and if he did, then he's even more dangerous. And don't get me wrong: I love the guy like a brother. Personally, I love him. But he came into our community and he used it as a kind of home base and none of us knew the full extent of what he was doing and as a result of his actions, the FBI came in here and turned a bunch of lives upside down. For some of us, they just ruined our lives.

"He thinks he's fuckin' Geronimo. I'm serious. He just has to let this go and move on. Even talking about this stuff anymore is putting too many people at risk."

Beginning in August 2003, it became clear that Rod and his radical colleagues had lost the tussle over what was and wasn't terrorism. That month, he gave a talk at a gay and lesbian center in San Diego for which he was later arrested. Rod had already served four years in prison for the Bite Back actions during the nineties, but when he reminisced on those days, U.S. attorneys decided his talk amounted to instructions for building incendiaries. No matter that no one actually made incendiaries from the contents of Rod's talk, nor ever intended to—the speech alone was a crime. Worse, due to provisions in the 2001 USA PATRIOT Act, it was terrorism. For his walk down memory lane, federal prosecutors threatened to put Rod in prison for as many as eighteen years under new terrorism sentencing enhancements. Very few people even knew this was possible. Rod certainly didn't. He took a plea for a year and a day and was in jail while I wrote most of this. The word terrorism had finally caught up to him and the movement.

By 2007, when he went to trial for the speech crime, at least ten eco-activists had received terrorism sentences—the first time such sentences were ever used for noninjury crimes by environmentalists, according to their attorneys—and many more were forced to give up information or face prosecution. Some of them had only tangential connections to the acts, all of which were property crimes they considered nonviolent. Several were colleagues of Rod's, and a couple were close friends. One of Rod's former supporters, Marie Mason, was sentenced in February 2009 to almost twenty-two years for arsons in Michigan similar to those that earned Rod less than a quarter of that amount. This is where we are today.

In the last few years, it has become almost routine for FBI officials and members of Congress to declare that the Animal Liberation Front and its more broad-based spin-off, the Earth Liberation Front (ELF), are "on a par with Al Qaeda." A couple of them said it to me directly for this book.

But there are differences that are impossible to overlook. Al Qaeda killed three thousand people in one terrible day in the United States; the ALF and the ELF have never killed or injured any people or animals in twenty years and over twelve hundred known incidents in this country. Recent attacks, such as the firebombing of a researcher's home in Santa Cruz that endangered his children, have unquestionably crossed the line into real terrorism, and that should not be glossed over. But there remains a problem of semantics that threatens to color the whole movement: To compare murderous jihadists to tree huggers like Rod and his colleagues—who do not target people—seems an insult to those who have died at the hands of Al Qaeda, or who are in an actual shooting war with them. Not to mention the intelligence of the American public.

Terrorism is now a subject I must address with most of the sources I've cultivated in the radical environmental movement, and a very strange one for hardcore conservationists like Dave Foreman who are veterans, vote Republican, and consider themselves patriots. When Rod pedaled away into the underground on that golden day in Venice, he took with him the facts that I needed to sort out what was terrorism and violence and what was not. Those facts comprise the story I'm telling you now.

ONE Iceland, November 1986

ROD CORONADO AND David Howitt sat in a clearing overlooking a whaling station on Hvalfjörður, an Icelandic fjord where that country's fleet brought whales to be butchered. It was a Saturday night, November 8, 1986. The two were eating a cold dinner they'd picked up in a supermarket forty-five miles away in Reykjavik—not the grand binge they had planned in the capital's top vegan restaurant, but in all their preparations they had failed to notice the restaurant's closing time. Night was falling as they listened to the radio coming through the open door of the rental car, enjoying what they assumed would be their last meal outdoors.

One of them had read that inmates in Icelandic prisons were put to work making cement sidewalk blocks. They joked about how they'd be the best sidewalk makers in the country.

They'd also be the two best-known environmental activists on the planet. They were both active crew members of the Sea Shepherd Conservation Society, but this was twenty years before Animal Planet's TV program *Whale Wars* would turn Sea Shepherd into a household name as radical defenders of whales and dolphins. The Iceland campaign was the breakthrough that would bring the group to international infamy. I've talked with them both about this action several times, and Rod himself wrote an account in 2005 in a radical journal called *No Compromise*, from which I cribbed some of these details. It's a well-documented tale, but without understanding Rod's role in Iceland, it's harder to understand the tactical and strategic evolution that came after.

Storm clouds moved across the pumice gray of the fjord as the two packed up to go. Only the car wouldn't start; they'd drained the battery. The whole day had been like this. They'd been planning it for months, but so many details were changing on the fly. Almost immediately they spotted a passing van and flagged it down.

It was risky, but they had no choice. Howitt's look wouldn't raise any suspicions. He was the model of the pale, brown-eyed Cornish tourist, ruddy in the winter cold, with a black watch cap covering his short thatch of brown hair. Rail thin, soft-spoken, and polite, he was the perfect agent: crafty and skilled, but also unassuming and, as a result, relatively forgettable. Coronado, though, made a lasting impression, with his big ears and smoldering dark smile. Anyone who saw him that night would be able to pick him out of a lineup. He was just twenty years old.

The van was full of Icelandic teenagers, who helped get the car rolling so the two could put it in gear and bump-start it. They parked the car again in a preselected hiding spot and pulled on dark rain gear, gloves, and ski masks. They strapped on fanny packs filled with tools as night descended and a marine squall broke into sheets of rain. They bent into the wind as they walked toward the station.

A workman on an excavator was digging a trench next to the whaling station, and Coronado and Howitt lay in the freezing rain for over an hour. When he shut down and quit for the night, they jumped up and produced a set of bolt cutters. Within moments, they were inside the empty facility.

Iceland is one of the great seafaring and whaling cultures of the world, and like their Scandinavian cousins the Norwegians, Icelanders had been whaling heavily throughout the twentieth century. They were still hunting whales in 1986, when the marine mammal's numbers were so depleted that the International Whaling Commission declared a worldwide moratorium on commercial whaling among all signatories to the commission treaty. Iceland is such a signatory, but was also one of three countries—the other two were Norway and Japan—that continued taking large numbers of whales for "research" purposes. Most observers of the so-called research whaling saw that the meat was being sold commercially and that little, if any, actual science was ever performed.

Which was exactly what had brought the two Sea Shepherd commandos to Iceland. Unlike a lot of mainstream environmental groups, Sea Shepherd had never positioned itself as a maker of environmental legislation; its members considered themselves enforcers of international law. Sea Shepherd captain Paul Watson had declared that Iceland was in violation of the Whaling Commission ban and that Sea Shepherd would police the country if no other agency would. Coronado and Howitt had been living in England and planning this attack for months.

The two activists were about the same age, and both men had been trained as diesel engineers on Sea Shepherd ships. At the whaling station, they put their tools to other uses. Inside the computer control room of the modern plant, they hammered at flashing banks of electronics with their wrenches and bolt cutters until the machines began to emit a hideous death growl. Leaving the nerve center a smoking ruin, they ducked into the ship's store, carrying out the most expensive pieces of repair equipment for the whaling ships and dropping them in the fjord.

When the pair located the administrative offices, they confiscated the record books showing the exact numbers of whales caught and when—proof that whaling had been ongoing under the ban— and then poured cyanic acid over everything that was left. They moved quickly to the six diesel generators that powered the station and crippled them. They smashed a set of precision centrifuges that spun whale blubber into a high-grade lubricant used in military applications such as missile production.

In a basement level of the station, they found the stash they had been looking for: a huge store of whale bones and offal that the whalers had to keep to comply with meat usage requirements. In reality, they had sold what could be sold, and this was just the leftovers.

The crates were stacked high inside huge refrigeration units. Howitt attempted to pull them out with a forklift, but the machine ran out of propane, so they wedged open the reefer doors and damaged the refrigeration units themselves so the meat would thaw and spoil. They were out to destroy everything they could.

A bewildered foreman who ran the station would recount on international news programs the next morning that the entire facility looked like it had been the target of an air raid.

The big night, however, was far from over. Coronado and Howitt dashed out of the plant and back to their car, sweating and grimy, and navigated their way over roads slick with black ice to Reykjavik harbor, an hour away, where their principal targets floated, spartan, in the lashing rain.

Iceland's whaling fleet consisted of four modern 175-foot, 430-ton hunting vessels, *Hvalur* (Whaler) 5, 6, 7, and 8. When Rod had first seen them upon entering the country almost a month earlier, tied together at their mooring, he had said they looked like the Four Horsemen of the Apocalypse. Coronado and Howitt had been watching the ships for weeks and knew that a night watchman was on board the one farthest from the dock, with his bottles of Brennivin, a strong Icelandic schnapps. One of the ships was in dry dock. That left two empty, vulnerable ships.

Without hesitating, they pulled on their ski masks and walked down the dock, leaping onto the deck of *Hvalur 6*. Howitt clipped the lock to the engine room with the bolt cutters and then quickly searched the ship to make sure it was empty. As he made his tour, Coronado piled into the fully lit engine room and began lifting deck plates, uncovering the valve that regulated the amount of seawater used to cool the engine. Howitt returned, announcing that the ship was empty, and together they heaved on wrenches to loosen the sixteen nuts that held the valve cover in place. As the nuts loosened, seawater shot out of the bolt holes and began spraying around the room.

Just as they were about to bounce over to *Hvalur 7*, the valve cover started to pop free, and with a little encouragement it blew. A geyser of water erupted into the room and completely soaked the two as they scrambled for safety. The water would fill the engine room and then the rest of the ship, sending it to the bottom of the harbor. They quietly leaped over to *Hvalur 7*, removing its valve cover and freeing a geyser there, too.

At five A.M., the two walked off the dock, throwing their tools in the water. The whaling station was in ruins; two ships were rapidly sinking. They'd seen nothing of the night watchman. They stripped off their ski masks as they walked to the car and calmly pulled away, headed straight to the airport for a flight to Luxembourg. They'd already checked their bags.

They were almost immediately pulled over by Reykjavik police. Coronado was incredulous. *No way*, he thought, *they can't be that good*. They ordered him out of the car and into the backseat of their cruiser. Howitt remained in the rental car, staring straight ahead. The two cops chatted in Icelandic for a bit, then turned and asked Coronado, "Have you drinken any alcohol tonight?"

Giddy with relief, he said, "No, I don't even drink!," which was a lie, but the cop then asked if he could smell his breath. Coronado complied and the officer dismissed him, wishing him a safe trip.

Back at the car, Howitt admitted he'd almost made a run for it, but decided to wait for a sign from Coronado. They both marveled over the poor cops who had let them go; they had stopped two of the most destructive saboteurs ever to hit Iceland, literally dripping with evidence, and had let them slip away. The two made their flight without incident.

Having hitchhiked from Luxembourg to London, where Rod's sister, Cynthia, was living, the two exhausted men picked up a copy of a morning newspaper. There it was on the front page: "Saboteurs Sink Whalers." Rod flipped to the story and saw an outrageous photo that still stirs feelings of pride and rage today, depending on where your sympathies lie: *Hvalur* 6 and 7 resting on the harbor bottom, listing a bit where they settled, just the superstructures and tall crow's nests and radar units peeking up above the opaque waters. Coronado and Howitt laughed and hugged each other in the street, elated to have succeeded and to have escaped with their freedom.

The Icelandic Ministry of Justice called it an act of terrorism, but Sea Shepherd was ready to expose the potential illegality of Iceland's research-whaling program. Paul Watson immediately took credit for the act, confirming that Coronado was one of the saboteurs but telling the *New York Times* that he couldn't name the other saboteur because he was worried that Howitt would be extradited from England under the Thatcher government's tough new antiterrorism legislation—which had been passed in the wake of truly violent and even murderous acts by animal rights extremists in Britain. Watson hadn't coordinated the attack, he said, but he had given his young charges some guidelines: the two men had been ordered not to use weapons or explosives.

In 1988, Watson flew into Reykjavik and demanded to be tried for the attack. He was arrested, but after some deliberation the government decided not to risk even further international scorn over flouting the whaling ban. This tactical alignment with international treaties, using publicity to shame countries engaged in unpopular or unlawful slaughter, has kept Watson out of prison for more than thirty-five years.

He also knows it's a dispute that might never be settled. Within two weeks, *Hvalur* 6 and 7 were refloated, though the whalers claimed two million dollars in damages. The owner of the salvage company told the Associated Press, "The boats popped up from the sandy harbor floor like a cork."

TWO Born in Wilderness

While we have no illusions that direct actions, such as this one, can by themselves bring about the end of Canada's role as a resource based economic and military functionary of Western Imperialism, we do believe that militant direct actions can have a constructive function as a springboard to the kind of consciousness and organization that must be developed if we are to overcome the nuclear masters.

—communiqué from anarchist antiwar group
Direct Action, after detonating a bomb at the Litton
Industries defense plant in Toronto, October 14, 1982

Of course, this book is for entertainment purposes only. No one involved with this project in any form encourages anyone to do any of the things described herein. We are all fat and out-of-shape (and would rather drink beer and watch TV at home than go out in the nasty, old outdoors). We're just hoping to make a buck with this book.

—Dave Foreman, introduction to the first edition of
Ecodefense: A Field Guide to Monkeywrenching, *1985*

ROD'S OLDER SISTER, Cynthia Coronado-Brown, just remembers woods. She so disliked the family's weekend routine as a girl that she doesn't know the names of the camps where they used to go. They were up in the Western Sierra, she said. Rod's older brother, Ray III, said that one of them was in Pinecrest, California, a high mountain town full of cabins and campgrounds on pristine Lake Pinecrest, at the gateway to the federally protected Emigrant

Wilderness. This was John Muir country, huge swaths of High Sierra lakes and granite bowls and ancient pines between Yosemite and Tahoe; once you were out of town, that wilderness would be accessible only by horse or on foot. Sometimes the family would even summer up there, but this was when Rod was a bit older. From where the Coronados lived in Morgan Hill, a bedroom community twenty-five miles south of San Jose, they could have been anywhere in the Sierras from Sequoia to Truckee in the space of three or four hours, so mountain country, from commercial campgrounds to high-alpine backcountry, was always waiting within reach.

Most Friday afternoons in the 1970s, the ritual in the Coronado household was the same: the kids' mother, Sunday, would have the camper packed and provisioned when their dad, Ray, came home from work. Ray and Sunday Coronado ran a company called Coronado Steel Corporation, which fabricated structural steel parts for heavy construction, and Ray was always ready to get away. Cynthia was the oldest child, then Ray III, and they'd both help pack up Rod, the baby. Often they'd drive through the night.

"We'd wake up in these fantastic places," Cynthia said. "Woods. Rivers. Lakes. Ha, ha."

There was always water, because Ray was a trout fisherman. The boys went fishing with Dad, while Sunday and Cynthia hung around the campground. No surprise, then, that as Cynthia became a teen-ager, she hated fishing. Not Rod, though. "He would have grown up with that," she said. "It was his whole life up until he was about eight, ten years old."

Rod is not vague at all about the details of those trips. By the time he was a teenager, parts of the Western Sierra were hardwired in his memory, and wilderness was a way of understanding the world. It was partly about the activity, the fishing and hiking and, later, hunting, but he also grew to love the feeling of being out in the pickup truck with his dad, the travel and the gear. Beyond the crowded public campgrounds, he saw glimpses of another world, one where all life, from the cold rivers to the red manzanita to the mountain lions, was its own neighborhood, and his own place in it was different. He saw that he was connected to something bigger, a wholeness, and that even the yard back home was a version of that wholeness. The wilderness became part of his self, a bigger Self; it felt personal and close. He wasn't aware yet that this could be a political or even a spiritual position. He just knew that he and his father needed it.

But he wanted to understand that wholeness, so he started to research. And when Rod got into something, from a school science project to a political question to wildlife biology, his siblings said, he went all in. You ended up hearing about his new passion at the dinner table every night as he tried to communicate every important detail.

He was also the sensitive one. Cynthia has kept a picture of Rod in his gear during rocket football years and always thought he looked out of character in it. Ray III played sports. He was going to be a businessman. But Rod just wasn't aggressive that way. As football and other sports dropped off, the fishing and hunting with Dad continued well into his teens.

Ray and Sunday Coronado were Mexican Americans, the third generation in their families to live in the United States. And with their fantastic surname, that of the Spanish conquistador who put what is now Arizona and the northern Mexican state of Sonora under his thumb in 1540, Francisco Vásquez de Coronado, they were the very model of assimilation. When pressed about their ethnicity, they just called themselves Mexican Americans, and if you asked them where they came from, they would tell you: California.

But they were also Yaqui, a Mexican indigenous tribe, and this became more and more important to Rod as he got older. His parents had differing reactions to their Native American ancestry, a consciousness that evolved over time.

Sunday spoke of it often, never letting the children forget. But Ray was more interested in the here and now of their life in Morgan Hill. Sunday's mother was a full-blooded Yaqui from Sonora, Ray's was part Yaqui and from Arizona, where some Yaqui people settled after centuries of war with the Spanish, the Mexican government, and even the United States. The Yaqui were originally from the Bacatete Mountains in Sonora, and occupied the Río Yaqui watershed, an area that was also sometimes home to the more infamous Apache. The Yaqui share some of their militant guerrilla history. The Yaqui's was a warrior society that formed to resist the conquistadores of the 1500s and steadily carried on a war of liberation against all comers—right up through participating in the uprisings in Chiapas in the early 1990s.

Growing up, all three of the Coronado kids were aware of this history, and the story that stuck with them was that of their great-grandmother, who survived an ethnic cleansing campaign (the Yaqui War) by the Mexican government in the early 1900s. Yaqui who survived government-led massacres were sold into slavery out of the port of Guaymas, and there Rod's great-grandmother stowed away on a ship bound for California.

Ray and Sunday spoke of their Yaqui resilience with some pride, but they were doing their best to honor the new life Great-grandma had found as an American. They didn't really participate in Yaqui culture. The family made frequent trips to Arizona and around California's Central Valley to visit family, but not necessarily to reconnect with the pueblo or to participate in Yaqui festivals.

The fact that they called themselves Ray and Sunday (rather than Reyes and Dominga, their Spanish names) says a bit about their attitude. Ray's focus was on the future and the good life. He was trained as a welder and started out as a partner in a wrought iron business, making ornamental iron. He always had other stuff going, though; he went to San Jose City College and even comanaged a hair salon with his wife. He eventually launched his own steel business and became the first licensed Hispanic steel contractor in the state, shifting away from the ornamental to structural steel parts for everything from homes to highways. For instance, Coronado Steel did a lot of work on Bay Area freeways that collapsed or suffered damage during the 1989 Loma Prieta earthquake. He hustled; he made good money so his kids could live the American dream. That was right out front in Ray's personality, so much so that Cynthia once wrote a college paper about it. He was conservative, and his own father, Reyes Coronado Sr., was a minister.

Rod, as was his habit, did his own research on his native heritage. When he was twelve, he read *Geronimo's Story of His Life*, the autobiography of the infamous Apache war chief. In it, Rod recognized some part of himself. This is where his own people were from, how they lived, what they looked like. Soon he also discovered Forrest Carter's moving, indelible, fictionalized account of Geronimo's war campaigns, *Watch for Me on the Mountain*. That's a book that stays with a man all his life.

When he was fourteen, Sunday gave Rod a copy of Dee Brown's *Bury My Heart at Wounded Knee*. She told him, "These are our people's stories. Being Yaqui makes you part of that." They aren't tales of joy and peace. Brown worked from historical documents to present the settlement of the western United States from the perspective of the Native Americans during what were usually referred to as the Indian Wars, from about 1860 to 1890. Reversing the popular mythology about bloodthirsty Indians, *Bury My Heart at Wounded Knee* is a disturbing record of murder, betrayal, and greed by settlers and the U.S. government, and though it was widely decried when it was published in the 1970s, most of its premises have been borne out. The book forever changed Rod.

Cynthia left the United States for England right after high school, wanting to work in the music industry. She stayed for twelve years. Rod's father has always been uncomfortable talking about Rod's activism, and the few times I spoke with him, in the mid-nineties, his voice dropped down to a low murmur at times, but he respected his son's passion. "It's always been the naturals of the earth. That's the thing that has attracted his attention," he told me in 1994, one of the last times he would grant an interview regarding Rod. "We noticed this many years ago, before he became politically involved with the various groups."

Rod had other political interests, too, and Sunday went so far as to accompany him to protests. Cynthia recalled that when he was still too young to drive, he went to a protest at the Lawrence Livermore National Laboratory, a national security lab about an hour east of their home. This, she said, was not something that would interest her mother, but she drove Rod out to the lab so he could participate. "I don't know if she waited in the car or what," Cynthia said.

Without knowing the term, Rod was an adherent of an ecological philosophy called deep ecology. First identified with the work of Norwegian philosopher Arne Næss, deep ecology is a belief that all living things have equal value and, by extension, share equal rights as part of a living whole. In this worldview, the entire planet is treasured as a system, rather than only specific forms of life. This biospheric egalitarianism clashes sharply, of course, with the prevailing culture, which values humans and their appetites over wolves or trees or living systems like rivers. Most of Rod's heroes in groups like Sea Shepherd and Earth First! were very taken with Bill Devall and George Sessions's *Deep Ecology*, a new primer that came out in 1985. This book made a lasting impression on a generation of activists.

In a lot of ways, the philosophy was a more efficient expression of beliefs already common to the progenitors of American environmentalism. Aldo Leopold's famed "land ethic," for instance, makes a nice description of deep ecology: "A thing is right when it tends to preserve the integrity, stability and beauty of the biotic community. It is wrong when it tends otherwise."

Rod understood this intuitively. His sense of a larger Self included everything that lived, even when he was taking it for food. And when that Self was threatened, he couldn't leave it alone.

Saving the whales became his first obsession. Ray did take him out on the Pacific on deep-sea fishing trips, so perhaps it started there, but the mainstream environmental movement of the mid-seventies was also beginning to push hard on whaling when Rod was about ten years old. The issue came alive for him, however, when he and the rest of the world watched fantastic, heroic TV images of Greenpeace out on the Pacific battling whalers in their little inflatable boats. Here was a cause even Geronimo could get behind.

It isn't hard to see Rod's 1986 Iceland attack not only as the ultimate expression of the thirteen-year-old Save the Whales movement, but also as the apotheosis of a tactical and strategic shift that had been bubbling up through the environmental movement for more than a decade. Coronado and Howitt recast whaling as a violation of international laws, which forced governments around the world to finally pay attention. Still, Coronado and Howitt were only second- or third-wave environmental radicals. So many eco-warriors had come before them.

Established in 1969 by peace activists and Sierra Club members in Vancouver, Greenpeace was originally called, somewhat anticlimactically, the Don't Make a Wave Committee, a reference to the tidal waves anticipated to be generated by the United States military's nuclear weapons tests in Amchitka, in Alaska's Aleutian Islands.

More genteel, well-established conservation organizations like the Sierra Club and the Audubon Society, which was already seventy years old at that point, could organize their tens of thousands of members to protest the radiation release, fund studies on affected wildlife, or lobby Congress, but they could do little to physically stop the tests. The Don't Make a Wave Committee, however, advocated direct action: activities that shut off the problem at the source, such as strikes, demonstrations, or, in this case, sailing. As the U.S. military planned a test at Amchitka on a weapon with reportedly 50 to 250 times the force of the bomb dropped on Hiroshima, the committee planned to sail a boat into the blast zone and stop the test. It christened its rented boat *Greenpeace*.

It was a suicidal plan that worked like a dream. The activists' first voyage, in September 1971, caused the military to cancel the test. On their second foray, they were still a thousand miles away from the blast zone when the bomb was detonated, but immediately thereafter the United States announced that it was halting all tests on Amchitka, and it quickly restored the island to its former status as a bird and wildlife sanctuary.

The world conservation community took notice. As author Rik Scarce writes in his excellent book *Eco-Warriors: Understanding the Radical Environmental Movement*, "It was a phenomenon that the old conservation groups had rarely, if ever, experienced: victory through failure! The crucial differences were the Committee's use of both direct confrontation and the media. The two are essential qualities of today's radical environmentalism."

When Greenpeace first began using these same direct action tactics to protect whales in 1975, it hit on a combination so dramatic and emotional that a generation of kids like Rod were converts for life. There they were in their first intervention, the Greenpeacers in their fast, two-man inflatable boats, the same Zodiac boats we saw on *The Undersea World of Jacques Cousteau,* buzzing around Russian whaling ships in the rough North Pacific, positioning themselves between the harpoon guns and the sperm whales surfacing over and over to breathe as they fled the ships. It was pitched and deadly combat; as explosive-tipped harpoons whizzed over the activists' heads, twice sinking with a sick thud into giant cetaceans only a few feet from the meddling rafts, the public awoke to a slaughter it had only known from books like *Moby-Dick*. Greenpeace's stroke of genius was to broadcast its life-and-death struggle on prime-time TV. This is the strategy still used to great effect by Sea Shepherd today.

In fact, one of the three Zodiac pilots in that first Greenpeace confrontation was twenty-three-year-old Paul Watson, who, according to his own account, had concocted the plan with Greenpeace leader Robert Hunter. At one point, Watson's Zodiac drifted only yards from a harpooned sixty-foot bull sperm whale as it thrashed in its death throes, beating the sea to a bloody pink foam. The roaring beast—whose kind was well known to attack boats in a rage—raised its mighty head and jaw out of the water to tower above Watson's tiny vessel, and the two of them stared at each other, separated by only a few yards, eye to eye. Watson's whole world changed in that moment. He was certain that the whale understood his mission and, in its last gesture, was communicating its pain. From that day forward, he dedicated himself to the protection of all marine life.

In 1977, however, the organization proved that it wasn't quite as dedicated to Watson's increasingly militant methods. Greenpeace would not damage property, steal, or otherwise break the law to interfere with its adversaries, but Watson had a different interpretation of the law.

He was on the Greenpeace board of directors by 1977 and was tasked with disrupting the clubbing of baby harp seals on the perilous Labrador Front ice floes just off the coast of Newfoundland. Watson is from nearby New Brunswick himself, so the campaign was something of a homeland defense. During the confrontation, he grabbed one of the sealers' clubs, tossed it in the water, and moved pelts they'd already gathered. He then handcuffed himself to the winch cable used to drag the pelts to the sealers' ship. He got more than he bargained for: The winch operator fired up the machine and intentionally dragged Watson across the ice, then raised him ten feet into the air and smacked him against the ship. Then he dropped Watson in the Arctic slush and hauled him out again, repeatedly. Eventually, the belt that held the handcuffs broke, and Watson plunged into the frozen water. He was dragged out, hypothermic, and after a half hour of watching him fall in and out of consciousness, the sealers grudgingly saved his life by letting him spend the night in the warmth of their ship.

Throwing the club into the water was a violation of Canadian law, and for that Watson was expelled from Greenpeace. Robert Hunter later described Watson as a "mutineer."

Watson formed Earth Force later that year, before changing the group's name to the Sea Shepherd Conservation Society. In 1978, he purchased a well-used, 206-foot, 779-ton trawler with donated money from philanthropist and author Cleveland Amory, the founder of Fund for Animals, an organization that runs sanctuaries for rescued animals. Watson rechristened the ship the *Sea Shepherd* and went after an infamous Cypriot-registered whaling ship called the *Sierra*. When he found the *Sierra* in the Atlantic in mid-1979, he did not hesitate but rammed the ship, cutting an eight-foot gash in its hull and forcing it into Lisbon, Portugal, for repairs. The *Sea Shepherd* was then accosted by a Portuguese warship and impounded in the same harbor. When Portuguese officials demanded that Watson turn over the ship as reparations for the attack, the *Sea Shepherd*'s chief engineer scuttled it. A few months later, divers loyal to Sea Shepherd fixed limpet mines to the hull of the just-repaired *Sierra*, which they knew to be empty, and sent it to the bottom of the harbor, too.

Rod joined Sea Shepherd as a supporter when he was twelve or thirteen. He'd contacted other organizations, including Greenpeace, but only heard back from Sea Shepherd. He'd saved up his allowance and sent two hundred dollars to the organization, earmarked for fuel on a trip to stop Canadian sealers. That meant something to Watson. Cleveland Amory might have paid for their ship, but the society was constantly broke. Watson wrote Coronado a personal note of thanks.

Saving sea mammals did not, however, turn Rod against hunting and fishing with his father. Even as Cynthia and Ray III entered high school and began to distance themselves from what the older brother once called their parents' "tunnel vision . . . about business, money-type stuff, making a living," turning instead to dating and weekend partying, Rod continued the outings with his father and later took up bow hunting. By the time he was sixteen, his dad was letting him and a few of his buddies disappear on their own for up to a week at a time into the Sierras, stalking deer and more generally practicing their survival skills.

Ray III was amazed that his dad let Rod go. "At sixteen, I know I had about a two-hundred-foot chain on my bumper. I wasn't going any further," he told me in 1994.

"Now, [Rod's] beliefs are like his beliefs back then," Ray III said. "You eat what you kill. I can remember them getting back, telling stories about how they barbecued this, or they'd accidentally kill this, so they'd have to eat it. They experimented with, like, eating snakes and whatnot. From sixteen, seventeen, they would go out there and catch fish and live off that, you know?"

Rod's real moment of departure came in 1984, when he took a high school graduation trip to Vancouver with his parents. Sea Shepherd was operating there at the time, and he got his chance to meet Paul Watson. He told Watson he was out of high school and ready to join, and Watson responded, "You can start right now." The crew's new ship, the *Sea Shepherd II*, had been impounded by Canadian officials, so they were painting educational murals in town called the Whaling Walls. Rod told his parents he was staying, so they left him there to work a few days, then picked him up on the way back to California.

It would be easy to say a radical was born then, but really he'd been one for years. He passed up college to join Sea Shepherd full-time the following year, at age nineteen. Clearly bright enough to excel in school, Rod liked to joke that he only went to college to commit crimes, mostly against animal laboratories. Scuttling those two boats in Iceland was his graduation to the big time.

Paul Watson was Rod's first mentor, but he wasn't his only one. A year after Sea Shepherd sank the *Sierra*, a terrestrial analogue to the oceangoing movement was developing in America's desert Southwest. It wasn't an organization, per se, but rather an idea, called Earth First!, and it would quickly become infamous in the United States—and irresistible to young Rod.

It's worth noting that Earth First! announced its arrival to the conservation community with a joke, a grand and high-concept joke, which set the tone for the network's inspired, dangerous but often hilarious actions. This joke was one of the reasons I liked reporting on them so much. It was the middle of the day on the spring equinox of 1981 when four men and a woman strode out onto Glen Canyon Dam, the massive "invading alien," as movement guru Edward Abbey described it, that had hacked off the free waters of the Colorado River and created Arizona's Lake Powell. The five carried a large cylindrical object between them and unceremoniously heaved it over the side of the dam. As it fell, it grew, a thin black plastic "crack" as long as a football field, unrolling and settling down the face of the dam. The great concrete arc looked like it had suffered a fissure. At a makeshift press conference, the activists called the action "The Cracking of Glen Canyon Damn" and called themselves Earth First!

For Earth First!, it was the fulfillment of a prophecy. Abbey's beloved 1975 work of comic fiction, *The Monkey Wrench Gang*, begins with a rumor that the gang is going to attack that particular dam, which symbolized, at least for Abbey, much of what was wrong with America: a country with a deep spiritual connection to wilderness incrementally and steadily killing off the wild, killing off the mighty Colorado that had dug the Grand Canyon, just to make way for more malls.

Abbey saw the wilderness as the last refuge of real Americans and wrote about an irascible and well-armed tribe of stewards who believe that bears and coyotes have a right to the land and are worth defending "by any means necessary." This is no leftist communal dream or argument for government control of resources; the mischievous vandals who star in Abbey's book favor an unfettered and even anarchist America. That's the cosmic joke, a little dark, at the heart of Abbey's book: his Monkey Wrench Gang members are essentially ultraconservative, and their overriding judgment is that there are just too damn many people and bureaucrats everywhere for America to go on being America. It's a formula that puts outlaw eco-radicalism on a par with patriotism, and the punch line comes in hanging the necessary dam-cracking on a quartet of Americans straight out of the 1950s, like Abbey himself. In the untamed Vietnam vet George Washington Hayduke III, the querulous, billboard-burning surgeon Doc Sarvis, his Bronx-born cowgirl-feminist nurse Bonnie Abbzug, and a "Jack Mormon" river guide named Seldom Seen Smith, Abbey created a set of comic book heroes that challenged every flattop-wearing sheriff in cactus country to find something in there he didn't like. The gang was based at least partly on real saboteurs who called themselves the Tucson Eco-Raiders and operated in Arizona in the mid-1970s.

That book became the founding myth of a movement.

Dave Foreman was just the kind of guy to respond to Abbey's cranky vision, a former southwestern regional representative of the Wilderness Society, a Republican and a native of Albuquerque, and a bow hunter to boot. He was the type of old-school white-guy Teddy Roosevelt–Gifford Pinchot conservationist who liked his wilderness camping with steak and whiskey. The crack he helped roll down the dam also symbolized his break with mainstream environmentalism, which came about as a reaction to a large-scale U.S. Forest Service survey called the Roadless Area Review and Evaluation (RARE II).

The 1979 RARE II survey cataloged America's roadless wilderness and recommended tracts to preserve as federally protected wilderness under the 1964 Wilderness Act. Foreman looked on, sick with dismay, as the mainstream environmental groups fell all over themselves trying to look moderate and subsequently, only one quarter of the eighty million acres under study was actually preserved.

These results were outrageous, but they were also typical. The so-called Group of 10 organizations that comprised the core of the mainstream environmental movement—including the oldest and most established groups, like the Sierra Club, the Audubon Society, the Wilderness Society, the Izaak Walton League, the National Wildlife Federation, and the Natural Resources Defense Council, to name a few—had lots of members and stacks of cash but very little taste for outright confrontation.

Foreman was grappling existentially with this issue when he took off for a camping trip to the Pinacate desert in northern Mexico in April 1980. With him were four other "rednecks for wilderness": oil roughneck and former Yippie Mike Roselle, Wyoming Wilderness Society rep Bart Koehler, Friends of the Earth's Wyoming rep Howie Wolke, and former National Park Service ranger and Sierra Club rep Ron Kezar. Out under the stars, they fomented and drank lots of beer. But on the way back to Albuquerque, a real plan emerged: identify the core swaths of wilderness in North America that would preserve the greatest amount of biodiversity, then use direct action to keep that territory wild. They wanted to cause a stir because of the glacial pace of change; however, they also thought radical action might help the Group of 10 look more moderate and do better in Congress. The five friends called themselves Earth First!—exclamation point included.

Sounds like just another environmental group, except for one crucial distinction: they weren't an organization—they were a disorganization. They had no employees, no office, no budget. Every participant in their actions would be responsible for paying their own way, so the assembled force itself would have nothing to lose. No big donations to protect, no hierarchy to arrest. They would be made up of decentralized cells that might or might not know one another. Their credo: "No compromise in defense of Mother Earth."

Well, one compromise, actually, and a necessary one: like Paul Watson, who would become friends with Foreman, Earth First! would practice strictly nonviolent direct action.

Depending, of course, on your definition of violence. The fictional Monkey Wrench Gang burns billboards, runs the developers' bulldozers off cliffs, and dynamites a coal train. This kind of Luddite "monkeywrenching" became the Earth First! calling card. Foreman advocated widespread (but strategic) ecological sabotage in a manifesto he wrote for the *Progressive* magazine in 1981, and very soon Earth First!ers put his ideas into practice.

It started out mildly enough. The first EF! national gathering, called the Round River Rendezvous after the summer fairs, or rendezvous, attended by Native Americans and settlers in the frontier days, was held in Wyoming's Gros Ventre Wilderness on July 4, 1980. When a road was surveyed for oil exploration in the Gros Ventre in 1982, Roselle, Foreman, and a couple others "unsurveyed" the road by pulling the stakes. Of course, they were also doing the things other conservation groups do, like holding public meetings and filing complicated lawsuits. The road was laid out again, and when EF!ers went back for that year's Rendezvous, they pulled all the stakes again. Abbey himself, who had become the godfather of the group, was also out there yanking them.

The sabotage quickly escalated. Any piece of property that stood for eco-destruction was fair game, from heavy logging equipment like feller bunchers to National Forest Service offices themselves. Foreman even wrote a book about it in 1985, *Ecodefense: A Field Guide to Monkeywrenching*. The book, which is still available everywhere today, including Amazon, contains thorough and thoughtful how-tos on just about everything a monkeywrencher might want to wreck, from spiking trees and burning machinery to sabotaging scores of different species of heavy-industrial equipment, including airplanes, to destroying traplines and making smoke bombs. What you won't find in there is how to make actual bombs or how to use any kind of weaponry. What you will find are constant admonitions to protect the life and well-being of one's adversary, as in this passage from a section about disabling snowmobiles: "Remember that snowmobiles are often driven by overweight, out-of-shape, poorly-prepared wimps, who may be put into a life-threatening situation if their snowmobile is disabled miles from civilization. *Be very conscious of the situation you may be creating and be concerned for the safety of the snowmobiler*" [emphasis in the original].

The most interesting parts of the book, however, are Foreman's eleven bullet-pointed billboards on the philosophy of what monkeywrenching is and what it is not. They form something of a mini-manifesto on the whole movement and include the following:

- MONKEYWRENCHING IS NON-VIOLENT

   Monkeywrenching is non-violent resistance to the destruction of natural diversity and wilderness. It is not directed toward harming human beings or other forms of life. It is aimed at inanimate machines and tools. Care is always taken to minimize any possible threat to other people (and to the monkeywrenchers themselves).

- MONKEYWRENCHING IS NOT REVOLUTIONARY

   It does not aim to overthrow any social, political or economic system. It is merely non-violent self-defense of the wild. It is aimed at keeping industrial "civilization" out of natural areas and causing its retreat from areas that should be wild. It is not major industrial sabotage. Explosives, firearms and other dangerous tools are usually avoided. They invite greater scrutiny from law

enforcement agencies, repression and loss of public support. (The
Direct Action group in Canada is a good example of what monkeywrenching is not.) Even Republicans monkeywrench.

Earth First! put out a newspaper, the *Earth First! Journal*, that was
a must-read publication for people like me who needed to know
where the action was. It was produced by a collective that moved
around the country and is still produced that way today. Scores of
different cells popped up all over the United States, and the name
Rod Coronado would quickly become familiar to all of them.

THREE Conservationists and Anarchists

THE WORST THING about Rod's Iceland action was its total effectiveness. Although the ships were eventually repaired, the damage to Iceland's reputation was severe (the country quit whaling for several years after 1989), and the only repercussion for Sea Shepherd was that Paul Watson was declared persona non grata in Iceland. Few of the Sea Shepherd campaigns drew such bright lines, and Rod found it difficult to continue some of the group's regular work—such as patrolling for dolphin-killing tuna seiners in the Eastern Tropical Pacific and posturing against drift netters and sealers—without really doing much damage. Being part of Sea Shepherd involved a lot of steaming from place to place looking for ways to frustrate big killers, but few opportunities to really knock them out. Without getting yourself killed, anyway.

At a 1987 direct action conference in Sacramento, where Rod delivered a public talk about the Iceland action, he met Jonathan Paul, an activist his age who shared his vision of nonviolent guerrilla action. As the two talked, they realized they were interested in many of the same wildlife issues in California, and agreed that the solutions might require more than protests and letter-writing campaigns.

Jonathan was four months older than Rod but was not as experienced in sabotage or direct action. He had a few actions under his belt, however, and he was very results oriented. What he'd seen in Rod's Iceland action was a tactic that produced real results.

Jonathan was about Rod's height, a few pounds heavier, with a round, friendly face and long brown hair. He was somewhat cautious by nature but had a sharp tongue; he could be acerbic and withering, wearing down his opponents with a kind of venomous condemnation. He was young and he was dead certain about his beliefs. Increasingly, he was motivated to back up his big talk with big action. He came from a privileged background. His father was an investment banker with Morgan Stanley in Manhattan and a conservative Republican; his mother grew up in England with the benefits of inherited wealth, then moved to America to become a social worker. Jonathan and his two older twin sisters grew up on a farm in Massachusetts, where Jonathan decided at age fifteen to become a vegan. Unlike Rod, who became a vegan while working with Sea Shepherd, Jonathan didn't really understand this as a political act at first. He just didn't want to kill animals. He was all set to go to college, maybe even Stanford like his sister Caroline, but found himself drawn into the activist trade.

He was hardly the black sheep, however. From 1992 to 1997, his sister Alexandra bounced up and down the California beaches as Lieutenant Stephanie Holden on *Baywatch* and used her fame to bring attention to environmental causes—including her brother's when he was locked up or needed media attention for his campaigns. Her identical twin, Caroline, was one of the first women hired into the San Francisco Fire Department, an experience she details in her 1998 book, *Fighting Fire*. She would also fiercely defend her brother, even as he became more radical.

As soon as they met, Rod and Jonathan started talking about defending endangered wildlife.

In 1987, California was in the process of re-legalizing the hunting of desert bighorn sheep, which had been rescued from the brink of extinction and taken off the Endangered Species List. The issue had come to the attention of mainstream environmental groups, Fund for Animals, and radicals like Earth First!, and they all had their own strategies for addressing it. But Rod and Jonathan's was the most direct; they knew they could easily disrupt the hunts, and, at that time, it wouldn't even be illegal. Just extremely dangerous.

So, with the help of some Earth First!ers and Fund for Animals, Rod and Jonathan launched a direct action initiative that would forever change big game hunting in the United States.

Hunt Saboteurs America, or the Hunt Sabs, as they called it, was one of the first American incarnations of a tactic that was well known in Britain. Hunt sabotage started there as early as 1824, when an antislavery activist named Catherine Smithies set up the Band of Mercy, a youth wing of Britain's Royal Society for the Prevention of Cruelty to Animals, which attempted to disrupt stag hunts and fox hunts in which the quarry was run down by dogs. Hunt Sabs was a tactic, rather than an organization, because there was no membership. But it was not sub-rosa: during their actions, they hoped to have press along and talk to the public. Once Rod and Jonathan's group got word of a hunt taking place in the new bighorn-sheep-hunting areas, the Hunt Sabs would gather a ragtag posse of activists from the Bay Area, Santa Cruz, Los Angeles, and the redwood coast and disrupt the hunt by squonking loudly on marine air horns, blowing whistles, blasting recorded music, and placing their bodies in front of the rifles.

For three years, from 1987 to 1990, Hunt Saboteurs America went after big game hunters who targeted mule deer, bear, mountain lion, and bison, and launched regular annual campaigns to stop the hunting of rare desert bighorn sheep and tule elk. Face-to-face confrontations with hunters who had drawn expensive, once-in-a-lifetime licenses to hunt these beasts had the potential to go very badly. The only reason it worked was that the sabs' commitment to nonviolence was made known in every possible way. No one ever got shot, but there were some misadventures.

On the first Mojave Desert bighorn hunt, for instance, Jonathan and a group of other sabs confronted some outfitters in their camp. When they approached, the hunters rounded them up and stuffed them into a horse trailer to wait for the arrival of the sheriff. The protesters were none too happy about it, but went passively as a way to prove they meant no bodily harm. One of the sabs was a well-known Earth First!er named Lee Dessaux, who lived in a fantastic tree house just outside Santa Cruz and was a principal contact for environmental action in that coastal area. Dessaux was also a bit of a wiseass, and he started to protest. When he dared to come out of the trailer—which evidently wasn't locked—one of the outfitters punched him in the nose and bloodied it. So he and the other sabs stayed in there a couple hours, trying to avoid a confrontation. Dessaux was scared and outraged, though, and continued to complain that he was being kidnapped. The outfitter, who was from Jackson Hole, Wyoming, considered it a citizen's arrest. He heard Dessaux yelling about how he was an Earth First!er and couldn't believe it, since he himself was something of an EF! sympathizer back home in Jackson Hole. In Wyoming, the Earth First!ers he knew were hunters. So he got on the horn to Howie Wolke, one of the five cofounders of Earth First! and a good friend. Recounting the story, EF! cofounder Mike Roselle, who also lived in Jackson Hole at the time, said the whole thing came off later as high comedy.

"And he says, 'I got this guy in my trailer, he says he's an Earth First!er. Have you ever heard of this guy?'

"And Howie says, 'What's he look like?'

"And he goes, 'Well, he's got a Mohawk and no eyebrows and, like, piercings all over his body.'"

At that time, Earth First!ers were a working-class, flannel-shirt-type crew; they were hardly rocking the punk aesthetic.

"And he's like, 'I don't know that guy.' Heh!"

Rod wasn't with the crew in the horse trailer, but he also thought it was odd, if not funny, saying, "We gave him shit about it, like, 'Well, did they have guns on you?' And Jonathan said, 'No, but we were scared!'" The sabs weren't trespassing, and California's brand-new 1988 hunter harassment law only threatened a one-hundred-dollar fine, so the sheriff eventually let Dessaux and the others go free.

When they first got back to camp, though, and Coronado saw Dessaux's injury, he was pissed. "Fuck this," he said, "let's go over there and talk to them," hoping to hammer out some kind of non-violent accord. They marched back into the hunters' camp around dawn the next morning, when they were still in their tents, but none of the hunters would talk.

On another hunt, a group of sabs got onto a hunter and dogged him for a whole day, staying just close enough to harass him. Finally, the guy was so frustrated that on an incline he drew his sidearm and fired two shots over their heads. A sab named Van Clothier shouted out, "Nyah, ya missed me!" and then kept right on with his pursuit.

"He didn't want to incite the guy to further violence, but he felt it would have sent a bad message that all you had to do was shoot over the heads of these people and they would back off. That would be very dangerous," said Rod.

The Hunt Saboteurs marked a transition in radical environmentalist culture, and not just because guys like Lee Dessaux had Mohawks and multiple piercings. They also came at environmental issues with a different ecological point of view. Up until the late 1980s, the dominant radical culture was the conservation-oriented "rednecks for wilderness" crowd that identified with *The Monkey Wrench Gang* and practiced deep ecology.

Rod and the Hunt Sabs, however, were also believers in animal rights. This was a much more prickly faction that found its bible in Peter Singer's masterful philosophical work *Animal Liberation*.

Lots of people read and loved both texts, of course. The difference was in the implementation: whether or not one should kill animals.

Deep ecology is a holistic philosophy that makes no apology for the existence of a natural food chain. In preserving the maximum biological diversity of a high mountain meadow, for instance, one preserves mountain lions. Mountain lions eat deer, groundhogs, and such, and a number of humans can eat deer and blue grouse there too, so long as the numbers are balanced so that every species is equally valued and can thrive. The practice of deep ecology is to protect true wilderness areas where all of the original inhabitants of the biome can be sustained, from grizzlies to prairie grass, and to keep humans from destroying these systems by overpopulating or by killing all the predators, such as wolves. The ideal is to protect whole ecosystems that don't need any human intervention.

Animal rights theory agrees with much of this, except the part about humans eating deer or grouse. Singer's *Animal Liberation* deals with some obvious aberrations in the food chain as it exists now on Earth, such as factory farming and product testing on animals, and says it's hypocritical to save animals in parklike preserves while torturing and killing them elsewhere. His dispassionate, coolly academic thesis asserts that if we extend the philosophical arguments upon which we base societal rules like, say, English common law or the idea of human rights, we find that nonhuman animals have the philosophical right to a natural life. Thus, eating animals is immoral, and torturing them in factory farms or using them in medical experiments or cosmetics testing is a crime. To not acknowledge their rights, Singer's theory goes, is speciesist.

Even if it weren't immoral, Singer goes on to argue, the idea of a balanced system anywhere on the planet is beyond our grasp. His proposal is that we need to stop eating animals and go vegetarian— if not vegan—in order to save the lives of the human population left on Earth, not to mention the animals.

Many philosophers are already talking about animal rights as the next step in a progression from rights for some to rights for all, a progression including, in the United States, women's suffrage, the Civil Rights Act of 1964, and the current battles over gay marriage. It's a big jump, but several European countries have already taken remarkable steps toward granting rights to individual animals.

Rod had a foot in both camps. He had become a vegan in 1986, but not in response to reading *Animal Liberation*. Instead, he credits his conversion to a British punk song called "This Is the A.L.F.," with its rapid-fire delivery and doctrinaire lyrics:

> Animal lovers, vandals, hooligans, cranks; recognise the labels? They say we don't care about human beings. We say all sentient beings, animal or human have the right to live, free from pain, torture and suffering. They say because we are human and speak the same, we matter more. Is our pain and suffering any greater or lesser than that of animals? Human v. animal rights is as much a prejudice as black v. white or the nazis versus the jews an affront to our freedom.

The song was by an anarchist punk band from the U.K. called Conflict, and Rod waded into the band's ethos looking for more information about anarchism as an organizing principle. He wasn't the only one. With well-educated, highly politicized, and popular bands such as the Clash at the vanguard, punk rock music was pumping messages to any kid who would listen in the 1980s, and anarchism stood out from the mix as an alternative to the perceived failure of party politics.

Coronado and friends like Dessaux were particularly focused on anarchism's application to ecology, or what was called green anarchism. It wasn't a belief in violence or chaos; those were just fun buzzwords to throw around. In practice, this form of organizing was basically the precursor to the "buy local" movement: its proponents favored making decisions and providing for services through small, local governance. Many American thinkers, like Thoreau, for instance, have had anarchist roots. The first philosopher to call himself an anarchist, French writer and politician Pierre-Joseph Proudhon, in the

1840s publicized his belief that "anarchy is order"; he considered anarchism a form of government or constitution organized around the idea of municipal ownership, which he and others referred to as the "commune."

The decentralized cells that had come to typify the radical environmental movement were perfect examples of this. The Hunt Sabs and Earth First! didn't believe in forming giant environmental groups with thousands of members to change policy. Bureaucracies were too easily compromised. Instead, it was the idea of green anarchist thinker Murray Bookchin and others to gather decentralized communes into a type of confederacy and thus wield large amounts of democratic power.

As much as his seminal work was a model for the green anarchist movement, Bookchin disagreed sharply with guys like Coronado in at least two ways: One, Bookchin did not believe, as Coronado did, in destructive direct action; he thought this was too easily confused with violence. And two, many anarchists of the punk era also put the individual before any larger social goal. In this new incarnation, one's personal identity as a transgendered, tattooed lacto-vegetarian was more important and worth fighting for than any larger social goal like, say, the right to vote, which was so much more difficult to organize.

Bookchin and others excoriated this tendency as a total failure. In his 1995 essay "Social Anarchism or Lifestyle Anarchism: An Unbridgeable Chasm," he wrote,

> The bourgeoisie has nothing whatsoever to fear from such lifestyle declamations. With its aversion for institutions, mass-based organizations, its largely subcultural orientation, its moral decadence, its celebration of transience, and its rejection of programs, this kind of narcissistic anarchism is socially innocuous, often merely a safety valve for discontent toward the prevailing social order . . . Lifestyle anarchism takes flight from all meaningful

social activism and a steadfast commitment to lasting and creative projects by dissolving itself into kicks, postmodernist nihilism, and a dizzying Nietzschean sense of elitist superiority.

The original wave of Earth First!ers had similar reservations about the growing influence of anarchists and lifestylers. In 1990, Dave Foreman disassociated himself from Earth First! because he felt the movement was becoming more about identity politics and less about biology.

"All you have to do is look at the *Earth First! Journal* that I edited in the eighties and what it is today," he said in our recent interview. "The style, the culture, the politics, it's all different. Sorry, folks, your personal problems are not the point. Animal rights is dedicated to preventing the suffering of individual animals, and while I think that's a worthy goal, it's certainly not conservation. Which is more concerned with species and ecosystems."

It was a major fissure, and Rod and Jonathan recognized they were headed into lonely territory. Paul Watson didn't even believe in animal rights. I've sat in several broken-down Central American yacht club bars with him while he devoured a steak. He doesn't think it's right that the United States government allows cattle to destroy federal rangelands at the expense of buffalo, wild horses, and other beasts—he calls domestic cattle and sheep "meadow maggots"—but as long as it's on the menu, he doesn't mind eating it.

The Hunt Saboteurs campaign to stop the sport hunting of California mountain lions—a major sab initiative until the passage of Prop 117, which halted the hunts in 1990—was one place where the two worlds intersected. Earth First!ers who ate meat were still very much against the killing of predators because it upset the biological and deep ecological hierarchy that helped regulate populations of prey species. If there were going to be bighorn sheep, for instance, there also had to be mountain lions to keep them in check. Without those top predators, the entire system broke down.

"There were Earth First!ers who were there, who were meat eaters, who didn't mind hunting but didn't like predator hunting. And we all still worked together," said Jonathan. "The Hunt Sabs was when Earth First!, that crowd, and the animal rights crowd— and some of this kind of urban, anarchist-type squatter people who worked on those issues too—we all came together. And us hardcore animal rights people were starting to go to [the EF! Round River] Rendezvous and hanging out in the Earth First! scene. And we started getting more educated about the ecological thing."

"That's when we really started seeing a new element get in," said EF!'s Mike Roselle. "And it was a mixed bag, because those guys were action junkies. I mean, they were brave, and they were capable, and they were passionate and determined. And so a lot of the actions we did, we did together. Although when they did most of their animal actions, we didn't really join them. There were a lot of people who were sympathetic to the opposition to the sheep hunt, on biological reasons, not so much on cruelty or antihunting reasons."

Marked differences between the two groups would remain, most notably concerning veganism and the treatment of animals, but more and more the tactics continued to merge.

"I don't think there was a big divergence across the board on the tactical issues," affirmed Roselle. "Except there were some of the folks that [Rod and Jonathan] were hanging out with that really thought that it was OK, even violence against humans, intimidation, threats—stuff that we'd call terrorism today."

That so-called terrorism was being carried out by the Animal Liberation Front, then a new resistance movement that was leaking into the country from the U.K. It involved an all-out assault on property and clandestine action, both of which appealed to Rod and Jonathan. In 1987, they started their own crew, the Western Wildlife Unit of the Animal Liberation Front.

The ALF was the brainchild of their Hunt Saboteur hero, British radical Ronnie Lee. Lee started his hunt sabotage group in 1971 in Luton, England, and tapped into ancient memory by originally calling it the Band of Mercy. The group, eventually called the Hunt Saboteurs Association, slashed the tires on hunters' cars and smashed their windows. They left notes explaining that the attacks weren't personal but warning that they wouldn't stop, either. Lee and colleagues ushered in a new escalation in tactics when they set a fire on November 10, 1973, that partially destroyed a new Hoechst Pharmaceuticals animal-testing laboratory near Milton Keynes. They went back and finished the job a few days later, burning down the rest of the place. It was the first known use of arson by modern animal rights extremists, and in its communiqué to the press, the Band of Mercy called itself a "nonviolent guerrilla organization dedicated to the liberation of animals from all forms of cruelty and persecution at the hands of mankind."

Lee went to prison for twelve months in the mid-1970s for an attack on Oxford Laboratory Animal Colonies in Bicester, and when he got out, he upped the ante. He wanted something that would strike fear into the hearts of his enemies, and so, in 1976, he began calling his group the Animal Liberation Front.

The Animal Liberation Front is what is called leaderless resistance: it requires no membership, no dues, no contact with other ALFers. Anyone can be a member. Some attempt is made by a volunteer Animal Liberation Front Press Office in both the United States and Britain to advocate nonviolent principles, but the whole point is to champion high-profile and clandestine destruction, including arson and sabotage.

By 1982, even Ronnie Lee couldn't hold back a rush toward violence, however, and British animal rights activists began making overt attempts to injure or even kill people. A group called the Animal Rights Militia (ARM) sent letter bombs to officials, including British prime minister Margaret Thatcher. ARM is distinct from the

ALF in that its activists refuse to follow nonviolence guidelines. In 1985, ARM activists car-bombed two animal researchers.

The Animal Liberation Front hit the United States soon enough. PETA executive director Ingrid Newkirk wrote a book about an American policewoman named "Valerie" who went to England to be trained by Ronnie Lee and brought the ALF back home. In 1981, a group of seventeen macaque monkeys that had been removed by police from the lab of Dr. Edward Taub in Silver Spring, Maryland, were snatched from state custody and whisked off to Florida in one of the first acts for which the ALF claimed responsibility in this country.

The acronym ALF really began to mean something in the United States, though, in 1984, when members broke into a head-injury lab at the University of Pennsylvania, caused seventy thousand dollars' worth of damage, and grabbed videotapes made by the researchers themselves. The tapes showed technicians laughing as severe head trauma was inflicted on conscious baboons. Though the lab argued that it was doing everything according to National Institutes of Health standards, the public was outraged; the facility was closed, the head veterinarian was fired, and the university was placed on probation. This ALF action shocked the biomedical community and was supported by many environmentalists and animal rights activists alike as an example of necessary action: the footage exposed the researchers to the moral judgment of the public, and there would have been no legal means to get it.

The ALF was formed to frighten its enemies, and in its rhetoric—if not its tactics—it very quickly took on the characteristics of a guerrilla military faction, especially in Britain. Law enforcement in the United States was very concerned when British ALF spokesman Tim Daly told the BBC in 1987, "In a war you have to take up arms and people will get killed, and I can support that kind of action by petrol bombing and bombs under cars, and probably at a later stage, the shooting of vivisectors on their doorsteps. It's a war and there's no other way you can stop vivisectors."

Rod and Jonathan's Western Wildlife Unit never endorsed these comments, and they insisted their war was limited to property damage and nonviolence. But this kind of inflammatory rhetoric had law enforcement—and the public—on the alert.

On the night of April 16, 1987, members of the Western Wildlife Unit jumped a chain-link fence at the University of California at Davis and set fire to the under-construction John E. Thurman Veterinary Diagnostic Laboratory, causing $4.6 million in damages. It was the first arson attributed to the ALF in the United States, and Jonathan later admitted he had been the getaway driver in this crime. Rod won't say whether or not he was actually involved in the action, but he does admit to detailed knowledge of the event, and he wrote about it in a pamphlet, *Memories of Freedom*, coauthored by his entire Western Wildlife Unit cell.

"The decision was a strategic one," the pamphlet states. "Public support was nice, but alone it had rarely saved animals [*sic*] lives. All those letters to Washington DC wastepaper baskets were proof of this . . . The campaign of maximum destruction, not minimum damage to the equipment of animal abusers had begun, and with it came a new element of the animal rights movement never before seen in the U.S."

The Western Wildlife Unit next struck on Memorial Day 1987, when it freed two hundred wild horses that had been rounded up in northeastern California to make way for cattle grazing on public lands. Coronado had originally been approached for this action by Cleveland Amory, who had in mind an aboveground protest spearheaded by Fund for Animals, but when Amory's attorneys advised him that his organization couldn't be directly involved, he threw some money to Coronado and told him to "go for it anyway."

"It was one of the most beautiful actions I've ever been involved with," said Rod, "taking down all that fence and then watching those powerful horses charge back into the wildlands in the moon-light."

Next, Rod went back to UC Davis to free turkey vultures used in poison studies for the U.S. Department of Agriculture's Animal Damage Control programs—programs that would become favorite targets over the next few years. Then came the liberation of beagles used in pollution studies at UC Irvine. The tactics began to spread, with a rash of fires breaking out all over California. Before the end of 1987, a group calling itself the Animal Rights Militia took credit for a fire at San Jose Valley Veal and Beef Company in Santa Clara, and then another at the Ferrara Meat Company in San Jose, and the ALF took credit for a fire at a poultry operation in Santa Clara. Other groups got into the act: an offshoot of Earth First! took credit for a 1988 fire that completely destroyed a livestock auction yard in Dixon, California, and the simultaneous attempted firebombing of the Cali-fornia Cattlemen's Association offices in Sacramento. In one highly coordinated 1989 raid, ALFers who may or may not have been the Western Wildlife Unit simultaneously broke into four animal re-search labs at the University of Arizona in Tucson, burning one lab and an administrative office and carting off twelve hundred mice, rats, rabbits, guinea pigs, and frogs.

The years 1988 and 1989 saw the most dramatic increase in ALF attacks, hunt sabotage, and EF! monkeywrenching in the history of the radical movement. The 1987 UC Davis fire—which put the FBI and the Bureau of Alcohol, Tobacco and Firearms (ATF) on the trail of the Western Wildlife Unit—awakened a militancy in the move-ment, and actions exploded across the country, undertaken by peo-ple Rod and his cell had never met and would never know.

Actions attributed to the ALF conformed to a policy of nonvio-lence toward humans and all living things, and that was a line Rod and Jonathan swore they would never cross. But that didn't restrain everyone. On November 11, 1988, a thirty-three-year-old New York City woman named Fran Trutt was arrested while planting a

radio-detonated pipe bomb in the parking space used by Leon
Hirsch, head of United States Surgical Corporation, in Connecticut. The company had been criticized by animal activists because it
used dogs to demonstrate its surgical staples. The powerful bomb
was wrapped in nails and designed to kill. Trutt was affiliated with
a little-known group called Trans-Species Unlimited, but no matter the name—or the fact that the act was condemned by every
other known eco-group—the bust confirmed law enforcement's
worst fears, that this peaceful movement might develop into something more lethal. Luckily, the plot was stopped before the bomb
was detonated.

Roselle pointed out that the ALF's campaign was becoming a
classic netwar: it just put the idea out in the air, in the pamphlets and
in stories printed in the *Earth First! Journal* and other radical
publications—and later on the Internet—and whole sets of tactics
and propaganda were picked up and used without any central organization at all. The whole radical movement suddenly appeared to
have an underground guerrilla component, and that's just what worried the U.S. Department of Justice.

FOUR **The End of the Monkey Wrench Gang**

DURING THE LATTER half of 1989, I was in Arizona witnessing what seemed to be the end of the Monkey Wrench Gang. The funny part, anyway. I had been writing about Earth First!, and I got to Edward Abbey's beloved Sonoran Desert just as the Department of Justice started classifying them as dangerous terrorists. Their days as lovable but mischievous vandals were over.

I realized this on a late-summer day in 1989 when it was over 112 degrees in Phoenix and I was inside an air-conditioned room in the Maricopa County Jail, interviewing a saboteur named Mark Davis.

"There I was, cutting torch in hand. I had burned about halfway through one of the legs," said a smiling Davis. "Agents just came out of everywhere."

I stopped the recorder then and whispered that he probably shouldn't be telling me that he had actually committed this crime, at least not on the record, since he didn't yet have a lawyer. It was just a bit of legal advice. The leg in question belonged to a huge steel pylon supporting high-tension electrical transmission lines to the Central Arizona Project, which brought water to the golf courses and tract housing of the desert. Davis was thirty-nine years old at the time, a sunburned, wire-haired athlete who was in the habit of running barefoot through the desert mountains and who was missing the tip of his nose from when a dog had bitten it off in childhood. He was proud of his action, but others following his story were worried about the way this act of sabotage was going to be presented at trial. Because one of the three other people standing at the base of that pylon was an undercover FBI special agent named Michael Fain.

Some cheered the discovery of FBI infiltration as evidence that their direct action movement was becoming legitimate, that it was now beyond high jinks. Radical zines such as the *Earth First! Journal* and *Live Wild or Die!* suddenly took on a new importance. Others were sure the government would use evidence of radicalism to criminalize the entire mainstream environmental movement, and big players such as the Sierra Club had to pick their line carefully.

Carl Pope, the executive director of the Sierra Club, told me as much at a social function in San Francisco not long after Davis's arrest. Our conversation was off the record, but what Pope told me would soon become the mainstream's standard line: he supported some of the goals of people like those in Earth First!, but his membership couldn't be associated with acts many Americans considered criminal or violent.

Dale Turner, who was then the assistant editor of the Tucson-based *Earth First! Journal*, told me, "There are a lot of Earth First!ers living free, living close to the earth, who find it difficult to realize how anyone could be against that. It's hard to convince them that this is real. Big Brother is here."

The political context had flipped, too: The Reaganites were pushing back against the environmental movement, and pushing back hard. In 1981, President Ronald Reagan had come into office declaring himself a "sagebrush rebel," a direct reference to a fight over the use of public lands in the West that had begun after the first Roadless Area Review and Evaluation (RARE I), in 1972. The Sagebrush Rebellion was a reaction by livestock, mining, and off-road-vehicle interests who were enraged to see the RARE process end in more federally designated wilderness that was off-limits to their pursuits. So, while guys like Dave Foreman were upset that too little wilderness had been preserved by RARE I and II, the sagebrush rebels fought a bitter legislative fight—spearheaded by Utah's Senator Orrin

Hatch and, later, Reagan's interior secretary James Watt—to put more public land in private or state hands.

The Sagebrush Rebellion also ushered in the so-called wise use movement, a pro-industry backlash against environmental regulation that cast Sea Shepherd and Earth First! as prime examples of environmentalism gone bad.

Ron Arnold, radical environmentalism's sworn and mortal enemy, was the father of the wise use movement. Smart, fearless, and a deft if overly pointed writer, Arnold was originally known to environmentalists as James Watt's biographer. In 1989, he published an antienvironmental playbook called *The Wise Use Agenda*. He's happy to take credit for turning both Earth First! and the Animal Liberation Front into terrorists in the public eye. I've interviewed him quite a few times over the years, and he's always been honest and passionate and never lets me forget that he coined the term *eco-terrorist* in a series of articles in *Reason* magazine in 1983.

Ron Arnold's definition of an eco-terrorist was Dave Foreman. Or Rod Coronado.

FBI special agent Michael Fain drifted into Prescott, Arizona, in 1988 calling himself Mike Tait and fairly quickly fell into a radicalized environmentalist community that had taken root in the juniper and manzanita scrub at the base of the Bradshaw Mountains. It was an area rife with climbers and river rats and Goldwater libertarians; local Prescott College had earned a reputation for its excellent Environmental Studies program and a popular Adventure Education major. Fain had come to town to investigate a spate of high-profile sabotage in the state, including a bold attempt in 1986 to shut down Phoenix's Palo Verde nuclear power plant by shorting out the power lines. A group called the Evan Mecham Eco-Terrorist International Conspiracy (EMETIC), ironically named after the former governor of Arizona, was known to be operating in the area and had taken credit for cutting through chairlift towers at the Fairfield Snow Bowl ski area. It seems that radical action had reached a critical mass in southern Arizona, and the FBI had finally moved in to stamp it out.

Fain had very good intel, it was discovered, as he worked with a local informant who was later paid for his services. The agent soon zeroed in on Peg Millett. The sister of writer Kate Millett, author of the groundbreaking 1969 essay "Sexual Politics," Peg was a cowgirl, wilderness advocate, and an employee at the local Planned Parenthood office. She was also openly identifying herself as a part of Earth First! and was the only member of EMETIC who knew Dave Foreman.

Earth First! was the real FBI target. It seemed obvious, even at the time, that EMETIC wasn't. EMETIC didn't exist. It didn't have an office, or a newspaper, or a book written by Dave Foreman called *Ecodefense: A Field Guide to Monkeywrenching*. Earth First! had those things, even if the newspaper only had four low-paid employees at the time. Earth First! was vulnerable because it was out in the open, attempting to spread its message to the American public.

The FBI also seemed to have a distinct agenda, besides catching EMETIC. The agency name given to this operation in 1987, as revealed in documents released in 1996, was THERMCON, short for Thermite Conspiracy. Thermite is an incendiary compound often used to melt iron oxide for welds on railroad tracks, or by the military as a firebomb. The idea that Earth First! was using thermite, though, was apparently a bit of wishful thinking on the part of the federal government. In Mark Davis's trial, it would come out that Fain tried to coach Davis on the use of thermite, but Davis's preferred tool was the propane torch. The introduction of explosives had a special resonance for the Department of Justice, as it could then qualify an event as an act of domestic terrorism. THERMCON was the first time that Earth First! was investigated as a domestic terrorist movement, which involved more than fifty agents under the direction of a counterterrorism task force.

If Earth First! was the general target, Dave Foreman was the specific one. Peg Millett, then, was the connection. Fain already knew that Davis and Millett had downed the ski lift towers (Millett later admitted it), but rather than act on that information, he used them to rope in Foreman, who had no connection with them. After romancing Millett over the course of a year, coming just shy of having an affair with her (she was married), and winning both her trust and that of the exceptionally wary Davis, Fain helped hatch the plan to take down the power lines to the Central Arizona Project irrigation system. Fain picked the spot and bought the supplies, and he also made sure his Chevy truck was filled with weapons when it was found on the site, a classic agent provocateur.

Fain finally met Foreman and had him sign a copy of *Ecodefense* for someone in EMETIC. This tenuous connection between Foreman and EMETIC was the only one that held up in court.

Then came the night of May 30, 1989, and the new version of the Monkey Wrench Gang drove up to the electrical pylon, comprising Mark Davis (as Hayduke), a soft-spoken biologist named Dr. Marc Baker (as Doc Sarvis), Peg Millett (as Bonnie Abbzug), and Special Agent Mike Fain (as Seldom Seen Smith). In fact, he was less than seldom seen: he disappeared. As Davis cut the tower and Baker looked on, Millett and Fain went in separate directions into the desert night to keep watch. A flare then popped high in the sky, presumably sent up by Fain, and agents swarmed in. None of the monkeywrenchers ever saw Fain again.

THERMCON was the beginning of a government counterinsurgency. A more militant era had begun.

The movement was about to go the way of the American Indian Movement (AIM), the Black Panthers, and the Reverend Dr. Martin Luther King Jr.'s Southern Christian Leadership Conference. The FBI program used to destroy those groups was called COINTELPRO, which stood for Counter-Intelligence Program, and its stated goal was to "expose, disrupt, misdirect, discredit, or otherwise

neutralize" the activities of groups deemed to be politically dissident. Now, twenty years later, the feds looked to be doing the same
thing to the radical environmental movement.

The same night the trio was busted in the desert, Dave Foreman
was pulled out of his bed at gunpoint. He later pleaded to a misde-
meanor in a complicated deal that kept all five conspirators from incriminating one another. The fifth alleged conspirator arrested was
Davis's girlfriend, Ilse Asplund. More than two dozen other EF! sym-
pathizers were either subpoenaed or questioned, and movement
houses were raided in Washington State, Montana, Arizona, and
Colorado. The idea of massive conspiracy charges swept through the
network, but, at least this time, nothing came of them.

"They were clearly after Earth First!," Foreman said. "If you
look at the history of the FBI in trying to disrupt and destroy
dissident groups . . . especially in the light of COINTELPRO
operations . . . that's what they do."

Wyoming attorney Gerry Spence, who had successfully sued
Kerr-McGee oil company in 1976 over the death of whistle-blower
Karen Silkwood, flew down to Tucson in his private jet and took
Foreman's case pro bono. He explained that the case of the Arizona
Five, as they were now known, was a battle of principles. "In the
Monkey Trial, the great trial of Scopes and Darrow, the issue was
about ideas," he said, referring to the legal battle over the theory of
evolution, which still resonates today. "Here, the issue that we're
dealing with is the very survival of the Earth."

FIVE Global Investigations

REVOLUTION MADE THE wild azalea hot with fragrance and the heart bloom. By the end of 1989, Rod and Jonathan had rented a house with a few friends in Scotts Valley, a progressive mountain town deep in the redwoods just a few miles up Highway 17 from Santa Cruz, and the house was their commune, their Bloomsbury. Some days they couldn't believe that they actually lived in this place; it was a five-bedroom pad with a hot tub and redwood trees jutting right up through the deck and into the coastal mountain air. They paid fifteen hundred dollars a month for the whole place and split it five ways. Jonathan was working for a carpet-cleaning business in Santa Cruz, and Rod had a standing invitation to work for his dad in nearby Morgan Hill. They were always broke but somehow had just enough money for weed and co-op potatoes and a case of beer.

The place rang with music, but it wasn't all Rod's Crass, Conflict, and Chumbawamba. He was the only one in the house into anarchist hardcore, and Jonathan was more partial to the Grateful Dead. In fact, other than the time Rod's housemates dragged him to see the Dead in Eugene, Oregon, in 1990, or when they went to hear Earth First! troubadours like Joanne Rand, he never saw concerts with them. They were more into radical folk like Billy Bragg and Michelle Shocked—and even pop groups like the Eagles. Jonathan would try to turn Rod on to stuff like Edie Brickell and the New Bohemians.

They were twenty-three years old and living the double life of the guerrilla fighter: during the day, their circle comprised mostly Hunt Sabs and members of another organization they had put together for local actions, the Progressive Animal Rights Alliance, (PARA), which, according to the alliance's Web site, worked to educate people about animal cruelty. PARA worked on issues like factory farming, hunting, and rodeos and opposed these things through public demonstration.

At night, Rod and some of his friends were the Western Wildlife Unit of the ALF.

As the crowns of the redwoods raked the stars out of the fog, they sat in the hot tub with girlfriends and comrades and fugitives and curious students from UC Santa Cruz, passing the puff, talking strategy and revolution. It was a lot of bed-hopping, but Rod shared his room with his girlfriend, whom we'll call Jan, and they were tight. Still, between them lay the knowledge that their relationship was never as important as the cause. Or at least, that's how Rod viewed the arrangement.

Jonathan had a different approach: he rarely brought his steady girlfriend to the house. He didn't want his worlds to mix. He tried to maintain a relationship by splitting his time—and passion— equally; when he was on a campaign, he was gone completely, and when he was back, he was with his girl and otherwise unavailable. This irritated Rod. For weeks at a time, Jonathan was just not around. Rod was always ready to go, even if it meant a breakup with Jan. Rod and Jonathan's relationship, like the movement itself, was volatile.

In 1989, Rod went off to do a solo action that would give him a new direction. He'd been asked by a group back east to investigate a fox farm outside Pittsburgh, Pennsylvania, and he flew there alone. He drove out to a remote rural location on his first day in town and crept into the woods with a video camera. He knew it was the right place when he saw the tall wooden fence behind the house, so he crouched in the brush for an hour in a light rain, until he was certain all was quiet. It was the middle of the day, but he felt safe as he scrambled over the fence and dropped in among the residents.

Rows of elevated cages stretched across the enclosure, each with a wooden house inside, and the place held a total of about forty foxes. Upon seeing Rod, they began the rapid pacing that researchers call "stereotypical" behavior, and every once in a while one would let fly a piercing bark that rang across the farm. Rod had been asked to look into the place because of allegations of abuse, and he saw pretty quickly that—no matter what else he found—these animals were suffering from the same psychological maladies that haunted all caged animals. Bits of fur formed a pathway inside each cage, a testament to thousands and thousands of turns with nowhere to go, each trail a visible manifestation of neurosis and frustration. He walked up and down the rows, videotaping the occupants up close as they paced and sniffed at him through the wire.

Fur farming is only about one hundred years old, and during the 1980s and 1990s many farms still started by livetrapping wild animals. That meant these caged predators carried wilderness in their genes, and even farm mink are much less domesticated than cows or pigs. The foxes' obvious struggles against the cages left Rod depressed and enervated. Back in California, he decided to enlist the Western Wildlife Unit to free them. The whole cell then flew out to Pennsylvania, but the trip was cut short. The group made a fairly unusual strategic move in contacting a local ALF cell to help with handling the animals, but once the local cell saw the farm, with the house only a few steps from the fox enclosure, it backed out. The Pennsylvania crew wasn't used to going in without inside help, and it didn't like the idea of spending many nights of surveillance making sure of the farmer's routines and security measures. So the raid was scrubbed.

Rod was disappointed because the video he had shot belonged to someone else, and it never saw the light of day. He was fed up with dead ends. He and Jonathan acknowledged to each other that they had become "mercenaries for the movement," doing dirty work for other public organizations. Membership-based groups like Friends of Animals (FOA), PETA, In Defense of Animals, (IDA), and Fund for Animals followed the movements of the Hunt Sabs and often jumped in to help fund some public aspects of their campaigns. Advocacy groups had hired Rod and Jonathan to do banner hangings and to carry out civil disobedience campaigns for media impact. But if they were writing a check for bail money, they'd also take the credit, trumpeting to the media about how IDA had stopped a bison hunt or saved the tule elk, rather than the Hunt Sabs, which was an issue for both Rod and Jonathan.

The pair struck on the idea of forming their own freelance agency called Global Investigations. Jonathan had been a photographer since he was fifteen and had been shooting during the Hunt Sab actions, but he wanted the images to elicit more outrage, like the footage of the head-injury lab at the University of Pennsylvania. For a fee, they would get images no other video crew could get; they could even sell images to the mainstream press.

In May 1990, the green was coming upon the West in layers of incandescent new grass and bruised blue hepatica and lupine and fast rivers. Tall cumulus still black with spring rain tumbled over the tops of the passes. Rod and Jonathan rolled along in Jonathan's beige, mid-eighties Ford Ranger pickup, jubilant to be on the road, on a mission, camping and covering expenses to boot. It was Global Investigations' first assignment. Despite Jonathan's naturally downbeat assessment of the human race, he was something of a foil to Rod, with his relentless push to the next destination. Jonathan was tolerant of the road and insisted on breaks, on making detours to parks and eating and drinking in the most broken-down diners and jackalope dive bars. Rod would be more likely to strike up conversations when they stopped in those places, but if he had his druthers, they wouldn't stop at all. They brought along a stash of all their favorite cassette tapes, and the pot smoke streamed over the roads behind them.

Rod and Jan had sold the idea of Global Investigations to Priscilla Feral at Friends of Animals, in Connecticut. His principal contact at FOA had been Betsy Swart, who had coordinated some civil disobedience actions with him when she'd been with In Defense of Animals. Swart declined to be interviewed for this book, as she doesn't work for Friends of Animals anymore, but Feral was very clear about the assignment: the organization wanted to expose living conditions on the 660 fur farms then in operation in the United States, and it was interested in the most grisly footage they could get. Some well-known footage of anal electrocution of foxes in Europe had caused outrage there, and she needed something of that nature.

Feral said there was no long-term hire, just a promise to pay the expenses of videotaping one particular farm. Coronado's version was that it was a standing offer. He said that he hadn't done the research yet and that he and Paul were to be paid ten dollars an hour to do research on multiple farms until they found the footage they needed.

"There was no employment scenario, no fee," said Feral. "If there were expenses, we would have paid them. Most of these people operate on a shoestring budget."

"After that one meeting here, I never saw him again," she noted. "They came to *us*."

The first fur farm on their list led them to a remote Montana town and a winding dirt road where, at one point in a bend, they could see cages below a hill on which a mobile home stood. These weren't the long, low mink barns they'd expected of a big fur operation—mink barns were really just long, skinny roofs and open sides, sheltering hundreds of wire cages side by side. But they decided to check it out anyway, parking the truck in the woods some distance away and pulling on their disguises. Whenever they went out on investigations, Jonathan said, they wore green trousers and tan cotton shirts to pass as California Department of Fish and Game rangers. It wasn't an actual uniform, and they didn't have badges and shirt patches, which was pretty much a dead giveaway, but they did have Fish and Game hats. Their cover was that they were biologists tracking hawk migrations from California.

They hiked a big circle around the trailer to where they could see the cages with binoculars. Even before they could see them, however, the smell told them the cages weren't empty. With cameras rolling, they approached and found a wolf pup, a wolverine, a mountain lion, a coyote, and a number of foxes. These weren't domestic farm animals but wild creatures that had been captured; Rod found out later that this was a business that loaned wild animals for nature films, amongst other commercial uses. There were less than a dozen animals in total, but the sight of these powerful creatures pacing in dilapidated wood-and-wire cages made Rod and Jonathan sick. The coyote never even budged. He just followed their every move with his lowered eyes, hunched over in defeat.

This was something new for the two liberationists. Every impulse told them to open the cages and flee. But they had agreed beforehand that they couldn't do that; freeing the animals would put every fur farm in the state on alert, and they'd have a tougher time getting the footage they needed. The depressed gaze of the coyote was an absolute indictment. Rod and Jonathan immediately felt they'd made a pact with the devil, and that feeling would stay with them for the duration of the Global Investigations project. Animals would be helped by this work, they reasoned. But the animals on this farm would most likely die in cages.

They didn't get much time to snivel. On their retreat, they were detected by the trailer resident's dog, which charged down the hill barking wildly. Rod and Jonathan both sank back into the brush, hoping that no one looking down from the trailer would be able to make out human figures hiding there. The dog continued barking a few feet away from them until someone finally emerged from the trailer and told it to shut up. Frustrated, the dog relented and went back inside. Jonathan and Rod just lay there staring at each other, their hearts pounding in their ears.

The guilt accumulated fast and pushed them to make this work, to make the project successful. They moved immediately to the next place on their list, another rural operation called Fraser Fur Farm in Ronan, Montana, on the Blackfeet Indian reservation. On the way, they stopped and FedExed their tapes to FOA headquarters. This would be their routine after every stop. The tapes weren't evidence of a terrible crime—trespassing, at worst—but they were proof that someone was casing fur farms for further action, and their discovery would put the whole industry on alert, so the two didn't want to get stopped for so much as a traffic ticket with these tapes on them.

They couldn't get too close to the Fraser farm but did get some footage from where they lay, hidden in the fence line. The other Montana addresses they had either were too risky or had been abandoned for some time. There may have been 660 of these farms nationwide, but they weren't easy to locate. Furriers were under fire in the press, and farmers weren't hanging their shingles out for all to see. Rod had located a few U.S. trade publications, such as *Fur World* and *Fur Rancher*, as well as numerous French-language Canadian fur journals, and had begun poring over them. Some of them had advertisements for breeding operations in the back.

On the way back to California, however, they were thirty miles east of Salt Lake City on I-80 when they passed through the town of Coalville, Utah, and there they stopped dead in their tracks.

From the road, they saw what they had to believe was the biggest fur farm ever, acres and acres of barns. They pulled over to investigate and discovered other farms as well. The town is ringed by high mountains on the backside of the Wasatch Range, a small community high and cold, and its economy, which had once run on a vein of coal there, now clearly ran at least partly on fur. The biggest farm, which Rod and Jonathan had seen from the interstate, had

about 180 fox cages right along the highway that they could investigate without being seen from the farmer's house, as they were shielded
from view by mink barns. Parking the truck in town, they unloaded
their mountain bikes and rode along the shoulder of I-80 back to the
farm. They ditched the bikes in the brush, crossed a railroad track,
and quickly scurried behind some farm equipment, then over the
short fence and into the fox enclosure.

After a safe interval, they broke out the cameras and went to
work.

"It was the middle of the day, and we started filming the foxes,"
said Jonathan. "I come around the rows of pens for foxes, right, and
I look down the aisle, and there's this dog, a black lab looking right
at me. We locked eyes. Luckily the wind was going towards me,
and I bolted right away. And the farmer came out, and he started
feeding."

When the farmer arrived, the dog turned his attention to his
master. The man got on an ATV rigged with feeding equipment,
pouring a thick protein gruel from a tank through a hose. He came
on them too fast for them to split, so they had to hide. Rod leaped
behind a plow. Jonathan rolled under an old dump truck parked in
tall grass.

"I was dressed in all green. But he was literally five feet from me.
And I was lying under this truck the whole time, not moving, with
that whole fight-or-flight thing, like, 'I could just run now,' but I
knew I couldn't. I never saw the dog again, luckily. But the farmer,
he drives around with his ATV, and I could see his feet. He was feeding all the mink inside, and we zipped out and did our filming and
bolted out."

But what reason did these farmers have to be suspicious? He was
doing what he did every day, and security had never been necessary
there. The fences were just to keep the animals in. In a couple years,
this same farm would be on high alert, and some of the facilities they
visited would have security systems and weapons at the ready. But

on this day, all the residents of Coalville would remember was a couple of mountain bikers riding along the edge of the highway who looked like they were from out of town.

Rod had already begun to wonder just how long he was going to confine his work to simple videotaping.

SIX "We're Sitting Ducks, Now"

MAY 24, 1990, broke as a more lighthearted day in the revolution for the residents of the house in Scotts Valley. Jonathan, Rod, their friend Avi Baum, and another Santa Cruz local we'll call Russell, who was a key organizer in PARA, got stoned in the hot tub and then tried to write some songs on a few electric guitars they'd recently acquired in a half-serious attempt to form a rock band.

Musicians often stayed at the house. Folksy balladeer Joanne Rand, who was a regular at Earth First! Round River Rendezvous campouts, had stayed there. Later that afternoon, they were expecting a house visit from EF! troubadours Darryl Cherney and Judi Bari, who were going to play that night at a forest-defense benefit that the house had helped set up in Santa Cruz. Coronado had first met Cherney in 1987 on an EF! action to oppose California mountain lion hunting. Now Cherney and Bari were spearheading an ambitious forest occupation they were calling Mississippi Summer in the Redwoods, or more plainly, Redwood Summer.

The formerly family-owned Pacific Lumber Company (PALCO), in California's Humboldt County, had been taken over by a Texas corporation called Maxxam, which had begun clear-cutting old-growth forests in an unapologetic push for a quick profit. Bari, who was a carpenter and a union organizer with Industrial Workers of the World—the Wobblies!—felt that the only way to get the world to care was to get thousands of tree huggers into the forest to bear witness to the destruction. Back in 1964, after the federal Civil Rights Act was passed, civil rights groups sent "freedom riders" to Mississippi to support black residents who were being murdered, raped, beaten, and arrested as they signed up other new black voters. Bari and others dared to compare that situation to what was happening in California's North Coast forests in 1990. The last stands of old-growth redwoods and Douglas firs, some of which had been standing there before the birth of Christ, were needlessly going to the blade when other stocks were available. A statewide referendum to stop the cut was on the ballot, and all they had to do was slow the saws until November.

Jonathan had gone up to the North Coast to sit in on one of the Redwood Summer organizing meetings and had decided it was too mainstream for the Scotts Valley house. In fact, they'd taken to calling it Deadwood Bummer, because the organizers were committed to soft mass actions—marches, forest occupations, rallies. Redwood Summer was advertised as nonviolent and family friendly. It wasn't hard to imagine the endless consensus meetings at camps in the woods. It also wasn't hard to see that some of the hippies would be subjected to violence by incensed PALCO employees and locals. Rod thought the organizers were "leading lambs to the slaughter." Still, there was a good chance the protest could generate a media feeding frenzy, and he and his crew respected Cherney and Bari and supported their recruitment efforts.

In 1989, around the time the FBI's THERMCON investigation was trying to take down Dave Foreman, Cherney put out a funny little cassette album called *They Sure Don't Make Hippies Like They Used To!* The drawing on the cover of the cassette, which could have been the cover illo from any issue of the *Earth First! Journal*, showed a man holding a monkey wrench and a woman with a gas can in green Earth First! shirts walking away from a burning bulldozer.

One of the songs off that album, "Spike a Tree for Jesus," was played in movement houses up and down California throughout the winter of 1989–90, including Rod and Jonathan's.

> *Now as Jesus he hung on that cross there*
> *It was not some thing that he liked*

And his last words were father I would not be here
If all of the trees had been spiked!

Of course, driving sixty-penny spikes into old-growth trees to thwart chain saws was not funny at all to the people whose job it was to cut them down. One twenty-three-year-old worker in a Louisiana-Pacific mill in Cloverdale, California, suffered a broken jaw in 1987 when his big mill blade shattered on a spike, sending metal shards into his face. When done respectfully, spiked stands were supposed to be marked with spray paint or another such indicator so that lumberjacks and mill workers would know to avoid them. Often they weren't marked at all.

The Cloverdale incident seemed to legitimate violence against all tree spikers. Up in Montana, where Rod and Jonathan had been videotaping, Republican congressman Ron Marlenee had advised loggers at a 1989 campaign rally to "spike an Earth First!er."

Bari had renounced tree spiking, and she and Cherney hoped to put a stop to this escalation of violence. Cherney was a thirty-five-year-old Woody Guthrie type with a jangly guitar and a mass of curly hair who played most of his messages for laughs. He was from around Garberville, a mill town in Humboldt County, and he was dead serious about his mission to save the big trees, but he clung to comedy as a way to get folks to listen.

Bari was forty, and her dream was not only to unionize the sawmills but to radicalize them with an environmental consciousness that would make stewardship a top priority in the woods. She was a talker and a haranguer and a hero to many near her home in the mill town of Willits, California, where she lived with her two young daughters. She was a frequent collaborator with Cherney and played a sloppy, meetinghouse fiddle with a big grin on her face as if it had been drawn there by R. Crumb.

The Scotts Valley house was rocking with the boys' own attempts at movement music when they got a phone call from the concert's primary organizer. Something had happened to Bari and Cherney, he said. There wasn't a lot of information, but something serious had happened. The show was postponed until a later date. The guys in the house didn't have enough information to know whether they should be concerned or not. About an hour later, there was a knock at the door. Avi Baum went to answer it.

"Rod, there's a sheriff at the door who wants to talk to you," he said nonchalantly as he reentered the room.

"Fuck you," Coronado said, laughing.

Baum laughed too. "No, seriously, there is a sheriff's deputy at the door."

Coronado poked his head out the door and saw a deputy peering into their kitchen window.

"You Rodney Coronado?" he asked.

"I am," Coronado said reluctantly.

"Were you expecting a Judi Bari and a Darryl Cherney to visit you here tonight?"

"Yeah. Why?"

"Were you aware that a car bomb went off in the car being driven by Ms. Bari and Mr. Cherney today?"

Rod went pale. He asked if they were injured. The deputy said that both of them had gone to the hospital with serious injuries. Then he began asking questions. What did Rod know of their trip to the Bay Area? What were they doing there? Who were they staying with in Berkeley the night before? Reeling from the news and trying to figure out what this bombing might mean, if it was true, Rod unself-consciously answered the officer's questions. Until he started digging a little too deep.

"Whose truck is that out there? Is that Lee Dessaux's truck?"

"No," said Rod, snapping back to reality. "That's Jonathan's."

"Can you tell me about your own whereabouts around noon today?" the deputy asked over his notepad.

Rod was now fully alert like he'd just had oxygen shot into his brain. "I'm sorry, I can't really talk to you anymore about this," he said, moving back inside and shutting the door on the deputy. The sudden turn in the questioning had told him exactly what was happening: if Bari and Cherney had really been car-bombed, the police were going to use the investigation to shake down the entire movement. Instead of searching for the bomber among loggers, antienvironmentalists, union busters, or some other opposition group, they were probably going to try to pin it on the eco-radicals.

And that's exactly how it went down. Within a few hours, Bari and Cherney were arrested and charged with carrying explosives, a claim so clearly contradicting the evidence that the Oakland district attorney and the United States Attorney's Office later had to drop the charges against them. Bari was arrested while still in intensive care clinging to life. Cherney got treatment and was arrested during questioning.

Bari and Cherney had attended a boisterous meeting the night before at a movement house in Berkeley occupied by members of Seeds of Peace, an outfit formed during the 1986 Great Peace March for Global Nuclear Disarmament. Seeds would provide the kitchens, toilets, and other logistical support for Redwood Summer. They met until the small hours, and the musicians got a late start in the morning for Santa Cruz. Bari was driving her white Subaru wagon, and Cherney was riding shotgun. As they pulled to a stop on Park Boulevard near MacArthur Boulevard, in East Oakland, the car hit a pothole, and the entire vehicle suddenly lifted off the ground and popped in a huge explosion.

A pipe bomb had been placed under the driver's seat and was detonated by a motion trigger. Bari had been sitting on it the entire ride. It was wrapped in finishing nails that were driven through her body, as was a seat spring. Her pelvis was shattered, and she had internal injuries. The rumpled car seemed to settle right into the pavement, with huge holes blown through the floorboard and the front seat. A Seeds member named Shannon Marr was just in front of Bari in her own car, close enough to feel the Subaru suddenly puff outward everywhere, as if it had been instantly inflated by a gargantuan, noisy shout. Window glass flew hundreds of feet in every direction. Inside the car, Bari was conscious, and Cherney, who was temporarily deafened in one ear and had numerous lacerations across his face, told her over and over how much he loved her and that she was going to live. Bari said later that she didn't believe him.

Strangely, the Oakland police were on the scene within minutes, and Special Agent Frank Doyle, the chief bombing investigator for the Bay Area office of the FBI, was right behind them, the first federal agent to arrive. Only two months before the bombing, Doyle had led a paid training seminar for Louisiana-Pacific employees near Bari's hometown, in which he had built pipe bombs right in front of them, giving them step-by-step instructions. Given the speed with which the FBI was on the scene of the car-bombing, it was almost, said Bari's attorney Dennis Cunningham, like they had been standing nearby "with their fingers in their ears."

Bari hovered near death for days but eventually pulled through. Permanently disabled, she was not expected to walk again but beat the odds and learned to get around with a cane, before succumbing to breast cancer in 1997. Five years later, in 2002, after a court battle that lasted eleven years, a jury found that the Oakland Police Department and the FBI had purposely ignored real evidence and instead concocted a web of false evidence and lies to the press in an effort to frame the two tree huggers. The disgusted jurors, some of whom told the press later that the FBI and the Oakland police had continued to lie to them on the witness stand, awarded $4.4 million to Cherney and Bari's estate.

In the hours after the bombing, Coronado and the others in the Scotts Valley house didn't have a lot of details, but the only thing they could believe was that someone had tried to kill Bari and Cherney. Scores of people involved with the movement could have told you on that day, with great certainty, that the two didn't advocate bombing and would not carry their own pipe bomb in their car— including the Seeds of Peace members, who were forced to sit on their lawn for hours in handcuffs while the FBI turned their house inside out, carting away computers and address books. But who would have placed that bomb? Coronado's first thought was not of one of the Stompers, a pro-timber group that had sent Bari and Cherney death threats. His first thought was of COINTELPRO.

Rod Coronado was an Indian. In 1990, there weren't too many politicized Native Americans around who didn't know that the FBI's COINTELPRO had murdered Indian activists and destroyed the American Indian Movement in the early 1970s. And in Oakland? The city had been home to the Black Panthers, and the FBI and the Oakland Police Department had collaborated under COINTELPRO to orchestrate fantastically complex—and thoroughly documented—snitch-jacketing and undercover campaigns, frame-ups, and raids that had resulted directly in the deaths of Black Panther Party members and helped drive that movement underground in the late 1960s and early 1970s.

"I thought, 'We're sitting ducks, now. They know who we are, and they know where the movement is headed,'" Coronado said. The deputy had come straight to their house, known his name, Paul's, and Dessaux's. There had been a lot of articles in the *Animal Rights Reporter*, a now-defunct national newsletter dedicated to the animal rights movement, about how industry groups were ramping up the rhetoric against groups like the Hunt Sabs, naming them specifically as targets of violence.

"We were aware of what had been done to the Black Panthers and to AIM, and we saw this could be the first moves of stuff being done to *us*. It was time to put up or shut up. And I wasn't going to be able to do that living comfortably aboveground, smoking pot and playing music with the most high-profile activists in town," Rod said.

He felt he had a target painted on his back, and the Santa Cruz activists had already come to the attention of the feds.

On April 22 of that year, Earth Day, heavy electrical power lines had been toppled in nearby Watsonville, just south of Santa Cruz, in a direct action by an unknown group. Released communiqués from

the Earth Night Action Group—a play on the name Earth Day—
explained that the action was meant to dramatize dependence on
coal- and oil-burning power plants that poisoned indigenous people's
lands and contributed heavily to CO_2 emissions. The feds reported
to the press that they recognized the Santa Cruz area as a hotbed for
eco-radicals and that they had connected the crime to the Animal
Liberation Front—but no one ever came to question Rod about it,
and he denied having anything to do with it. And still, here they
were at his door. He wasn't afraid to have them try to pin the power
line incident on him, because he didn't do it. But he was afraid that
agents would just send a message, or discredit him, by planting a
bomb on him. He didn't own a car at this time, but he wondered
every day after if Jonathan's truck was carrying that bomb.

To add to the paranoia, similarly suspicious bombings were happening in Britain. During June 1990, two car-bombings attributed
to the ALF targeted animal researchers in the U.K. The first bomb
slightly injured a veterinary surgeon. The second fell off the car of a
university psychologist and critically injured a thirteen-month-old
child. Both were of a type the ALF never used, and the press office
condemned the attacks, saying they were the work of provocateurs.
A few days later, a huntsman in Somerset was arrested for bombing
his own Land Rover in hopes of discrediting the ALF. On top of the
Bari and Cherney news, lots of people wondered if some kind of international counterintelligence campaign to discredit the radical
movement had begun.

Coronado wasn't afraid to escalate his tactics, but now he felt
someone was forcing his hand. Agents had set up Dave Foreman in
Arizona. Someone had tried to kill Cherney and Bari, and law enforcement seemed to be protecting the bombers. For months, he had
felt himself getting pulled toward more militant action. Now he admitted that nonviolence was no insurance against being murdered in
this line of work.

SEVEN

The Triumph of Jim Perez

LATE SUMMER WAS on the cottonwoods when Rod walked into the Montana Department of Fish, Wildlife and Parks office in Kalispell, and introduced himself as Jim Perez, a small-time rancher from Redding, California, who was interested in getting a start in the fur industry. He was looking specifically for breeder foxes, he explained. He had a buyer for fox fur and had heard there were good breeders in this area. The uniformed officer working the counter there was a wildlife biologist named Bruce Campbell, and the two of them struck up a friendly conversation. It just so happened that Campbell also raised fur animals, though he raised mink, bobcats, and lynx, he explained, and on a much smaller scale than others in the area.

Campbell was easy to like. Coronado took to him right away. His obvious expertise regarding wildlife made him a font of information, and Coronado was like a sponge. In any other context, they would have become friends, and to a certain extent they did. After an hour of conversation, Campbell noted that he knew of a few farmers in the area who bred foxes, and he jotted down their contacts, wishing "Jim" luck in his quest. As Coronado left the office, he was so excited he couldn't help breaking out with a huge smile.

Rod had already been in Montana for about a week, traveling with his colleague Russell and staying at the Kalispell home of a Sea Shepherd colleague. On this trip, he was trying a new tactic: Global Investigations would have to take false identities and meet farmers face-to-face.

All summer, he and Jonathan had tried to get their footage without confronting farmers directly, and the summer had been mostly a bust. There had been excellent scouting: Jonathan had donned his Fish and Game hat and gleaned fur-farm contacts from a feed shop called Northwest Fur Breeders Cooperative in Edmonds, Washington, and the two of them had traveled all over rural Washington and Oregon following leads. But there wasn't much to show for it. In June, they had tried to find the experimental mink farm at Oregon State University in Corvallis, but had found only the chicken barns. At the farm of Clarence Kyriss in Sweet Home, Oregon, they had gotten great footage of caged mink that had cannibalized their tails as a result of stress, but it just wasn't dramatic enough. Besides, Jonathan was so nervous about getting caught that he didn't want to use the light on his camera very much or stay on-site very long, so each of his video clips was only about fifteen to twenty seconds long.

Rod had also taken more than a month out of the campaign to pursue a privately funded campaign of his own in Louisiana, a very serious attempt to liberate six of the famous Silver Spring Monkeys from a heavily fortified primate-research center in the swamps near Lake Pontchartrain. He had spent many nights inside the compound and was increasingly infuriated by his inability to find the specific animals among the four thousand or so primates in captivity there. Everything was pushing him closer to the brink of dramatic destruction, but he was still holding out. He wanted Global Investigations to be a success.

He never stopped obsessing over footage of killing and skinning. With fall coming on hard, he thought he'd get what he needed in Montana.

Rod had already paid a few midnight visits to a big mink farm in the Bitterroot Valley south of Missoula, which also had foxes, as well as an operation raising sixty to eighty bobcats owned by Cole McPherson near the tiny township of Lolo, but he still wasn't getting an insider's view of the industry. Friends of Animals had made it plain: what they really needed was something horrific and shocking— literally shocking.

Rod was there with Russell because he doubted he could get that footage with Jonathan. Rod felt his longtime friend was not only too worried about being caught but also too impulsive and sensitive: What if they were invited to dinner and the farmer decided to throw some steaks on the grill? Jonathan, admittedly, wasn't going to be able to stand by while an animal was killed. He would have to intervene, even if it meant blowing their cover.

Russell was a good replacement. He didn't do much of the videotaping, but he was a reliable lookout and projected an aura of calm competence, exactly what Rod needed. He could take care of everything else.

And so, the stop at Fish, Wildlife and Parks in Kalispell. Jim Perez would need to move fast and establish himself in the local community in order to film the pelting season, which started right around Thanksgiving.

Campbell had unwittingly given this effort a huge boost. Rod recognized one of the addresses he had given them, the farm of Stu Fraser in the nearby town of Ronan. Rod and Jonathan had surreptitiously videotaped that operation on their first trip to Montana last spring. Now, however, Rod and Russell had an introduction. They jumped in their van, which they had borrowed from a Sea Shepherd pal in Seattle, and drove to Ronan, a tiny crossroads straight south on Highway 93. There they stopped to call the number from a pay phone.

Stu Fraser got on the line and said he wasn't raising foxes anymore, but only mink, bobcats, and lynx, the animals Rod and Jonathan had seen on their prior late-night visit. Rod said he was interested in those, too, and added, "Bruce said you had a pretty interesting operation. Would you mind if we stopped in to get a few pointers while we're in town?"

"Come on over," said Fraser.

Soon they pulled into Fraser Fur Farm. Russell seemed calm, like this was nothing out of the ordinary, but Rod was uncharacteristically rattled. At least one of the men he saw working on the farm wore a sidearm, and the place looked like an armed camp. Of course, it wasn't; it was just a bunch of farmhands moving up and down long barns holding thousands of mink. But when they looked at him, he felt their eyes were full of suspicion and threat.

He was imagining things. No one was raiding American fur farms in 1990, and the ALF was a bunch of freaks who only attacked university labs in liberal bastions on the coasts. Besides, he and Russell were both generally able to separate the fur issue from the farmers who made this their livelihood: they could still have a civil discussion with a man like Fraser, and even like him. Rod walked up to the first worker they encountered and asked for Fraser. He took them up to the main house, where Fraser greeted them on the porch.

They shook hands and immediately fell to talking. They hoped to get into fur farming, Rod said, dropping Campbell's name as if they were old friends. Fraser was equally casual and, like Campbell, seemed to trust Rod just enough to get friendly. Rod asked if they might look around, and though this was slightly unusual, Fraser led them on a tour.

Lynx were the first thing on Rod's mind. He'd never seen them in captivity up close, and he wanted to see how such large, private cats dealt with such tiny cages. And how they might be sprung. As they stood in front of the first cage, Rod noted, "This big female here has a kind of deformed foot."

"That's because it was in a trap," Fraser explained. These weren't domestic animals; he had started with wild stock, livetrapping a few lynx in the nearby Mission Mountains and bringing them back to his ranch to breed. The toes on this one had been broken in a steel-jawed leghold trap. The thought of the lynx being not even one generation out of the wild made Rod's heart turn. This big female had memories of freedom. She backed into the corner of her cage and gave them a fierce stare as they approached, growling softly.

Rod asked about the market value of lynx and why Fraser raised them instead of foxes.

"And how do you kill them?" he asked finally.

"With a .22 to the head," Fraser said.

When Campbell's name came up again, Fraser said he'd sold the biologist a few bobcats and also a breeding pair of lynx. Rod asked about the price for bobcat pelts, and Fraser was pretty dismissive, saying that it didn't actually pay much to raise them for fur but that there was a secondary market for them as pets that was doing OK. In total, he only had about twenty-five bobcats and fifty lynx.

But he had eight thousand to ten thousand mink. It was a massive operation. They walked the barns as "Jim" grilled the man about the color phases he was breeding for—mostly the superdark brown-as-black variety that was a specialty of the North American mink industry and was marketed as "blackglama" mink. Again, the agitated animals dashed and spun in the cages as the men came by. As Rod kept asking questions about what exactly constituted the highest-quality pelt for market, Fraser steered the tour into the pelting room to show him for real.

Standing amid the skinning and drying equipment, Fraser asked his son-in-law to grab a mink. He donned his heavy gloves and returned in a minute with a squirming, fighting little predator trying to get his needlelike teeth into his captor. He lifted it close to them as Fraser ran his hand over the fur so they could see the downy, super-light hair that lay beneath the outer "guard" hair. As soon as that down was gone, it would be time to pelt out.

But that was still months away. Rod and Russell had been there more than an hour and decided that was enough for one day. As they left, Rod promised to be in touch about buying some breeder animals from Fraser soon.

They checked out a few more farms and made notes. Later, over a camp-stove dinner, the two were high on the idea that they'd successfully infiltrated the industry. They also agreed that this measured, farm-by-farm investigation had another upside. At each one, they would make notes about how it could be sabotaged: a section of fence that could be cut, for instance, or easy entrances to locked barns. If the videotape didn't have the desired effect in Congress or with the public, they'd be back.

Returning to Kalispell, Rod rang up Bruce Campbell again, and Campbell invited the pair to visit his home in Lakeside, just south of Kalispell on the northwest shore of Flathead Lake, where he ran his own fur operation.

Later that day, they found Campbell out in his mink barns, which were much smaller than those they'd just seen at Fraser's place. Campbell had about three hundred mink and, in a separate barn, four bobcats and the two lynx he'd purchased from Stu Fraser. As at other farms Rod had visited, the six cats were held in welded wire cages about five feet square.

Once again, Rod found that Campbell was easy to like. He was a career wildlife biologist, and he confessed to Rod that he'd given up hunting some years earlier for personal reasons but still clung to his fur operation out of interest in breeding and raising the animals. He was an avid outdoorsman—and what an outdoors! The Flathead Valley was high and wild, the air filled with the drone of busy summer insects and the winds sweetened by pine as they swept down off the surrounding Salish, Mission, and Flathead mountains. In 1990, Lakeside was a little stopover of about fifteen hundred people on Highway 93, one of the gateways to Glacier National Park to the northeast, and a cold blue smell of lake water suffused the summers there.

The three of them talked about the breeding of Campbell's mink, the quality of their fur, the state of the business, and where Campbell sold his pelts. They also talked about the incredible hiking and mountain biking opportunities in Lakeside and Kalispell, some favorite trails, camps, and even political issues regarding Fish, Wildlife and Parks. Most important, Campbell invited Rod and Russell to come back in December to videotape that year's mink pelting. It wasn't electrocuting foxes, but it was still a huge victory.

Rod stopped at a pay phone in Lakeside and rang up another contact Campbell had given them, Gered Huggans of the Huggans Rocky Mountain Fur Company, in Hamilton, about 150 miles south, and arranged a meeting with him the next day. By now, Rod was getting good at the pitch, and Jim Perez was starting to feel like a familiar spirit in the local fur-farming scene.

The next day, Rod and Russell said their good-byes to their friends in Kalispell and headed south on Highway 93 to Missoula, an important college town in the world of radical environmentalism and home from 1990 to 1993 to the offices of the *Earth First! Journal*. The Wild Rockies Earth First! offices there were a base of operations for many of radical environmentalism's best-known names, including representatives of Earth First!, Greenpeace, and several predator projects and forest campaigns. The place was crawling with Rod's colleagues.

On this trip, however, Rod may have stopped in to say hello for a few minutes, but the visit was brief. By the afternoon, he and Russell were well south in the old mining town of Hamilton, a small city of three thousand or so and home to a couple biomedical facilities, including Rocky Mountain Laboratories. Rod had discovered in his research that the lab was often used by fur farmers to conduct blood tests on farmed mink in an effort to control blood-borne diseases that could wipe out entire farms. This was an important link in the mink-breeding system, and Rod had put it on his list as a potential target.

When Rod and Russell arrived at Gered Huggans's large farm, he offered to show them around the place. Like Fraser's farm in Ronan, Huggans's was a massive operation with thousands of mink and several full-time employees beyond Huggans and his family. As the three men talked, they strolled down row after row of mink cages and later toured the fox pens. They lingered by the pens and talked for a while about the peculiarities of fox breeding and the market for pelts before moving over to the pelt-processing barn, where most of the employees of the Huggans Rocky Mountain Fur Company were busy with the day's feed and with the pelt-drying equipment. With winter right around the corner, the most important part of their annual crop cycle was coming up fast.

Like others Rod had talked to, Huggans was friendly and unassuming. Once or twice in their discussion, he mentioned that fur prices had declined because of the interference of "the animal rights people," but he seemed comfortable with Rod and Russell. They had established a friendly rapport by the time they left.

After mailing the last of their videotape to Friends of Animals, Rod and Russell pointed the van back to Seattle and then rolled through Redding in Russell's car. Rod took some photos there of a stranger's ranch that he intended to pass off as his own place, where he and Russell were going to raise mink and foxes.

There were weeks to wait for pelting season, and relationships in the Scotts Valley house were strained. Rod and Jonathan were doing most of their work separately. Plus, Rod and Jan had broken up, and he had moved into a smaller room. While he was in Louisiana, she had been on a bison campaign in Montana and had kissed a man there, and he couldn't deal with it. But there was more, and he knew it: she wasn't engaged in this antifur campaign, and that made her less attractive to him in ways he felt he couldn't help. Campaigns turned Rod on. Jan understood this—the same thing had just happened to her in Montana—but Rod suddenly didn't feel that committed to fixing this relationship. He was increasingly preoccupied with Global Investigations, and that left him a bit isolated, too. Jonathan and Russell turned their attention to the Hunt Sabs and the

1990 fall hunting season, which was now upon them, and though Rod was eager to get out in the field with them, he was on a different track.

They'd planned to disrupt a youth deer hunt that fall near Clear Lake, a large lake north of San Francisco that lies between Mendocino and Napa counties. Rod was hosting a visitor at the time, Alexis Gill, a seasoned fox hunt saboteur from Britain who was also anxious to help on the deer hunt. Gill was the sister of a British woman who had helped them start Hunt Saboteurs America and was an experienced hand.

The two drove up separately and, on arriving at the Hunt Sab camp near Clear Lake, found a kind of sprawling party going on. Lots of people were drunk, and the next day's action was disorganized. There were eighteen people in camp, but only Coronado and Gill got up in time to actually disrupt the deer hunt. They decided to be their own affinity group and took off early in order to beat the hunters into the field. They didn't encounter any of the other saboteurs the entire day. Without having the backup necessary to do a more audacious action, the pair picked out a group of hunters and shadowed them all day, interfering with their hunt and ensuring that they didn't kill anything.

Back at camp, they found out that those people who did eventually go out in the field ended up getting lost and never even made it to the hunting grounds. A group of them laughingly recounted their misadventures as they took a wrong turn and walked en masse onto private property, where they were quickly confronted by landowners. No one was prosecuted, but no one sabotaged any hunting, either, and they cracked some beers to celebrate.

Rod quit the Hunt Sabs that day. It was the last straw. He didn't want to be the guy with no sense of humor, with no love of the party, but things had grown too serious for this. He didn't want to become embittered. Hungover anarchists and hippies wandering around on private property were going to get someone shot or at least ruin the reputation of the movement they'd worked so hard to build. Judi Bari was still in a wheelchair, and Darryl Cherney was waiting for his hearing to completely return, and any one of these people might be next.

Back at the Scotts Valley house, Rod got a call from Bruce Campbell on a voice mail service he used to keep up his ruse among the fur farmers. Anyone calling that service would encounter only wannabe fur farmer Jim Perez. Campbell said he'd be pelting out his mink at the end of the week. Pelting was time sensitive and he couldn't wait. Rod had only a couple days to get there.

Neither Jonathan nor Russell, though, was up for it. Both had plans to go to the Mojave Desert to participate in the annual sabotage of the desert bighorn sheep hunt. Rod and Jonathan's strained relationship finally reached a breaking point.

"You can't go up there now," Jonathan argued. "The bighorn sheep sab in the Mojave is our top priority. It's always been our top priority."

"If I don't get this footage of the pelting, the whole year of video work is basically lost," Rod countered. "I can't go to Montana without you. I don't have a car. I don't have a camera."

"I don't think that's our priority. Those animals up there are going to die no matter what. But in the Mojave, we can save bighorn sheep."

Rod grew hot and frantic. The two men shouted at each other. Rod accused Jonathan of abandoning the work they'd hired on to do as Global Investigations, of supporting a lifestyle instead of effective action. Jonathan accused Rod of undermining the Hunt Sabs. Even while he was saying these things, Rod knew he'd lose this argument. Jonathan was hardheaded; once he was set on a course of action, it took a lot to divert him. Plus, the car and a lot of the camera gear were his.

Rod had only a day to sort this out. He could get his hands on another video camera, but he still needed to find a car to make it to Montana. The only people he could hit up for a car and a camera that fast were his folks.

He didn't hide his intentions from Ray and Sunday. They had stood by him when news broke about his sinking Iceland's whaling ships, and they had heard about Bari and Cherney's car-bombing on the news; they knew little about what he did day to day, but they knew that Rod and his peers were engaged in a controversial brand of nonviolence. He had rarely asked for anything. When he needed money, his dad gave him a job with the steel company, never a hand-out. This time, it was an emergency, and he told them about the footage he wanted to get in Montana; whether or not they knew he was getting it under an assumed identity is unclear. By the next day, he had a 1985 Subaru wagon and money for a 35-millimeter still cam-era. He borrowed a video camera from someone else.

That night, he lay awake wondering how he was going to inter-view Campbell from behind the camera. He really needed a partner, both for getting footage and for security reasons.

Out of the worrisome spinning of his mind arose a desperate, wonderful idea. During the summer, he had gone up to Ashland, Oregon, to chill out after the car-bombing and to visit some friends in the woods. Two activist friends we'll call Tom and Jessica had hitchhiked across the country from New York City; Jessica was pregnant, and they had decided they wanted to have the baby in the supportive small-town environment of Ashland rather than bustling NYC. Avid fans of anarchist punk music and environmentalism, they had been introduced to Rod by a mutual friend in Sacramento who had also turned Rod on to some of his favorite highly politicized punk bands, like Flux of Pink Indians, Rudimentary Peni, Crass, and MDC. Tom and Jessica lived in a one-room cabin on the edge of Ashland in a kind of hippie ghetto made up of cabins and trailers and shacks in the trees. During Rod's last visit, they had all driven out to the gorgeous Applegate River valley to picnic, swim in the river, and enjoy the country.

There had been a woman with them that day—we'll call her Shelly. Tom and Jessica wouldn't be up for this kind of radical action, but Shelly had told Rod that if he ever needed help with an animal campaign, he should call on her. It might have been just a casual remark. He didn't even know how to reach her on the phone. But she was new; she was perfect. Before he fell asleep, he decided to swing through Ashland on his way to Montana and find her.

EIGHT Neck-Breaking in Montana

THE NEXT EVENING, Rod, weary and red-eyed after driving four hundred miles from Scotts Valley, walked into an Ashland restaurant looking for a friend who worked in the kitchen. The first person he ran into was Pearl (not her real name).

"Oh, he's not working tonight," she said with a big smile. She was a gorgeous girl, probably seventeen, with remarkable hair and a radiant personality. She wore a hippie dress, and lit up the faces of the other customers as she moved through the place.

"Well," he hazarded, "Do you know one of his friends named Shelly?"

"We just moved into a house together," Pearl replied, offering to take Rod to the house after her shift.

Later, she led Rod up a hill to a two-story Victorian, which she shared with Shelly and another young woman who had grown up in the Ashland area, whom we'll call Mila. They found Shelly scrubbing out a bathroom, music blasting. She laughed and stood up, smiling. The roommates were not yet settled into their new living situation, and the atmosphere was a little giddy.

"Can I talk to you alone?" Rod asked Shelly, interrupting the happy banter. He needed to get to Montana and had to know if she was coming.

Shelly excused them and shut the bathroom door.

"What's up?" she asked.

"You said that if I ever needed help, I should just ask you," he started, "and I need help now in the worst way." With nothing to lose, he laid out his plan. Even as he talked, it felt preposterous.

Before he could even finish, though, Shelly cut in. "Rod, I'm there. I'm down. I will do whatever I can to help you."

Shelly drove the Subaru through the Columbia River Gorge in a torrential rainstorm while Rod slept, exhausted. She mentioned that she didn't have a license, but he was too tired to care. In Spokane, they picked up a cheap purse at a department store and cut a small hole in it, so they could videotape the fur farms surreptitiously if they had to.

At the Idaho border, they stopped for a night in a hotel and slept like Huns. In the morning, they drove straight through to Lakeside, where they rented another motel room before getting in touch with Bruce Campbell.

He told them to come over right away. He was already skinning.

A light snow was falling outside as they walked into Campbell's barn and into a scene of small-scale slaughter. Rod and Shelly were still rattled from the road, and the first thing they saw was Campbell, dead mink in hand, standing amid a pile of skinned, lank little pink-gray carcasses. Rod began to feel uneasy, and the feeling grew.

"Hey, hello," Campbell said to Shelly. "I'd shake your hand, but I don't think you'd like it too much."

Rod felt the welcome was warm and genuine, and Campbell didn't seem to mind Shelly's presence at all.

"Do you mind if we videotape this?" asked Rod. "Russell couldn't be here because of a family situation, and I know he's going to want to see how this is done."

"Sure," Campbell said, "knock yourself out." He picked up a dead mink from a small pile he'd already made.

"Well, it's not the prettiest thing in the world, but this is how it's done," he added, looking at Shelly. Rod was anxious, but he started in with a battery of questions, Shelly started taping, and Campbell took a pair of ordinary garden shears and clipped off the mink's feet. Then he hung the little weasel in a rack that positioned the body upside down. Cutting near the anus, he slit the pelt along the hind legs until he could pull out the tailbone and yank the entire pelt off in a downward motion like pulling off a sock. Then he chucked that skinny little bag of bones at his feet and grabbed the next one.

When he was done with the pile and the naked carcasses were freezing on the ground, he said enthusiastically, "Let's go get some mink."

As a way to cover his discomfort, Rod offered to help, and Campbell handed him a five-gallon pail. All three walked out to the mink cages.

Striding over to the rows of cages, Campbell wrestled out a mink with his heavy leather gloves. The animals were in a rage and screamed furiously, musking everywhere, the smell of death. He held the head in one hand and the tail in the other, and as the squirming animal tried to get away, he pointed the head away from him and worked his hand under its chin to bend the head back until the mink's vertebrae popped and the squealing stopped. Rod felt his own body flush with rage. It was all he could do to hold himself in check. Every once in a while, as Campbell repeated this process, a mink would wriggle free and quickly sink its needle-sharp teeth into one of the protective gloves, and Campbell would curse and fight to regain control.

"Sometimes when those little buggers bite you, it really feels good to hear that neck pop," he said, somewhat out of character.

Campbell was completely unfazed by the presence of the video camera, and he kept up a steady flow of banter with Rod as the bucket grew heavier and heavier with dead mink. More than once, a mink suddenly flopped out of the bucket and tried to get away, with its jaw broken instead of its neck. The biologist snatched it up off the floor and quickly finished it off, making sure this time to snap its neck.

At one point, one of the terror-stricken predators squirmed free and ran straight at Rod, and by instinct he reached down and pinned the animal to the ground with his gloved hands.

"Thanks, oh, thanks," said Campbell. "He would have gotten away. They can really run once they get going."

A few flakes of snow drifted before Rod's eyes as he realized in that moment he'd made a mistake. A profound, life-changing mistake. "Let me get him," said Campbell as he wriggled the mink out from under Rod's grip. All he would have had to do was let that one get away, and that would have been something. More, Rod knew he should have come the night before and set them all free. He should be stopping Campbell from opening the next cage. But these creatures were going to die so that Rod could make a videotape. It was the ultimate betrayal of both the animals and himself.

"I felt as if the mink knew who I was, knew that I was different from the other humans who were imprisoning them, and yet I did nothing to interfere with their deaths," Rod said later.

"My rational mind told me that, in the world of mass media, filming their suffering was so much more effective than interfering with the slaughter of a couple hundred mink, that I might make a greater impact on the larger industry. But that was my mind talking, not my heart, and my heart was screaming and breaking at that very moment, telling me to do something, anything, to stop that horrible suffering."

But there he was, holding the bucket. He was not who he professed to be.

"Everything that I was in my whole life, everything that had separated me from others and led me to a life committed to making a difference, was telling me that day that I had made a huge compromise. When I was twelve and saw Paul [Watson] on those ice floes in Newfoundland, it was his actions I wanted to emulate, not the others who were simply filming. That's what I had promised to do. I had betrayed those I had given my life to represent."

The air grew more dense with screams and acrid musk. Rod

noticed that the loudest screams weren't coming from the animals in Campbell's hands, but from those next in line, who emptied themselves in a last flush of terror like animals on the killing floor of a slaughterhouse.

Rod felt hollow and shivered in the cold. He was down to moral reserves; he had tried so hard to compromise with the political world, but now there was nothing left to lose. He was holding the bucket of dead mink as he turned to those still alive in their cages and made a silent vow.

"I promised myself and I promised those mink that I had witnessed die that I would do everything humanly possible to destroy the industry that had destroyed them," he said. "And I meant it, too. I would make them pay."

All the while, Shelly kept rolling. Somehow, they both decided to finish the job.

When the bucket was finally full, Campbell said he still had to skin all these mink before their bodies froze in the cold. They went back to the skinning floor and kept videotaping as he skinned a few more. But by then, Rod had taken all he could take. He was absolutely sick with guilt. He could see that Shelly had had enough too.

"Well, Bruce, I think we're going to leave you to the rest of this. We didn't even get a chance to check in to our motel," said Rod, stripping off the gloves.

"Yeah, we just drove straight through," said Shelly.

"Plus, we want to go visit Stu Fraser, too, before the day's out," Rod added. "I'll give you a call later."

Rod and Shelly thanked Campbell profusely for all he'd taught them and set up another appointment for later that week. Then they raced to their motel and connected the video camera to the TV to review the footage, propelled by guilt and anger to make sure that they'd at least got the shot. They almost regretted that they had. When the neck-breaking footage appeared on the screen, they both burst into tears. Safe in the confines of the motel room, they let it all out. It wasn't just the sheer barbarity of the images. Rod was crying over his own betrayal. He didn't want to face that he'd let this happen. And he was surprised by a wave of fear that hit him as he thought about what was to come. A new road had opened up before him, and he couldn't even tell Shelly about it. In those moments standing before the cages, he had seen where this would lead. Destroying this industry would not mean passing legislation. He would blow it off the face of the earth—using any tactic that didn't physically harm any animals or people. Sabotage. Theft. Cleansing fire. Whatever it took. He would stretch the definition of *nonviolence* to its breaking point. In the hotel room, he realized that this could only end badly—in prison, for sure, maybe in his own death.

He was preparing to go to war.

Rod turned the camera off and immediately called Betsy Swart at Friends of Animals. She was thrilled with the description of the footage. She said it would cause a sensation.

"Was it honest? Absolutely," said FOA's Priscilla Feral. "They went in and filmed the guy, who thought they were on the tour, and he was boasting about his mink, and it was all legit."

But both women pressed for more. Footage of ranchers electrocuting foxes was a public relations coup, and they still wanted that. Rod hung up and gathered his strength again. From what he understood, every fur farmer in this corner of Montana was pelting this week. He and Shelly had to get right back to it. His war would start when this job was done.

Within the hour, they met Fraser in his pelt-processing barn, where about five men were busy skinning mink the same way Campbell had.

"He wanted to videotape us skinnin' mink and stuff, and we told him, 'No, you can't,'" said Corey Richwine, Fraser's son-in-law, who was there when Rod turned up with Shelly and later became sole owner of the farm. The Frasers were skittish because just before

Christmas of the previous year, a thief had broken in and shot a couple of their bobcats for the fur.

"So Rodney asked, 'Are you worried about the animal rights guys?' And my father-in-law, he says, 'No, we keep a twelve-gauge shotgun loaded, and if we hear anything, we start shootin'. And we have big dogs, too,'" said Richwine.

The two interlopers were in too deep to pull out now. Fraser was a good-natured fellow with a big, hearty laugh and an easy manner. Spirits were high, and there was a fair amount of joking going on. One of the workers told Rod and Shelly about one time when they were skinning mink and the animals hadn't been sufficiently gassed (the Fraser farm killed its mink with carbon monoxide); a few of the animals already had their feet clipped off and were in the middle of being skinned when they started waking up. "You can imagine the horror," the man laughed. Rod and Shelly laughed too. They didn't know what else to do.

They recounted the neck-breaking they'd seen at Campbell's place, and Fraser said that wasn't what the industry considered a "preferred humane practice," adding, "Well, come on out here and see how it's done properly."

Fraser's son-in-law was driving the mobile killing chamber. The box was about four feet long and three feet high with a door at the top, and it was filled with wood shavings. As carbon monoxide hissed from a gas bottle, a worker wrestled out a screaming mink and slam-dunked it into the box. Its tiny heart racing, the creature quickly suffocated, which left the pelt in perfect condition.

Richwine explained to me why they used gas. "Because we had way more to do, and we were licensed with the Fur Farm Animal Welfare Coalition, and to have our pelts registered as a humane pelt, they suggested that we use that method."

Rod noticed that Shelly was pointing her purse at the gassing operation, and he quickly looked away. He tried to deflect any attention from her and give her some cover by engaging Fraser and his son-in-law in conversation. They followed along for about thirty minutes as one mink after another was dispatched, and then Fraser invited the pair into the house to warm themselves with a cup of hot coffee.

They sat over steaming cups in a house well armored with rifles and pistols hung here and there. They fell into a conversation about the future of fur farming and threats to the industry, which inevitably led to talk about the animal rights movement. Fraser joked, "If I ever caught any of those animal rights people on my property, I'd grind them up into mink feed!" They all laughed over that one, Rod the hardest of all.

He excused himself to go to the bathroom, where he checked the tape in the microcassette recorder he had in his breast pocket, making sure it was on. When he returned, Shelly was in the middle of a rant against the animal rights movement. She had concocted a story on the spot about how her father's life had been saved by an experimental medical procedure that had first been tried on lab animals. Medical research was one of the most contentious issues in the battle over animal rights, and groups such as iiFAR (incurably ill For Animal Research) and the National Association for Biomedical Research were very good at distributing information, so it was bound to connect. It was fairly easy for Shelly to fake this line of argument, but still, Rod was impressed.

He knew these stories had their limits, though, and they had to keep the visit short. They could both feel an impending invitation to dinner. After this day, having to down a chunk of steak or meat loaf would have literally been too much to stomach. Rod eased up from the table, saying that he and Shelly had one other farm on their list, so they had to keep moving. He didn't feel the connection with Fraser that he felt with Campbell, and both he and Shelly breathed more easily when they were walking back to their car.

It was late afternoon when the two left the Fraser farm, and they arrived at their next location just as the farmers were leaving, a husband-and-wife team. They were courteous enough to hold up their exit for a bit and chat at the gate. It was a small operation, with maybe four rows of fox pens, each row holding about a dozen animals. Standing in the cold wind, the farmers indicated that they were done killing for this season and their pelts were already drying.

Rod quickly got the two talking about their methods. They didn't use anal electrocution, they explained. They found it easier to just stand on the foxes' chests until they suffocated. That didn't mess up the pelts at all.

Strangely, when Rod and Shelly mentioned they'd been on the Fraser farm, the husband recounted the story about the mink waking up with their feet chopped off, and both he and his wife were visibly upset by this. They didn't think this kind of suffering was right. Even a man who killed fully conscious foxes by standing on their chests had his limits.

Rod reached Swart on a pay phone the next day and recounted all the videotaping they had done. Swart began debating whether it was worth it to film more gassing. The conversation started to upset Rod. This was not what he wanted to hear. Finally, she told him that Friends of Animals was pursuing another avenue for getting the fox electrocution footage on the East Coast and that they should abandon their efforts in Montana.

Had it all been worth it? Rod began to despair. They had witnessed so much death and butchery, maybe for nothing. Why? Because their footage wasn't sexy enough for the six o'clock news. Rod was in a kind of fugue about it. They didn't know what to do next, whether to go home or attempt a liberation.

Rod remembered he owed Campbell a call, so he rang him next.

"Hey, I've been wanting to talk to you," Campbell said.

"Oh yeah? What about?"

"I've got a proposition. I know you want to get into the business, and I've really got too many mink on my hands here, so I'd like to sell you a couple dozen so you can start breeding them. Cheap. You won't get a better deal on breeders."

Rod saw the light. This was the way he could atone for those mink he'd helped kill. They talked a bit more, then he added, "This is a very generous offer, Bruce, thank you. Shelly and I are standing on the street in Butte. Let me talk to Shelly and Russell and get back to you."

They were excited by the idea of saving a few of these mink, but neither one of them wanted to give Campbell even one dollar that was going to be put back into the fur operation. So, right there on the street, they cooked up a counteroffer.

"Bruce? It's Jim again. Yeah, listen, I've got an idea that might take yours one better."

"OK. I'm all ears."

"Well, we'd like to buy you out."

The next night, they were in Campbell's trailer putting the final touches on the deal. He had resisted, but then started to get excited about the idea. He was in his thirties and single and ready to go back to school in Seattle. Rod's offer to buy out the farm was an opportunity to start over.

As Shelly cooked dinner—a pasta dish with a carefully camouflaged vegan "meat" sauce she had pre-prepared—they all sat in Campbell's small kitchen, cracked a bottle of vodka, and inventoried everything he had to sell. It amounted to sixty-six mink, four bobcats, two majestic lynx, enough feed to last a few months, rolls of wire, and all the mink cages, nest boxes, skinning racks and knives, and assorted gear. For that, he wanted six thousand dollars. They drank to it and then dove into their dinner, with Campbell commenting on how good everything tasted. The mood was high, and the little kitchen rang with laughter.

Afterward, Campbell wanted to take them out for coffee in Kalispell. "Jim" and he had become friends, and this changed the young radical as much as it changed the biologist. Before this research, Rod had found it more convenient to believe that anyone who would skin a mink for profit was murderous or, at the very least, ignorant. That kind of categorical dismissal was a defense mechanism that made activist life easier for Rod, though it wasn't in keeping with his general tendency to like people, and he was relieved to find that he and Campbell could pursue a relationship based on humanity and respect. Both loved the wildness in animals and found joy in listening to the expertise of the other.

They talked late into the night, and then Rod and Shelly drove back to Missoula.

They set out for Ashland the next morning, and Rod felt lighter of heart. His war was on hold, but he had been given a new way to save lives, and he was grateful for the chance to redeem himself. There was plenty of time for destruction later. He started thinking about how he could rehab these animals. Their first stop was an overnight in Pullman, Washington, at the home of Rik Scarce, a Washington State University grad student in sociology and the author of *Eco-Warriors: Understanding the Radical Environmental Movement*, which had just come out that year. He and Rod were well acquainted, having shared extensive interviews and notes for the writing of that book. In Pullman, Rod explained to Scarce some of what had just transpired with Campbell's farm and got on the phone to supporters in Southern California looking for money. He also hit the university library for rehabilitation tips. The Global Investigations project was over. He'd gone to Montana to dismantle fur farming, but he was coming back a farmer.

NINE The Sanctuary

THE TRANSMISSION WENT out in the Subaru just about the instant they hit Ashland, and both Rod and Shelly were relieved to be back in safe quarters with Pearl and Mila. Rod got on the phone to Friends of Animals, certain they'd be able to help him buy Campbell out. After all, buying his inventory wasn't illegal. But the phone call left him feeling like the mainstream movement had kicked him in the balls.

Priscilla Feral not only refused to put up any money to buy Campbell's animals, but was angry Rod had even suggested it.

"Here are the two things I didn't like about that scenario," she told me. "I didn't like rewarding somebody for unloading their animals. If he was going to get out of the business, I didn't want to reward him financially for that. Second, if you get these mink and let them go into the wild, there are unacceptable risks associated with that."

Releasing rehabilitated farm animals into the wild is illegal, and Friends of Animals had to be careful, because funding any illegal action could cost it its nonprofit status and hurt its membership numbers and fund-raising. Releasing farm- or lab-raised animals also carries a slight risk of introducing genetic mutation or disease into the wild population.

Plus, there was an image problem: They should have bought all the animals and saved them *before* Campbell pelted them out. This way, it looked like they had let it happen just to get dramatic footage. She had a point, but Rod didn't see it. He was gripped by the idea that the rescue, rehab, and release of an entire fur farm was a media coup. He thought they should film the whole thing and make a documentary out of it.

But there was an even deeper betrayal. Even if Friends of Animals couldn't afford to be connected with the purchase, even if it had to disavow ever supporting him at all, why couldn't it just quietly send him the money? It wasn't much bread, and it would save the lives of seventy-two animals. He felt he had earned it.

"I know he was frustrated—and I got it," said Feral. "It's really hard to do all this investigating and then just walk away. So then, what do you do? He wanted to bury this industry, but that's the job of advocacy groups who work in the public sector and get popular opinion behind the elimination of these places. So, no, I didn't assist, and I'm sure it ticked him off."

As Rod hung up, he felt his face flood with tears. He rushed out of Shelly's house, through the trees and bushes to an undeveloped hillside where he could hide in some manzanita scrub while he cried. He was shocked by how disappointed he was, but it wasn't just about the money. It was yet another break with the movement. His connection with the wild was driving him beyond politics, away from all the people he assumed would share his views. He was worried that his battle against the fur industry would eventually leave him utterly alone.

Within two days, however, he had borrowed nine thousand dollars total from California Animal Defense and the Anti-Vivisection League. He needed a commune, a sanctuary, and he just made it up on the fly. During the stop at Rik Scarce's house, Rod had phoned his pal David Howitt, who'd helped him sink the whaling boats in Reykjavik. Howitt's wife, Linda May, had crewed on the Sea Shepherd ship *Divine Wind* and had worked as a veterinary assistant rehabilitating rescued wild birds and mammals when she had lived in San Diego. The two of them lived on ten acres outside of Port Angeles,

Washington, deep in the rain forest of the Olympic Peninsula. They
had no house there, but lived in a refurbished school bus. Coronado
told them he was headed their way, but Howitt later told me he really had no idea what was coming until a large truck full of animals
arrived on their property.

In mid-December, Rod gathered his friends to help him collect
the animals. The bighorn hunt was over in California, so Jonathan
and a female friend, an Earth First!er, made themselves handy. Despite their earlier disagreements, Rod had asked for Jonathan's help,
and he had agreed to lend a hand. They traveled in Jonathan's pickup
to Pullman, where they rented a twenty-six-foot Ryder truck.

They drove through a steady snowstorm and by the next day
were standing in Campbell's driveway in Lakeside. They stayed overnight there, and Jonathan, too, really felt comfortable with the biologist.

"It was just the weirdest thing because Bruce Campbell is a really
nice guy," said Jonathan. "He wanted out of the business. He basically
said, 'I'm done with killing.' He had this wolf pelt on his bathroom
door that I asked him about. He said, 'Oh, that was this wolf that my
grandfather won in a poker game a hundred years ago.' I think he
knew that we were not potential fur farmers. I think somewhere he
knew."

Rod was worried about Jonathan and his friend blowing his
cover as Jim Perez, and was even more worried when they walked
into the barn to find about fifty skinned mink carcasses still frozen
to the floor. He could see Jonathan shooting alarmed stares at the
woman with them and knew he just had to keep him moving or
there might be an incident.

With the biologist to guide them, the three moved the mink into
ten-inch cages and stacked them in the truck with wood between
each cage so they wouldn't bite one another. Campbell produced a
blowgun and darted the cats with ketamine, an animal paralytic
drug. The wild, anxious felines didn't sleep, but gradually just lost

control of their motor functions. They were rolled into four-by-four cages and secured in the over-cab storage of the Ryder truck. Then the truck was lightly packed with nest boxes, feed bags, and a few bales of hay. The rest of the gear they had purchased—feed buckets, rolls of wire, skinning racks, watering cups, heavy leather gloves, the blowgun, and a package of veterinary drugs—was loaded into Jonathan's pickup. Campbell wrote out a bill of sale that would also serve as a permit for transporting this menagerie across state lines. As far as he knew, they were headed for Redding, California. Rod had even shown him pictures of his ranch there.

Campbell was packing too. In fact, he was leaving right behind them. Montana Game Farm #2113 was out of business, and he told them he had resigned his post with Fish, Wildlife and Parks in order to go back to school. Rod was thrilled to be facilitating this transformation, but he didn't really mind what the guy did as long as he wasn't killing mink or anything else. He found that his relationship with Campbell had followed a remarkable arc. They chatted a while, then said their good-byes and hit the road.

The Earth First! gal was at the wheel because she had grown up driving in snow and was the logical choice to navigate I-90 at night. By mid-afternoon the next day, they'd managed to back the truck down David Howitt and Linda May's muddy driveway before it got stuck.

Howitt and May weren't prepared for the number of animals that Coronado had brought to them, so they all began off-loading the mink cages into a makeshift tarp shelter, where they'd at least be out of the wind and rain. The cats were put in a separate area, away from the mink, under a corrugated metal roof.

That night, Rod, Jonathan, and their Earth First! friend withdrew to a hotel to dry off and get some sleep. The next morning, she and Jonathan split for California once again. Christmas was only a few days off, and they had other things to do besides care for these animals. That task would fall to Rod and, in actuality, mostly other volunteers who would arrive to work on what they all called "the sanctuary."

For the next week, Coronado and Howitt built a new shelter for the cats, and every night they all ate and slept in the bus. As they worked in the relentless marine cold of the peninsula, building with wood that froze every night, they passed between them a bottle of homemade coffee liqueur that one of the neighbors had given May for Christmas. The new cages were bigger than any the cats had had before and were built into a hillside surrounded by alder and fern, which screened the cages from humans and let the cats see only wilderness.

So began an exhausting mission that would require almost six months to be completed without ever having enough people, money, or resources. Rod would fiercely defend this project, as he intended to keep his promise. The first few months would involve little other than feeding and caring for the animals, so once the new shelter was built, Rod hitchhiked back to Ashland to get his Subaru out of the transmission shop and recruit some help.

The project needed a name, and Rod had begun calling it the Coalition Against Fur Farms, (CAFF). He opened a bank account under that name and secured Post Office Box 3095 in Ashland 97520, which was in the back of a shop called Ideal Drugs. He used the same box for communications with fur farmers, in which case he'd say CAFF stood for Country Aire Fur Farm. He used the other version on communiqués and stories he published in the environmentalist press. On January 3, 1991, the group issued a statement of purpose whose second clause read, "C.A.F.F. is in the business to put itself out of business. We see ourselves existing only long enough to end the practice of fur-farming."

CAFF was a public group with a public rehab project, so Rod's name became associated with the CAFF statements. Sometimes he was Rod Coronado; sometimes he was Jim Perez. His double life grew more complicated and more risky for everyone around him. At this point, he hadn't done anything illegal other than trespassing and releasing a few farm animals. But he knew fur farmers would not take kindly to his investigation; later in 1991, when the public began to suspect who he was, his voice mail would be flooded with death threats.

Rod had been back in the house in Ashland for one night when Shelly agreed to go work on the sanctuary. They all stayed up listening to Sinéad O'Connor's *The Lion and the Cobra* until it was time for Rod and Pearl to drive Shelly to the bus station for a midnight bus to Seattle. The next day, Rod retrieved his car and decamped for Scotts Valley.

Stepping into the house in Scotts Valley was like entering a different world. A dysfunctional, paranoid world. The hot tub bubbled, and there was a crew in the house getting stoned, but mostly what they talked about was the persistent FBI presence since the Bari and Cherney bombing. Helicopters hovered over the house with some regularity, apparently taking photos or video footage, and unmarked sedans shadowed them through the tiny burg. Any underground actions were shut down. Rod was only there to get his things and move out, and when he explained exactly what they were doing in Washington and why it was so exciting, he wasn't surprised that no one volunteered to help.

On his way back through Ashland, Rod picked up Shelly and Pearl's roommate, Mila, who had decided to volunteer. She was young, just nineteen, and told Rod as they drove through Grants Pass that she'd never gone on a journey like this without her folks. But she was a very confident young woman and was also a wit, with a great sense of humor that made her a joy to be around.

Living five deep in the bus, however, was not really a joy at all, especially in winter. Linda May soon came up with a solution. One of the customers at the health food store May managed in Port Angeles had a cabin she needed occupied while she went to India. It sat right on the Elwha River about ten miles out of town, and soon Shelly, Mila, and Rod moved in, along with a young man from Ashland we'll call Lonnie. Lonnie had a lot of construction experience and soon began building a new permanent shelter for the mink. During the entirety of the CAFF project, many people would come from all over the country to volunteer, sometimes for only a day or two, sometimes for months.

David Howitt only worked on the project for a couple weeks before leaving on a Sea Shepherd mission to the Persian Gulf, where the group intended to use the *Sea Shepherd II* to clean up oil spills caused by the Gulf War.

"Linda would certainly rather I didn't go. She wanted me on the property at that time. She did feel a bit wary about Rod's intentions. But I felt inspired by Rod, and I guess what I really felt I could do was get that boat to the Persian Gulf," said Howitt, laughing at his own ambition. The boat made it as far as Key West and was hung up by repairs. He was gone for almost the entirety of the rehab project.

May helped craft a rehabilitation plan for the animals, but she was also running a store, so Shelly took on the daily feeding chores. This was an unpleasant task for a vegan, but after the neck-breaking and other episodes it was nothing. They had brought frozen blocks of meat by-products from Montana, which were thawed and chunked up. Then she'd fill a five-gallon pail with dry mink pellets, mix in about ten pounds of the meat, and add hot water to make a gooey, bloody mash. The four bobcats and two lynx gobbled it down.

One of the strategies for breaking all contact with humans was to have a single person doing the feeding, but Shelly hadn't been on the sanctuary long when she had to leave. Mila picked up the job, and Shelly was replaced by a woman we'll call Emma, who was living in Portland and who eagerly volunteered to work with the animals. Emma worked as a cashier in a natural foods store and arrived with much-appreciated groceries.

Rod and Mila were often shoulder to shoulder doing the meat-slop and construction work of caring for these animals, and they eventually became lovers. Rod had a crush on young Pearl, but Mila was right there with him, a beautiful, funny brunette five years his junior and just trying on the depth of her commitment. The situation was so predictable he almost felt guilty. Rod knew it was part of the familiar pattern all his relationships had taken—even then, he suspected it would end when the rehab was over and the sanctuary torn down. He fought with himself over it, because he really did feel loved. Her love sustained him through poverty and bobcat claw marks and months of lugging heavy cages around.

Funds were low, and Rod continued to talk to Swart and Feral. Finally, they issued an ultimatum: they'd pay for the care of the rescued animals if CAFF would agree to send them to a licensed animal sanctuary in Texas. But the sanctuary wouldn't feed them live food, nor would they release the animals into the wild. This is where Rod's beliefs in biodiversity and deep ecology diverged from the notion of animal rights. All of these creatures were predators; he felt a clear responsibility to teach them to hunt live food again and to release them to live or die on their own. That was a deep ecology position, and the animal rights crowd wouldn't like it. But after a vote, CAFF decided to rehab the animals themselves and teach them all to eat live food.

It wasn't long before the animals were chomping through steady supplies of live mice, rabbits, and quail and no longer touched pellet food. The CAFF crew learned to draw blood samples from the animals and sent those to a private lab to test for infectious diseases. The animals got a clean bill of health. Between February and June, in an exhausting series of long hikes with heavy cages, volunteers helped videotape the former residents of Campbell's farm as they were released, two by two, into deep wilderness all over the state of Washington.

In February, Rod pulled into the parking lot at the Seattle Fur Exchange, one of the biggest fur auction houses in the world, with the intention of attending its annual mink auction in the guise of new fur farmer Jim Perez. He had $250 in his pocket from Swart and Friends of Animals to cover expenses. It wasn't illegal, and FOA could use information about the auction, the fur buyers, and the furriers they represented to find a weak link, an element of the industry that would be vulnerable to a targeted media campaign. The industry guarded information about its members to avoid such a campaign, and perhaps Rod could help FOA deliver the coup de grâce. For his part, Rod was also interested in delivering that coup in the form of sabotage, if public shaming didn't work.

The Seattle Fur Exchange was in Tukwila, a small town about six miles south of Seattle. The auction house—which has since changed its name to American Legend Auctions, reflecting its exclusive representation of the American Legend brand of mink—was founded in 1898 during the Alaskan gold rush and is the Sotheby's of the fur trade: the world's top buyers are there, representing furriers in Korea, Russia, Japan, Europe, and the United States, with an emphasis on foreign markets. The space is huge, forty thousand square meters, and is packed to the rafters with individual lots of carefully graded furs from just about every mink and fox farmer in the country.

As Rod sat in the parking lot, he saw men in expensive suits hustling, discussing their purchases and trades. He was a little nervous. He felt like he was walking into the lion's den. These people were pros, and he wasn't going to be able to bullshit them. He was wearing dress pants, a long-sleeved dress shirt, and shoes that would buy him some cover, but he knew he looked awkward. He wore a thin sport coat and carried an old leather satchel for his notes. He got his game face on and strode into the place, where he was welcomed by an employee named Joel, whom he'd talked to previously by phone. He knew Rod was new to the scene. "If anyone asks who you are," Joel said, "just tell them you're a friend of mine."

Rod's first couple of days were very odd, a lot of wandering alone among a small cadre of foreign buyers, mostly Asian, who were not particularly eager to chat. Foreign buyers prize American mink because of their typically high-protein diets, which produce glistening coats, a by-product of this country's intense factory farming. In other places, mink are usually fed fish meal, but in the States there are entire economies of cheap meat scraps to be had. Joel led Rod into a warehouse where more than two million mink pelts were hanging from mobile racks for potential buyers to sample. Each rack held about six hundred pelts.

At one point, it was obvious a group of men were watching Rod as they inspected pelts. Finally, one of them approached him.

"Excuse me, sir, but are you a buyer?" he asked.

"Oh, no, I'm a farmer just getting into the business," Rod said.

"You don't hear that much these days," said the man.

After Rod threw out the names of some of his Montana contacts, the men visibly relaxed. They invited him to inspect pelts with them and gave him a tutorial on how to grade furs. It took some time to master, but the technique was to run your hand against the fur, holding it up to the light to gauge the thickness of the guard hairs that gave the pelt that American sheen. Afterward, Rod felt comfortable enough pulling racks himself and handling bundles of pelts.

At night, Rod would slip into the hotels where the buyers were staying and camp out in the bars looking for company. Beer in hand, he jumped into ongoing conversations by asking if the buyers had any advice for a new fur farmer. More than once he was told, "Yeah, get out of the business." The fur market was under attack from antifur propaganda, they insisted, and it was tough for even established farmers to make a living. But that's about all they would say. They were suspicious of anyone asking too many questions; the animal rights people were everywhere, and they didn't want to spill any information that could be used against the industry.

By the third day, fur farmers from across the country had started to show up, and Rod finally had crowds of people to talk to. The presence of the new farmer caught the attention of Marsha Kelly from the Fur Farm Animal Welfare Coalition (FFAWC), an industry marketing group. Rod just about gagged on the name of the organization, but Kelly and her colleagues got one look at him and saw a golden opportunity. Here was a young farmer just getting started, smart, enthusiastic—the future. Rod's story about founding a new farm in Redding became the talk of the auction. A representative of the FFAWC was walking with Rod one afternoon and threw his arm around him, saying, "Jim, we gotta stop the animal rights people in this country before things get as bad as they are in Europe. They're burning down fur shops and releasing animals from farms." Rod nodded and pumped him for more information.

Eventually, the auction attendees were called into a "members only" buyers' meeting to which the public was not invited. Rod watched the entire gathering file one by one into a meeting hall, leaving the auction rooms almost empty. He felt awkward until Joel came out.

"Hey, you want to sit in?"

"What is it?"

"It's our big annual meeting. Come on."

They walked in mostly unnoticed just as Kelly launched into a tirade against animal rights as the number-one threat to the fur industry, drawing numerous cheers. The industry's anger was right there on the surface, and all week Rod had been absorbing it in conversation after conversation: good American farmers and furriers would be making money, he kept hearing, "if it weren't for the damn animal rights people." Kelly pointed out that the survival of the remaining 660 fur farms in the United States at that time depended heavily on the success of a university-based research network called the Mink Farmers Research Foundation (MFRF). The mission of the MFRF was to solve nutrition and disease problems and lower fur-farm overhead. It was funded by a 2.5-cent levy on every pelt sold at the auction. Important MFRF research was being carried out on an experimental fur farm at Oregon State University in Corvallis, she noted. Rod listened intently; he and Jonathan had visited Corvallis specifically to find this farm, but had failed to locate it.

He captured the whole session on a tape recorder in his pocket, but he hardly needed it. Rod was wide-eyed throughout the entire talk. His heart started pounding. The Seattle Fur Exchange was telling him exactly how to cripple the entire industry: hit the MFRF.

TEN Guerrilla War

LIKE IN A cartoon, the shadow moved only when Rod moved. Rod took two steps under the double darkness of oak trees at night, trying to walk lightly through the leaves, and he heard the tiny *chsh-chsh-chsh* of little feet. He flipped on his flashlight for a moment and looked behind him, catching two mischievous little eyes in his beam. A mink was following in his footsteps.

It was less than twenty-four hours after Rod and Mila had released the last bobcat from the CAFF project, early June 1991, and he was poking around on his own at the experimental mink farm at Oregon State University in Corvallis. There was a small white car in the driveway of a house about one hundred yards away, which he took to be the caretaker's, but the facility itself was quiet. The main building, a white-painted cinder block lab, was bordered by a wooden barn to the southwest and a bunch of short, open-sided mink barns under a grove of oak trees on its north side. The compound was within the city limits, but lay among the school's agricultural properties, just a half mile or so south of the main OSU campus.

Rod moved over to the fence and opened the gate, holding it ajar for his little friend. The mink edged cautiously forward into the world and then dashed for nearby Oak Creek, a tributary that ran into the Marys River. Along the Marys were city parks and wooded residential areas, plenty of habitat for an industrious young weasel.

Rod found a bathroom window propped open on one wall of the lab building and dropped in from the roof. His heart hammered in his ears as he checked for signs of security. Blinking lights, infrared sensors, anything. There were none. The lab had been there in some form since the 1920s, but had hardly ever been the subject of protest. The ALF did hit a University of Oregon lab in nearby Eugene in 1986, however, releasing 125 monkeys, rabbits, hamsters, and rats. Roger Troen, then of Portland, was convicted of burglary, theft, and conspiracy, and he got five years' probation, but three other activists arrested along with him were released without ever being charged. They were Bill Keogh, Jonathan Paul, and another of Rod's old friends who was active in the Sacramento-Davis area, Crescenzo Vellucci.

In the main room, Rod found what he was looking for: decades and decades of research protocols in binders, plus boxes and cabinets jammed with files. Great reams of it were nutrition and genetic work done for the Mink Farmers Research Foundation.

In the desk of Ron Scott, the manager and research technician in charge of the farm at that time, he found some grisly slides of mink suffering from encephalopathy, or severe inflammation of the brain, and another whose jaw had been broken. He pocketed a few of those and snatched a couple of documents for further reading.

Scott later confirmed that the farm was doing MFRF research at the time.

"Most of the research that had been done in the years prior to the event we're talking about was focused on nutrition," he told me. "So that particular facility was a little bit specialized in working with developing better-quality diets for fur animals and, as a secondary focus, was looking at utilizing meat by-products from poultry, fish, things that would have no other value than, say, commercial fertilizers. We had wonderful people in the Animal Science Department looking at the physiology of development, how hormonal systems go about creating seasonal changes."

The Mink Farmers Research Foundation was small, Scott acknowledged. There were probably only four researchers nationwide, and three of them worked at universities.

Rod hauled himself out the bathroom window, left it open, and lay down on his belly to look over the farm from the roof of the lab. He listened to the mink scratching in their cages down below and considered how relatively easy it would be to destroy this entire facility.

"In that moment, I told myself, 'OK, Rod, you could do this, you could shut this place down forever. You could declare war on the fur industry and deal them a crippling blow. But if you choose to do what you are thinking, your life will be changed forever. You will either be killed by some armed fur farmer while raiding his farm, shot by some guard, or go to prison,'" said Rod.

"I never imagined I would get away with it, because Jim Perez was a real person with a real face and a real name and it would all lead back to me, Rod Coronado. And then I remembered those mink and that day on Campbell's farm and that promise I had made, and I decided, yes, that I would keep it. I would do everything possible to destroy this industry. On the roof, that promise began to be fulfilled."

He dropped down and closed the gate on the mink barns, whispering promises to the approximately three hundred mink and one thousand or so new kits that were housed there. He crunched back through the creek bottom to the park where he'd left his car. Only days before, a requested donation of fifteen hundred dollars in cash had arrived for him at the CAFF post office box from a supporter known only to Rod. He planned on using the money to take down the MFRF, starting right here. The mink facility at OSU would never recover.

Two hours after leaving the OSU mink farm, Rod pulled up to a middle-class house in the suburbs of Portland. The house was on a double lot with a big garden and a tangle of flowering bushes and trees. It was a quiet street, and few area activists would have recognized it as the home of a radical environmentalist—the young woman who lived there might not even have identified herself as one. The front of the house was dark, and Rod followed a path of cement pavers through a wild spray of azalea to the backyard, stopping momentarily to enjoy the doorway of flowers. He was cautious. He wanted to avoid running into anybody, especially the girl's mother.

He slipped around to the back of the house and saw her through the window, a young woman we'll call Jill, playing her guitar and deep in concentration. He tapped on the glass, and she opened the window to the cool June night.

"Oh, hey! How's it goin'?" she said quietly.

Rod climbed in without saying a word and tossed the slides on the bed.

"Oh my god, what the fuck are these?" she said, looking at them in the light.

"We have to talk."

They drove to a local pub, where, over beer and a huge plate of fries—vegan bar food—they got reacquainted. He'd met her in Eugene during a protest action at the University of Oregon and she'd done some work on the CAFF sanctuary. Rod had stayed in touch when he could, which wasn't often. Despite her relative nonchalance when he appeared at her window, Jill was surprised to see him. Taking a huge risk, he started describing the work of the Mink Farmers Research Foundation and explaining why targeting OSU could diminish or even cripple the American fur industry.

He also said he knew that eventually he'd probably be named as a suspect, because of his high profile with CAFF, but he assured her that she could stay completely in the background if she wanted to.

It was quite a jump for Jill. She had engaged in protests and some Earth First! campaigning, but she'd never crossed the line into sabotage. She didn't give her answer right away. They sat at the table for a while staring into the bottoms of their pint glasses. Before the night was through, however, she was in.

Rod's operation required at least four bodies, and ideally none of them should know one another, so by morning he had set off to recruit the others. Michael was an anarchist Rod knew from Los Angeles who had relocated to an organic farm on the Oregon coast. He had undertaken a few fur-shop attacks in Southern California with the ALF, smashing windows and gluing locks. He'd also earned Rod's respect by once delivering a carload of shivering punks to a bighorn sheep Hunt Sab action in the Mojave. Rod drove out to see him at his cabin on the coast.

Over a travel mug of organic coffee, Rod described his mission and asked if he'd be interested. Michael nearly spat out his coffee. "You're nuts! They'll shit their pants! Of course I'm interested," he barked. They spent the rest of the day discussing the details and then passed the evening listening to Michael's collection of punk rock vinyl in the farm's main house, since his cabin lacked electricity.

The next night, Rod rolled into Berkeley and up to one of the big old wood-frame houses that typify the university area. Rod had met Tim at a street demonstration in San Francisco, when a group of black-masked anarchists had formed what was known as a "black bloc" of protesters—meaning a whole group who dressed alike and worked in solidarity to avoid being singled out and arrested—and had blockaded the Financial District. It had been the day after Earth Day. Tim had become a hero at that action when he'd slashed the tires on a San Francisco Police Department paddy wagon.

Life wasn't always that exciting, however. Down at his favorite local falafel house, Tim started grousing about the state of the movement, complaining about so-called radical politics devolving into questions of identity, which distracted from real change. Rod interrupted him with an offer to go after the fur industry.

Tim halted his rant and smiled. He knew Rod hadn't looked him up just to chat. Rod gave him a quick rundown of the action, which he said promised "maximum destruction, not minimum damage."

That last bit of anarchist cliché got him.

"OK, let's do it. I'm in!" Tim exclaimed. They made arrangements for him to meet the rest of the group in Corvallis later that month. And Rod was in the car, headed back to Portland.

On June 9, 1991, Rod, Jill, and Michael met at the Santiam River rest area on the I-5 in Oregon. While they waited for Tim to arrive, they went for a swim in the Santiam, basking in the warm June sun. They were all introduced to one another using fake names; it was just safer that way. Tim had borrowed a car, and he followed Rod's Subaru into Salem, about a half hour north of Corvallis. There they had a hotel room.

Jill had already purchased each of them a set of black clothes, which they'd later dump, from local thrift shops. She and Michael got to work rubbing down all the tools with alcohol, making sure to wipe off any fingerprints.

Rod, meanwhile, was making an incendiary device. Three, actually. The triggers were small, and each would fit in a six-by-six-inch Tupperware container. One wouldn't exactly call them bombs, since they weren't designed to explode, but only to quietly burn. He'd bought three one-hour kitchen timers from a Fred Meyer store and shoplifted battery clips, wire, and soldering equipment from a Radio Shack, where he'd also asked for and received a list of the radio frequencies used by police in Corvallis.

Instructions for making a similar incendiary could be found in the book *The Anarchist Cookbook*, which is still available on Amazon today. They could also be found in any number of other books, on Web sites, and at gun shows both then and today. Using epoxy, Rod glued two stripped electrical wires to the top of a kitchen timer just a fraction of an inch apart. On one wire, he soldered a nine-volt battery lead; on the other, a small automotive lamp, the kind of light-bulb used in a standard car taillight. Once the battery lead and the bulb were connected, he completed the circuit by soldering the remaining wire ends into a closed loop. The bulb would act as the igniter: Rod heated up the glass on the bulb with a cigarette lighter until it glowed and then dipped it into water, causing it to shatter. After picking the glass out with a needle-nose pliers, he glued in several windproof matches whose heads touched the now-exposed bulb filament.

The last step was to glue a nail to the clock hand. When it came around to the fifty-minute mark, the nail would push the two wire ends together, closing the circuit and lighting the bulb filament. That hot wire would light the matches, which would be stuck in a can of Sterno gel. The Sterno would sit under a two-liter plastic soda bottle filled with a mixture of oil and gasoline. The oil would stabilize the gas and keep it from exploding, making for a longer burn.

When two more similar devices were complete, Rod packed them all into Tupperware. He then filled three soda bottles with the gasoline-oil mixture and threw everything into his backpack. In a separate pack he placed three cans of Sterno and some fire sticks and fire paste, which he had picked up easily enough at camping stores.

Sitting in their hotel room over take-out food, the four ran over their plans again and again. The attack consisted of two separate break-ins, one to the lab and one to the barn, which held all of the farm's experimental feeds and mixing equipment for its nutrition research.

Michael, Rod, and Jill had the advantage of having done a trial run only a few nights earlier. They'd slipped into the lab, Rod's second time inside, to rifle through documents and secure any information they could find about the MFRF. Jill had found a breakdown of the operations budget for the farm and details of the funding from the MFRF. Rod was only a little surprised to find that the feed used by the farm was mixed and delivered by the Northwest Fur Breeders Cooperative in Edmonds, Washington, where he'd bought the meat and pellets for his own animals on the sanctuary. He had been in that building a number of times and had wondered whether the co-op was involved, as one of the biggest fur-animal food providers in the country. Now he had proof. OSU was able to run its program thanks to an eighty-thousand-dollar donation of feed from the co-op and an MFRF grant of forty-five thousand dollars.

"If we can destroy the feed in the barn, we could force the farm to lose the majority of its operating budget," Rod reasoned.

The barn was also about forty yards away from the mink pens

themselves, with the lab building in between. As long as the wind was right, the mink would be sheltered from the fire.

Jill had run into Corvallis and photocopied all the documents and then returned them to the lab the same night. They'd also kept a few copies of the lab's OSU letterhead, on which they'd print their communiqué.

A small handbook Rod had "borrowed" from the lab explained that the farm had a long and illustrious history in the service of agri-business. It was founded in the 1920s as a federally funded wildlife-research facility specializing in foxes. During the 1960s, the federal funding was replaced by funding from the state of Oregon's agricultural division, which represented fifty-plus mink farms. When the bottom fell out of the fur market in the late 1970s and '80s, the university had to turn to the farmers themselves for support, and by 1991 the farm was operating on a shoestring budget made feasible by the MFRF.

Which made it an alluring target.

When night fell, they checked the batteries in their flashlights and VHF radios one last time. They joked about being agents and double agents as they made sure each had a set of fingerprint-free tools, maps, and getaway money in their backpack, laughing about who would rat out whom. It was only safe to laugh because they were sure nothing like that would ever happen. Michael picked up an empty duffel bag for papers and documents they might steal. They also had video and still cameras for images they could release to the press.

"Try to find a group that you know you can trust / Plan more ambitious direct action, sometimes risky but a must!" Michael sang, launching into a song he knew Rod would like, Conflict's "This Is the A.L.F." They all knew the rest of the verse and shouted it out, releasing nervous energy: "Direct action in the animal movement is sussed and strong, and our final goal is not far off!"

This music had barely been heard in the United States, but Michael was like an anarchist jukebox. He knew all the bands that Rod had loved in Britain. The fact that everyone in the car knew the song suggested a whole underground of other potential ALFers, just waiting to put their pop anarchism into action. The four all knew who this song was about: it was about them.

Around two A.M. on June 10, Rod stopped the car near a school just south of the fur farm, and the three others piled out. He then swung around and drove about a mile to the sprawling OSU campus, parked the Subaru, unloaded his mountain bike, and pedaled back to the others. When he got there, he realized he'd forgotten the still camera. Michael offered to go back for it while Rod and Jill helped Tim get the lay of the place as they hid in a backyard garden.

Michael was gone a long time, and when he arrived, he was panting heavily. "I was seen by a neighbor, and he shined a light in my face!" he blurted in a whisper.

"Shit! What did he say?" Rod hissed.

"He asked me what I was doing on the school's property, so I told him I was hitchhiking and just looking for a place to sleep for a few hours. That seemed to satisfy him, and then I told him I was moving on, that I'd look elsewhere."

Jill looked at Rod. "What do you want to do? Should we postpone the action?"

Rod didn't want to, but it wasn't his call. "Well, I guess it's up to Michael to decide. He's the one who's been seen."

Michael ran his hands through his long hair and short beard. After a minute, he said, "I'll cut my hair and shave the instant we get out of here. He didn't get a good look at me." He hid the bike in the underbrush. "Help me find the bolt cutters. I dropped them when he walked up on me."

They returned to the nearby school yard and found the cutters after a short paw through the dark grass, then Tim took up his watch post. They all pulled on black ski masks and switched on their radios.

After a short bushwhack through the creek bottom, they were on the farm, and Michael went to work pulling all the breeding-record cards from the mink cages themselves. Jill and Rod went through the lab's unlocked bathroom window again and opened the back door. They were all aware that the man who had seen Michael was in a house only about one hundred yards away, and that the small white car once again sat at the caretaker's house about seventy yards the other way. The streets were empty, but the neighbors were home.

As Jill speed-rummaged again through the file cabinets in the main lab, a huge mass of discarded documents piled up around her. Rod put black plastic garbage bags over the windows in Ron Scott's office, then turned on the video camera's built-in light and began taping. Jill moved into the office, lugging the duffel bag and stashing documents, slides, and address books in it, and finally spray-painting "ALF" on the office wall. Rod grabbed bottles of ketamine from the refrigerator for future animal rehabs.

Deciding that they had the documents they wanted, they stopped searching and started trashing. The duffel bag had over sixty pounds of stuff in it, but there were still walls full of documents stored in boxes, most of them protocols and notes from hundreds of experiments. This single room contained all the research records since the farm had begun in the 1920s. This was exactly what they had come to destroy. Everything went on the floor and accumulated underfoot until it had become a small mountain. Lab glassware was smashed, and all the tables were upended. They trashed the place.

Rod broke the water line in the bathroom and flooded the entire building, turning all those paper records into mush. On one wall, they wrote in dripping red spray paint, STOP THE BLOODY FUR TRADE— MINK ARE NOT YOURS TO EXPERIMENT ON, and on the opposite wall, WE SHALL RETURN FOR THE KITS, meaning the one thousand baby mink in the cages outside. They also scrawled, NOWHERE TO HIDE A.L.F. IS WATCHING, FREEDOM FOR ANIMALS IS A RIGHT NOT A PRIVA- LEGE [sic], A.L.F., OLDFIELD YOUR [sic] NEXT (for widely published

OSU researcher and Mink Farmers Research Foundation head J. E. Oldfield), CONCENTRATION CAMP FOR ANIMALS, and OKAY RON THIS IS YOUR WARNING GET OUT OF THE FUR TRADE (for Ron Scott), among other messages. No one said they were poets.

Michael rushed into the lab building, carrying hundreds of breeding cards and record books he'd found in a small adjoining office. He had done an equal smashup job on that office and a refrigeration room. He huffed that he'd seen a woodstove where they could burn the cards.

"Let's just leave them in the barn with the devices," Rod said between slugs off a water bottle. "We've done as much as we can here. Let's get this stuff out of here and torch the barn."

Michael hefted the duffel onto his back, putting his arms through the straps, and Jill trailed him as they both moved into the creek bottom and were gone.

Rod pushed through a wooden door that led from the lab into the feed barn. Small tractors and feed mixers were parked in neat rows. He quickly surveyed the wood structure to find the best place to set a fire, then started piling wood nesting boxes under the base of a stairway for a kind of pyre.

Suddenly the radio crackled with Tim's voice: "We have a definite code yellow, possibly red alert."

Rod froze. As he stood panting in the darkness, he realized that if Tim had wanted Rod out of there, he would have given the code word, "scramble." Pulling himself together, he ducked outside and found Tim in the woods.

"What did you see?"

Tim was staring at the caretaker's house, where a bright floodlight illuminated the entire yard and the curving two-track up to the farm. "Michael and Jill were crossing that field, and the light came on and caught them right out in the open."

Rod thought about it for a minute. All was quiet. "They must have tripped a motion-detecting light," he said.

"That's what I think, too," said Tim, "because if anyone had seen them, they would have called the cops, and they'd be on their way by now."

Tim and Rod watched the house for about ten minutes, and the light finally went off. It turned out later that the caretakers *were* home at the time, but all Rod could do was trust that the two hadn't been seen.

"OK, I'm going back in," he said, disappearing back into the barn.

Rod set the three devices near one another under the stairs and dumped all the breeding cards there, too. Then he attached a nine-volt battery to each timer, setting them each for forty minutes, and placed the bottles of gasoline above them. Just enough time to get back to the I-5 and out of town. He left them ticking.

He stood up and took one last look around. It was three thirty A.M. He ducked back outside, and he and Tim hustled through the underbrush, peeling off incriminating layers of black clothing that was now covered in dust, vegetation, and mink musk, stuffing it into their backpacks as they moved. At the rendezvous, Michael and Jill waited for them with the car and the bike. Rod and Tim jumped in, tense. The car was silent. Within twenty minutes, they were on the I-5 and headed north.

As the highway passed over a river, Michael flung all their shoes over the railing into the dark waters. One of them, however, bounced off and lay on the shoulder of the I-5. They all laughed then as they drove on, imagining that this would be the big crime lead: one lone shoe lying on the roadside.

They stopped in Salem and retrieved Tim's borrowed car before pressing on to Portland. There, Tim and Michael would board separate buses to their respective homes, and Rod and Jill would find a hotel room and begin sifting through the bag of confiscated documents. But as they drove, Rod slumped in the passenger seat with the first light of dawn breaking over the hills to the east. Gazing out into the glow as it lit the green of new fields and far-off hills, he felt the beauty of the moment. In the eighteen straight months he'd devoted to fighting the fur industry, he'd never felt so good. No more complicity with the industry, no more strategic compromise. Just maximum destruction. As the adrenaline slowly leached out of his body, he was suddenly aware of cuts and bruises. He closed his eyes and slept all the way to Portland, thinking about the last words of the press release: ". . . actions by the A.L.F. will continue, until the last fur farm is burnt to the ground."

At last, he had himself a hot war.

According to the June 11 *Oregonian*, the feed barn was a total loss. It was never rebuilt. Damages were listed at $62,000 and later revised upward to $125,000.

"It's pretty upsetting, the FBI wandering in and telling you, 'Be aware of . . . packages at your house and any activity because these people may be targeting you personally,'" Ron Scott told me. "It does keep you wired up at a personal level. Your sleep patterns, because you think you're hearing things around your house. A lot of overtime hours, because there's already a shrunken-down labor force. I think I worked almost thirty days straight without time off. I'm sure my family would probably have had me home more."

Scott seems a kind man and is now long retired from the university. He was genuinely concerned about the idea that he might have been targeted personally, though he doesn't think now that he was. He doesn't seem outrageously angry at Rod, either.

"I don't think I got really focused on the issue of 'Are they right or are they wrong?' There are different methods of expressing your personal desires and trying to get change made, and the vandalism didn't appear to me to be an acceptable method for getting changes made."

The state legislature would immediately take up the issue and pass legislation making an attack on an animal enterprise a felony crime. Rod's timing, however, was good. The industry was in a downswing, and it was hard to justify running a program for the benefit of about fifty state farmers. The farm was cleaned up a bit but closed for good two years after the fire.

On the afternoon of June 10, Jill called the Associated Press and Portland TV stations KOIN and KATU and told them they would find videotapes of the OSU attack stashed outside their offices—in one instance, in a flower bed. They also distributed copies of the following communiqué neatly typed on OSU Animal Science Department letterhead:

On June 10th, 1991 the Animal Liberation Front (A.L.F.) broke into Oregon State University's Experimental Fur Farm in Corvallis, destroying the facility's equipment and data base and liberating mink imprisoned on the premises. The institution, founded by the mink industry, was targeted due to its role in the barbaric fur trade.

Members of the Western Wildlife cell of the A.L.F. found mink intentionally infected with diseases that cause intense pain and suffering, confined in cages barely large enough to turn around in. These experiments include activities that are aimed at controlling reproductive behaviour of female mink in order to control litter size, kit-raising and levels of fertility. Other experiments at the lab aim to increase fur farm profits by eliminating diseases that result from intensive confinement or native wildlife. One of the lab's primary goals was to lower the costs of confinement farming at the expense of the animals' psychological and physical well-being. This drive to increase the profit margins of fur farms is vital to an industry faced with plummeting sales due to public opposition to animal abuse and ecological devastation.

On July 5th, 750 3-month-old mink are scheduled to be subject to the same useless and repetitive experiments that have already resulted in the deaths of over 50,000 mink in the past thirty years. A.L.F. will not tolerate this arrogant, human-centered disregard for life and, should it continue, will return to OSU to end the torture by any means necessary.

The fur interests' current environmental rhetoric seeks to cover up the environmental devastation caused by their industry. Mink, in their original state, are wild beings filling a vital niche in their native habitat. Facilities such as the one at OSU seek to destroy the ecological integrity of these individuals in order to produce another "crop" to be "harvested."

The exploitation of female mink is symptomatic of a much deeper oppression, the oppression of the feminine. The mink are mere breeding machines in the eyes of their oppressors. A.L.F. challenges not only the OSU vivisectors, however, but the larger patriarchal domination and control of natural lifecycles. Vivisectors such as J.E. Oldfield, Cliff Thompson, Ron Scott, John Adair and Nancy Wehr are typical examples of the mindset that seeks to destroy the inherent wildness in animals, the earth, and, ultimately, ourselves. As women in the A.L.F., we feel the connection between the infringement of our reproductive freedom and that of the mink at OSU. For these reasons we seek to destroy their oppression as well as our own.

This action is a direct response to the exploitation and environmental terrorism committed daily by the fur industry. As long as the electrocution, gassing, and enslavement of animals for fur continues, similar actions by the A.L.F. will continue, until the last fur farm is burnt to the ground. Expect to hear from us . . .

ELEVEN The Fall Offensive

ROD AND JILL spent a couple nights in a hotel room in Portland, sorting through the documents pilfered from the Corvallis lab. They had committed the perfect crime, and no one was paying any particular attention to them. But Rod felt a clock ticking, like he had to hit more labs and farms before they got a chance to change the locks, hire security, or network across the rest of the Mink Farmers Research Foundation. They drove east out to Multnomah Falls to burn the paperwork they didn't want to keep. The rest they kept and hid in a storage locker, and they were again clean of all incriminating evidence.

By this point, Rod and Jill had become lovers. It was passionate; it was convenient; it was also a great cover. Rod couldn't always slip in and out of Jill's life without activist friends seeing them together or wondering what he was up to, and if they knew he and Jill were seeing each other, they made a point of butting out. When the two of them disappeared for two days or a week, they just told people they were on a camping trip or traveling to see friends.

Rod's already complex double life was getting dangerously tangled. After months of high-profile work on the CAFF sanctuary, which he'd written about in radical journals and for which he'd approached movement leaders for funds and activist help—and which openly identified him as working on mink and fur issues—it would look weird if he dropped out of sight entirely in the middle of an explosive new arson campaign targeting the fur industry. He needed to maintain his normal contacts in the eco-radical movement, even though he was sure that this is exactly where law enforcement would be looking for a suspect.

And if the feds were already onto him, he was putting everyone he knew at risk.

For instance, Emma, who'd worked for a time on the sanctuary, lived in what was then a well-known activist house in Portland nicknamed the Malka Ranch. It's not a movement house anymore, but it still sits on Southeast Clinton Street, near the Clinton Street Pub and the Clinton Street Theater, at the supergroovy little intersection with Southeast Twenty-sixth Avenue. The Malka was the hive of Stumptown Earth First!, which included several people who worked on the *Earth First! Journal*, and Rod—who had no actual home after leaving Scotts Valley—would hang out there sometimes.

Often, when he was feeling vulnerable, he'd sneak around the back of the Malka and tap on Emma's window. They'd go down to the Barley Mill Pub on Hawthorne for a beer and fries.

Other times he'd just embrace full contact with the movement, not knowing if he was bringing police attention down on them or if one of them was an informant. One night, Rod got a call on his CAFF voice mail from a Danish friend whom he'd met years earlier on a Sea Shepherd campaign. He was in a campground south of Portland and had called to see if Rod was anywhere in the state and wanted to meet. So he and Emma jumped in the car and drove to the campground, found his friend and a few others, and brought them all back to the Malka Ranch to party. They ended up having a late-night drinking session with some of the folks in the house.

This was close to the time of the OSU arson, and to Rod it really felt risky to be partying in a movement house. Still, he had to maintain CAFF as a legitimate, aboveground group and he needed the support of friends and allies to accomplish this.

*   *   *

On June 14, Rod and Jill left Portland and headed to Edmonds. The Northwest Fur Breeders Cooperative was a vast concrete building just a couple hundred yards south of the ferry terminal, built on the waterfront in 1947 to freeze fish scraps for distribution to its members. Rod and Jill ran by the place in the car just to get a look at it; the building shared a big, heavily trafficked parking lot with a popular wharf-side restaurant, so there was plenty of cover for hanging out in a car there.

The right thing to do was to watch the place for a few days, get to know the security routines, if there were any, and recruit a couple more people to help. But Rod was more impatient than ever. He felt foolishly confident, despite having only visited the place a few times to buy food for his animals. In the car, he convinced Jill: if it looked good, they were going in.

Others who had worked with Rod, who didn't want to be named, said this overconfidence made working with him unnecessarily perilous. "His security was sloppy," one former CAFFer said. "When shit started happening, the FBI tore our community apart. We didn't even know what he was up to. He was not mindful of that."

Jill had little choice. Her role was to sit in the parking lot and stand watch with one of the VHF radios. The couple went by a closed gas station so that Rod could fish a couple of plastic one-quart oil containers out of the trash, which he filled up with gasoline and oil. He picked up some Sterno and matches at a local Safeway. That was it. That was his device. Later, they sat in the parking lot.

"We're here," Rod said. "Nothing's ever going to be perfect. This is our opportunity. Let's just do it."

In the early hours of June 15, Rod emerged from the car in black clothing and walked across the parking lot to the co-op. He slipped behind some trucks parked near the loading bay, from which big tractor-trailers delivered the co-op's products all over the country. A delivery chute, used to convey the raw components of animal feed, ran right into the building through an ungated hole in the wall, and Rod easily squeezed his skinny frame through the opening. He moved unnoticed into the main warehouse building, past several empty offices.

He froze when he saw what he thought was a motion detector. A red light moved across its face, and it emitted a high-pitched frequency. After a minute, he cautiously moved around a bit, and when nothing happened, he reasoned that the sound was intended to scare off rodents. A place like this was certain to have a problem with mice and rats. It was only a guess; for all he knew, security could be en route, but he moved deeper into the building past pallet after pallet of bagged food, machines for mixing the mink pellets, large refrigerated units, and wood and paper bedding. In the northeast corner of the building, he found bales of paper bags and piled those up with bales of excelsior—or wood wool—wood chips, and new pallet boards. When he had his kindling, he set up a crude version of the incendiary he'd used at Oregon State University. This one worked the same, but a lit cigarette was the timer; it burned down until it lit the matches, which ignited the Sterno, which, in turn, fired up the plastic quarts of gas.

He ran back to an employee locker area near the conveyor, grabbed a can of spray paint he'd seen earlier, and sprayed FREEDOM FOR FUR FARM PRISONERS on the wall. He then went out the same way he'd entered.

He and Jill were outside Portland before they heard about the fire on the radio. It was massive and reportedly gutted the entire place. Damages were said to be $511,000 and were later set at $800,000.

The communiqué dropped off at KIRO radio station in Seattle and later various outlets in Portland said that the ALF's Western Wildlife Unit had planted incendiaries "with the hopes of causing maximum economic damage to an industry that profits from the misery and the exploitation of fur animals." Rod's note also warned of further acts of "economic sabotage." Accompanying the releases were video dubs of the June 10 OSU action and new tapes of masked ALFers burning documents and slides from the OSU raid.

When Rod and Jill woke up in a hotel room late on June 15, they were still anonymous. But by the end of the day, Rod, in particular, had put his neck in a noose.

The smart thing to have done, of course, would have been to leave Edmonds, maybe leave Portland for a while, and never look back. But these crimes had a political point, and Rod had an almost monomaniacal need for the public to understand it—a need to force people to look at the Mink Farmers Research Foundation and question what it did—and that drove him to some decisions that were less than smart.

On the evening news, "Jim Perez" appeared as the face of the Coalition Against Fur Farms. He offered himself up as an activist with experience rehabbing and freeing mink who could explain what the ALF were probably trying to do. This was a strange twist, since this was his fur farmer cover. He gave a series of interviews to Oregon news outlets, and to each he also offered video footage of CAFF releasing its animals into the wild so they'd see the positive side of the activism. He expounded on all he'd learned about fur farming and told them he supported the use of arson in the OSU attack, which drew a lot of outrage from viewers.

This is how I first met Rod. A few months after he gave those first interviews, we began talking on the phone. I knew him only as the spokesman from CAFF. But I knew him as Rod Coronado, as did many other people. He'd give CAFF interviews as Jim Perez, even appearing on TV under that name, but his writing in the *Earth First! Journal* and other radical publications appeared under his real name. So he was already partially exposed.

"We were hoping that we would do the anonymous press release and then other animal rights groups would step up to the plate and take advantage of the attention on these industries," said Rod, "and when they didn't, that's when I made the decision that I was going to do it. That decision wasn't based on, obviously, my security. I was twenty-four at the time. I wasn't thinking long term. Do the damage. Accomplish the mission. Damn the consequences. In hindsight, I would have never done anything like that."

When he talked to Sarah Hale at the Associated Press, she asked how he had received the ALF communiqués. Rod said, as an example, he had been told to go to a particular *Oregonian* newspaper box and there, on the bottom, was taped one of the ALF press releases. He explained that he had no idea who the ALFers were. If any of his recent contacts at fur farms or from the Fur Farm Animal Welfare Coalition had seen these reports, they'd have seen that Jim Perez was, in truth, an antifur radical. Local activists, however, knew immediately that Jim Perez was Rod Coronado.

It turned out that a few cops did too.

"In all my years, that's always been the Achilles' heel; the people doing the action also do the media. It's more evidence bringing them closer to you," said Rod.

For Oregon State Police arson investigator Richard "Dick" Schuening, those two roles were hard to separate. In conversations with other investigators, he would say that he had a gut feeling about Rod. Even though Rod had been doing his interviews and putting out CAFF press releases as Jim Perez, Schuening had him ID'd as Rod Coronado early on. He just didn't know the full scope of his activities—for example, that Rod had been investigating fur farms in Seattle and Montana. The FBI and ATF also started digging into CAFF and putting together some intelligence on its sanctuary in Port Angeles. It wasn't too long after the OSU fire that Schuening started referring to CAFF as "Rod and those two gals" in meetings and phone calls with other investigators. But those two gals weren't identified until March 1992—and even then, they were only two of the women Rod worked with on the sanctuary and were most likely not involved in anything more than the rehabilitation of the animals.

Still, Schuening was focused on Rod. Even if he wasn't the actual arsonist, he still might be useful: if Rod was close enough to receive communiqués, they might be able to use him to find the arsonists. Schuening's federal counterpart, Special Agent John Comery of the ATF, in Portland, was equally suspicious of Rod. His past record of smashing fur shops, jumping bail, and sinking whaling ships did nothing to discourage this line of inquiry. Schuening started putting together a dossier of photos that included pictures of Rod and would eventually also include those of other people who had worked on the CAFF sanctuary.

The press release from the Edmonds fire said that the co-op had been targeted because of its association with the fur farm at OSU. Dick Schuening and others were pretty sure these two fires had been set by the same people. Now it seemed they were on a spree. And the only activist in the country who was sticking his neck out to defend these fires was Rod Coronado.

News organizations treated him like a star, an inside source. He was good for ratings. Two days after the Edmonds attack, Rod was in a TV newsroom in Portland, and one of the reporters told him that the co-op fire had smoldered in the insulation and flared up again. He was using the news organizations to broadcast his message and to get inside information at the same time.

The co-op would eventually reopen, but the original concrete building was torn down in 1994. It would also change its name to Northwest Farm Foods Cooperative, partly to get rid of the word "Fur."

Images of Rod were not hard to get: the feds had several booking photos, and he was popping up in the news all over the Northwest. Schuening started showing Rod's photo around, and it didn't take long to get hints that he was on the right track. Witnesses in Corvallis had seen a man and a woman acting suspiciously in the vicinity of the OSU mink farm immediately before the attack, and they thought the man looked similar to Rod. It was not a positive ID, and it may have been Michael they had seen, but Rod's picture looked familiar. They could not positively identify the woman with him.

Investigators were also quick to deduce that other researchers and facilities affiliated with the Mink Farmers Research Foundation would soon become targets. Don Maupin, then the top investigator with the Washington State University Police Department, said he got a call from Schuening weeks before anything happened up there. WSU professor and researcher Dr. John Gorham was on the short list of those who had received grants from the MFRF, Schuening told Maupin, so look out. He also told him specifically to watch for Rodney Coronado and "two gals," then sent him a photo of Rod.

The June 24, 1991, issue of *Fur Age Weekly*, a leading voice of the fur industry, featured a cover story titled "Violence Marks 'Animal Rights Week.'" The story described the OSU and Edmonds fires, linked them to the ALF and a week of nationwide activism, and then included this tantalizing offer from the National Board of Fur Farm Organizations:

> The National Board is encouraging anyone with information concerning the two attacks to contact the investigating law enforcement authorities, and is offering up to $35,000 for information leading to the arrest and conviction of the activists who committed the crimes . . .
>
> The award fund was created by the National Board together with contributors from several other groups. No one who participated in either arson fire will be eligible to receive award funds.

This was simply a reward for information on the attacks, no different than other such rewards that are routinely offered—sometimes even backed by mainstream animal welfare groups wishing to show their disapproval of property damage. Over the next six months, however, Rod began to scrutinize this reward more closely. He wondered about the identity of the "other groups" mentioned in the article. He wondered how far a fur industry supporter might go to get that reward; one of them—even a government agent—could blow up a facility, causing injury to many animals or people, and plant obvious evidence that implicated Rod just to get the reward money. It was ripe for a setup. His anger against the fur industry grew as he realized that its reward might inspire a lot of bloodshed by people who were a lot less careful than he was.

TWELVE   Night of Stars Falling

IT WAS JUST after sundown in the rolling grasslands of eastern Washington, wheat country with big skies, when Rod and Jill donned dark clothing, stuffed ski masks in their backpacks, and headed out on a stroll. The night of July 26, 1991, was warm, and they walked out into the agricultural fields belonging to Washington State University just outside of Pullman, near the Idaho border. They skirted the university dairy farm, which sat opposite the school's experimental fur farm, looking at the lights of the buildings scattered in the low hills. They tried to figure out the distances they might have to carry rescued mink to a vehicle and scoped the whole layout from time to time with a pair of binoculars.

The fur facility housed experiments conducted by Dr. John Gorham, a key link in the Mink Farmers Research Foundation. Gorham worked on, among other things, a sickness called scrapie (pronounced "scray-pea"), a fatal degenerative brain disease that affects mostly sheep and goats. Scrapie is one of a class of transmissible spongiform encephalopathies (TSEs) that also includes mad cow disease and Creutzfeldt-Jakob disease in humans, which made this very important research. Because mink were susceptible to scrapie, they made good test subjects for studying the disease.

Gorham's federal research was funded by the U.S. Department of Agriculture (USDA) and the National Institutes of Health (NIH) as well as the MFRF, because it focused on several diseases whose study had an application in humans. For instance, the NIH considered his work on a mink condition called Aleutian disease to be a potential animal model for immune-complex diseases. He was also working on an error of metabolism called tyrosinemia and a genetic condition called Chediak-Higashi syndrome, which had killed twenty or thirty children at that time.

Rod and Jill walked the perimeter of the fur farm, emboldened by the apparent emptiness of the facility, which was encircled by an eight-foot chain-link fence. Finally, they both went up and over the fence and moved toward the mink barns, hiding in the shadows away from the road.

After a long wait to see if there was any security patrol, Rod went up to one of the mink barns, only to find the doors on both ends padlocked. That was unusual; he started to think there might be some heightened security in place already. He finally did find a place where they could enter the barns and then retreated. He figured there were about a thousand mink there. (Gorham, interviewed in 2008, said, "Oh god, no. I'm going to guess we had fifty." They may have been talking about two different agricultural facilities, but Gorham also admitted he didn't really remember the exact number.)

They were only there for a brief recon visit, so they quickly scrambled across the farmyard and back to the fence; Rod swung himself over and crossed the road, and Jill was struggling to do the same when she was swept by lights from an oncoming car.

She was caught in the beam right on top of the fence. The car kept coming, and she could only keep moving. Just as the car passed, she leaped from the top of the fence into some tall grass outside the farm. The car kept going, and Rod quickly dashed back across to her side of the road. They started walking toward campus, but Rod saw the car do a U-turn behind them and turn its lights off. As they walked, he scanned the road ahead with the binoculars and saw another car parked with its lights off directly in front of them. It was the police.

WSU police officer Bill Gardner was in the first car. Rod and Jill had tripped an alarm, and Gardner and his partner had been dispatched to investigate. He had seen somebody scaling the fence in his headlights, but he didn't stop because he was too concerned for his safety. He was in his first year on the force, and none of the WSU patrol cars carried long guns. All he had on him was a pistol. And he wasn't about to confront a possible eco-terrorist without a rifle.

"We saw something, a person, leaving one of the research areas," Gardner said. "And we sat and watched. And it was obviously somebody in to do some recon of the area. And we could not follow them out. They went out east across the wheat fields, toward Idaho, and we called for surrounding agencies to go out looking for cars, to pick people up on the highway. But we didn't get anything.

"We laid out in the woods and tried to be real tactical. We did not have rifles at the time. We thought that person did. We thought a lot of things, but we didn't ever verify anything."

Gardner's experience that night illustrates the fear that the ALF inspired in law enforcement officials, as well as the misinformation that was disseminated about the group: Gardner, who is now WSU police chief, is pretty sure he saw the person on the fence carrying a rifle. That never happened, according to Rod. "I can't for the life of me think why he thought we had a rifle," Rod said. Neither he nor Jill was carrying any kind of weapon at WSU. Not only would slinging a rifle have been incredibly impractical, but it was also against everything they stood for. Nor were they carrying long-handled bolt cutters or anything of the sort. What Gardner had seen were shadows.

Not to pick on Gardner, but the fact that he still believes this, seventeen years after the fact, is a problem. It reflects false intelligence that was flowing down from the U.S. Department of Justice. Gardner's department had been informed that the ALFers were killers.

"I didn't know much about ALF except that we were told that these guys are really professional," said Gardner. "These guys really are thorough. They're not crackpots. They're very dangerous. They will kill you if you find yourself in the wrong place. So be careful. That was pretty common rhetoric around the department."

This information had come to Gardner, as at other police

departments, from the FBI. But it was exaggerated. It was not supported by any known actions or observations in the United States. It
was an extension of reports that had come from Britain, where the
ALF and other groups were much more militant and openly advocat-
ing targeted killings and armed uprising, and had been transmitted
by the Department of Justice to law enforcement everywhere. But
the ALF in the United States publicly disavows the use of firearms,
and to date there has never been any evidence that any ALFer in the
United States has ever been armed.

No matter: the cops were spooked.

Rod grabbed Jill by the arm, and they had started walking the
other way when they heard the first car speeding toward them. The
lights of the second car, driven by Officer Nanette Kistler, turned
on, and it came toward them too, in an attempt to pinch them in the
middle.

Rod and Jill flung themselves off the road, and Jill went sprawling
into a ditch, landing in water and mud up to her waist. Rod hauled
her out, and they ran flat out across fields toward the dairy farm.
They headed away from their parked car and up into the hills. When
they stopped and looked back, they saw a pair of patrol cars with
their headlights trained on the fur farm, as the two university officers
searched.

The two fugitives kept moving across the farm, but the full
moon rose fast and left them totally exposed. The short grass of the
pasture gave them no cover, and within minutes they were forced to
crawl on their hands and knees through a herd of cows in order to
reduce their silhouettes against the sky. Soon police cars began driving the dirt roads, sweeping the hills with their spotlights, and Rod
thought for sure they would be spotted. One car came so close they
could hear the conversation on its radio and the pinging of gravel
under its tires.

While they lay peering through a vista of cows' legs, letting
their hearts settle, the two heard the cry of a coyote in the far-off

hills—then, surprisingly close, a chorus of yips and howls in re- sponse from below them, somewhere on the campus. Jill and Rod looked at each other in the moonlight, knowing without speaking that there were also coyotes in captivity that needed to be freed. Their WSU action was growing more complicated by the minute.

They had no idea just how complicated.

"I remember laying in the grass, thinking, 'What the hell? I don't have a rifle. And if one of these guys sees me and he does, and if it's true that they don't care, I could be . . .'" Gardner trailed off. "We didn't catch anybody. We just weren't equipped to. You just don't engage in a running rifle battle at those distances, in a routine patrol."

Running rifle battles. This is what Gardner thought it meant to confront the ALF. People who, at worst, might be carrying a pocket Maglite and a hummus sandwich. But the ALF did little to disabuse him of this fear. As dangerous as it was, the group members also thrived on it. This time, two of its members got away, and no one got hurt. But the stage was certainly set for someone to get shot.

By the time Rod was back in Portland, after the recon, the ALF campaign had turned the town inside out. As he crashed from place to place, he found that the buzz in the activist community was not about how aboveground groups should be supporting these actions, but about how the actions were going to harm more mainstream initiatives. Rod was disappointed by this. He kept his own counsel and never discussed the actions with anyone, working only on CAFF initiatives in public. A newspaper article following up on the Corval- lis raid reported that fur farmers were arming themselves against ALF attacks and were concerned that the ALF had documents with the names and addresses of all the working fur farms in the country. The new wing of the Western Wildlife Unit was quickly finding it- self a pariah and subject to possible violence.

Rod sat in a café in the Burnside section of Portland with one of his old friends, Joseph (not his real name). He needed to recruit new help for an attack on WSU and couldn't risk talking to any neophytes. He had to go to people he could trust. The two of them drank soy lattes and traded some movement gossip. Joseph was a very steady presence, a committed anarchist who saw no future in incremental legislative change. During the time Rod had known him, Joseph had always viewed environmental regulatory victories as crumbs from the oppressor's table, meant to restore faith in a corporate-owned legislative system and guarantee that no real change ever happened.

The recent spate of ALF attacks on fur research facilities, however, had nearly taken the edge off Joseph's withering cynicism. As he excitedly related what he knew about the attacks, he sounded downright optimistic. Here was evidence that activists were waking up. He thought this hardcore direct action made an emphatic point that people were growing frustrated by the pace of change.

Rod hinted that he knew the source of those ALF attacks.

Joseph's face remained impassive as he subtly glanced around. "That's what I had hoped this meeting was about when you first contacted me," he said.

Rod's reaction was one of both relief and alarm. He was thankful that his old friend was receptive to his guerrilla designs. But he also realized that Joseph must have already suspected that Rod was behind the recent attacks. Rod was standing out as a likely perpetrator among his own community and to the cops. For that reason, he maintained a no-phone policy when meeting with other activists, contacting people in person or by hand-delivered notes whenever possible.

He placed his trust in Joseph and laid out the connections between the WSU research and the MFRF, and why WSU's mink research was a legitimate target. Joseph listened attentively, then suggested they burn Gorham's offices, where he likely kept all his data. Rod shut that down, saying that Gorham's offices were in a school building full of students and guards. They'd find another way. Joseph was in.

Jill was staying with friends in town (staying with Mom wasn't working out so well), and Rod showed up on his bicycle, indicating that they needed to talk. They never spoke about the campaign in anyone's house because the hawk was out, and reward money could flip even a friend. So Jill hauled out her bike, and they pedaled over to the Burnside Pub.

They had a few laughs over some beers, and then Rod told her about the new recruit without giving away his name. She listened intently and then produced a file of research protocols she had unearthed at the University of Oregon library about the animal studies going on at WSU.

Rod and Jill would have been determined to free those coyotes no matter what the university was doing with them, but in fact they misread much of this scientific information. Rod would later publish in his own pamphlets and articles that the WSU coyotes were furnished by the USDA's Animal Damage Control program for a study of a parasitic infection called sarcocystis, which can affect domestic livestock. It was true that the coyotes had come from Utah State University, which had connections to Animal Damage Control. But Dr. William Foreyt, the WSU researcher who was using the coyotes, confirmed to me that he was studying salmon poisoning disease, which is lethal in both dogs and coyotes. Canids of all types contract the disease by eating raw Pacific salmon and trout, which carry a fluke that infects the host and releases rickettsia bacteria, which cause an infection. A related disease in humans is Rocky Mountain spotted fever.

"I was attempting to develop a vaccine for dogs, using coyotes as the test animals," Foreyt wrote in an e-mail. "There is no direct application to human disease, but indirectly, there are several important rickettsial diseases in humans where the vaccine development information could be applied."

Foreyt's study was privately funded, and he was only borrowing USDA facilities to house the coyotes. Animal Damage Control, he said, was not involved in the study in any way. The study also hadn't started yet, so the animals were still healthy. Today, Foreyt notes, there is still no vaccine available to prevent this disease in dogs.

Rod and Jill did their best to understand the animals they were dealing with, digging in university libraries to unearth what they could about every study, but in this case they were simply off the mark. Not that it changed anything; the coyotes were in cages, and they had to be released.

Rod got on the phone to writer Rik Scarce, still in Pullman finishing his sociology Ph.D. at WSU.

Rod had been interviewed by scores of reporters, writers, and academics over the years, but Scarce had deep knowledge of the movement and loved to talk philosophy. The two of them could sit around the kitchen table for hours and hash out the finest details of anarchism, deep ecology, and the role of a movement in a universe where the individual was supreme. During the recon trip to WSU two weeks earlier, Rod had spent a couple nights at Scarce's house, though it's unclear whether Jill had. (Scarce told me he had "no comment" on whether Rod's accomplices had ever stayed at the house.) Scarce had asked Rod if he'd like to house-sit sometime when Scarce was on vacation, since Rod was essentially homeless. Rod told him over the phone that he'd take him up on the offer.

In the first week of August, Rod drove Scarce and his family to the Pullman airport, asking lots of friendly questions about their travels. As far as Scarce and his wife, Petra Uhrig, knew, Rod was there doing research for CAFF rehabilitation campaigns. He couldn't help feeling some small dollop of guilt as he bid them bon voyage, knowing he might be making them the subject of intense federal scrutiny by the time they got back to their home.

Rod and Jill had also picked up a fourth ALFer on their way to Pullman, a woman from the Ashland area whom we'll call Marie. She was another onetime CAFF volunteer who had spent some time with both of them in the cabin on the Elwha River taking care of the mink and the cats. She was young, and she was new to this kind of action, but she was committed. Rod had spent time with her again among a group of friends in the bucolic Applegate Valley in July, after the attack on the feed co-op, and as he'd gotten to know her better, he'd gradually revealed his plan to hit WSU. She didn't know anything about Rod and Jill attacking OSU or the co-op, but when she heard about the animal experiments at WSU, she was eager to help.

With Scarce and his family gone, Jill and Marie dug for more research information in the university library while Rod toured the university farms again by mountain bike. He knew a lot of what he needed to know about Gorham's operation, but he was looking for a hidden lab he'd read about in a local newspaper.

Dr. Fred Gilbert was working to improve the efficacy of leghold traps designed to kill beavers, otters, and muskrats by drowning them. An article about his work in the *Spokane Spokesman-Review* had indicated that Gilbert was worried about an attack by animal extremists, and all the signage had been removed from his field lab. The only thing Rod had to go on was a type of fence shown in the newspaper photograph.

As he pedaled up a dirt path beyond the mink farms, he found a grassy hollow that held some buildings not visible from the nearby gravel roads, and next to one of the buildings he recognized a bit of fence from the photograph: it was the fence that surrounded the pool for Gilbert's animals. Without going any closer, Rod quickly moved on, figuring they'd come back at night and do some recon.

When he told Jill and Marie about the discovery, Jill suggested they check it out immediately. She'd almost been caught last time, but she was ready to dive right back in.

Long past midnight, Rod, Jill, and Marie climbed on their mountain bikes and coasted down through sleeping Pullman toward campus. This time, they each carried topographical maps, water, and enough money to get back to Portland if things went haywire. On the northern edge of campus, they locked up their bikes and slipped over a fence into tall grass, changed into dark clothing, and then glassed all around to make sure they hadn't been spotted. After the close call less than two weeks earlier, they reasoned that campus police would be on the alert, but their radio protocol, clothing, and tools seemed like real James Bond spy stuff in little Pullman, home to the National Lentil Festival.

When they found the single-story building Rod had seen earlier, far off the road, they sat together and watched it for over an hour by moonlight. There was the pool featured in the newspaper photo and a series of dog runs that they figured held the fishers, martens, and beavers used in Gilbert's research. Rod spotted small poles at each corner of the enclosure, which turned out to be elements of an infrared security system. Finally, they belly-crawled up to the west edge of the lab and studied the infrared beams. It wouldn't be impossible to get in, but it would be time-consuming and risky to bypass them.

They retreated to hide in the brush again, then made their way toward what they believed would be the coyote pens. Between Gilbert's facility and Gorham's Fur Animal Research Station, they'd seen a low building that looked like it was made up of a series of long caged pens. It was completely dark and without even a yard light. The trio crept up on it and were only a few feet away when they noticed the canine shapes waiting within.

Timid and frightened coyotes hugged the shadows in seven of the pens. Rod found that despite a small padlock on the gate, he could lift the latch just enough to get the door open. As he walked down the row of pens, the coyotes cowered as far away from him as possible.

Executing coordinated strikes would require planning, more planning than they could do in the field, so they walked back to their bikes in silence. They had to try to hit Gorham's offices on campus, the Fur Animal Research Station where he kept his mink, and Gilbert's wildlife unit. And now the coyotes. Jill, in particular, wouldn't leave without those coyotes.

Rod spent the next week sitting on a small hill above the parking lot of WSU's Bustad Hall, the College of Veterinary Medicine building where Gorham had his offices, watching the flow of people coming and going. The building was busy, but soon he knew the hours of the cleaning crew, the faculty, and a few industrious graduate students burning the candle at both ends.

On the final night of his recon, Rod slipped into the building just before the doors were locked at nine P.M. Unmasked, he trotted up to Gorham's offices on the third floor. He'd been in the building several times and knew the way. Next to Gorham's offices in rooms 337 and 339 stood a series of steel file cabinets, and Rod deftly leaped up onto them and pushed up a tile in the drop ceiling, peering into the darkness with a flashlight. A series of heavy steel pipes, probably a sprinkler system, ran through a man-size hole in the cinder block wall. Through that hole, one would be directly above Gorham's offices. That's all he needed to know.

On the way out, he examined the push-bar latch on the building's rear door. The catch could be rigged with short screws that would give way with a sharp tug. In minutes, he was back on his bike and gone. Later, the three saboteurs talked into the night, carefully mapping every one of their individual routines. It was three A.M. before they finally went to bed.

The next morning, they were awakened by Joseph knocking at the door. It was a relief to have someone else around with whom they could talk openly about the campaign. Neither of the women knew Joseph, and neither he nor Marie knew for sure that Rod or Jill had been involved in the Corvallis and Edmonds actions, so there was a lot that went unsaid. Rod never revealed Joseph's real name to the women. He would use a pseudonym.

While Rod made coffee and a breakfast of scrambled tofu and potatoes, Jill ran down the whole action plan to Joseph. He had just come in off the road, but he listened attentively and asked relatively few questions.

Lots of questions remained, however, and many of them centered on Gilbert's lab. The newspaper article about his work had mentioned a cache of videotapes there, which he'd refused to release, saying they were the property of the Canadian government. The Western Wildlife Unit decided they would love to get their hands on those tapes and whatever gruesome footage they contained, but none of them had seen the inside of his building. There was also the issue of the infrared security system.

On the morning of August 12, the foursome rose knowing that they'd probably be awake for the next twenty-four hours or longer, and that some of them might be in prison or worse by the time they were through. Rod knew that the action was too complex and they had too few people, even as he watched his cohorts wiping the fingerprints off their tools. But he wasn't about to pull back. He reasoned that a few people could achieve more than an army if sufficiently motivated. Delusion was as good a motivation as any, maybe better.

The skies offered an omen: the weather was clear and warm, and Perseid meteor showers were predicted. Rod hopped on his bike and coasted down to Bustad Hall to swap out those screws.

He locked his bike near the building's loading dock and moved to the door, quickly checking the upper floors for movement. Then, in the space of two frantic minutes, he produced a screwdriver and zipped out the two screws that held the metal catch, replacing them with short screws. When he was finished, he dashed up the stairs and made sure there were no unexpected changes to Gorham's office setup.

On a cart outside one of the offices sat a clear plastic cage that caught his eye. Seven or so mice scurried around in the wood chips inside, and the tags on the cage indicated they'd just been irradiated. Without thinking, Rod scooped up the cage and hustled down the stairs and out the door, closing it carefully to not dislodge the catch. It was an impulse grab. He'd stash the mice in Scarce's house and figure out what to do with them later.

Joseph drove through the dark streets as Jill, Marie, and Rod sat in silence with backpacks on their laps. It was clear that everyone was a bit frightened. Still, Rod thought to himself that he didn't want to be anywhere else. He was living for this. As they approached the drop-off point on the remote dirt road, Joseph geared down and used the emergency brake so he wouldn't illuminate the brake lights on the car.

"Radios to Channel 2," Rod said, leaping out. "We'll do a radio check when we're in place. See you in a few hours."

He, Jill, and Marie piled out into some tall grass and hunkered there for a short while to make sure their exit hadn't been noticed. They moved further away from the road and over some fences to a small stand of trees near Gilbert's lab. The radios were loud and clear, and they told Joseph they'd only call again for a pickup.

Near the fence surrounding Gilbert's lab, Rod found an eight-foot section of two-by-four lumber laying in the grass and slid it across the top of the fence to rest on a cage inside the compound. The infrared beam ran under it, at a height of about three feet off the ground. He climbed up on the fence and tested his weight on the board, then was distracted for a moment by bats flying overhead; to Rod, their squeaks and pips sounded like an alarm. He had just relaxed again when the radio crackled. "Police patrol," Joseph whispered on the other end.

Jill and Rod retreated back to Marie's lookout position and waited. The car passed on the road and did not stop. But they continued to wait to make sure it didn't double back, and in the process lost a lot of time. There were only so many hours until daylight, and they had so much to do. Gilbert's lab was the one area they knew nothing about and needed to search, so they reluctantly shifted the plan. They'd have to hit the other locations first, where they'd already been inside and had mapped out their steps, then return here if time allowed. Hoisting their bags, they began to jog down the trail.

The dew fell on the grass as they ran, and the meteor shower splashed streaks of light across the blue-black sky. Far off over the hills, they once again heard a lone coyote howl, answered this time by another, closer, and then the three prowlers were startled by the piercing wails of those in detention now only a few yards in front of them.

This was the moment to free them. Marie took up a watch position, and Jill began to cut the barbed wire that served as a secondary pen around the coyote facility. Rod pulled out a small set of bolt cutters, snapped the kennel's padlock, and, moving down the line, cut the locks on each individual pen.

Dark shapes moved around Rod as he worked, and he felt his mind open to these animals. Millennia of survival had gifted them with a brightness, a language that Rod felt enter him as a presence and that surprised him. He'd felt this with the mink and the cats on the sanctuary, but never before with coyotes. In many indigenous cultures, the coyote is known as the Trickster, the creator of the world, the untiring presence of God. He felt that intelligence now as he opened each pen and stood aside as its occupant fled.

Five of the six bolted for the hills, but one lingered, standing only a few feet outside the facility. It stood in the darkness looking nervously at Rod. He walked outside and tried to shoo it away, but it only leaped back a few steps and then stood its ground, insistent. Then Rod heard scratching from a part of the kennel he hadn't checked, and he realized there was one more. On the far side of the facility, he found a last occupant and cut it free, and as it bolted through the opened fence, the other wheeled, and together they disappeared into the dark ocean of grass.

Rod and Jill gathered up Marie, and the three of them ran to the Fur Animal Research Station. Rod and Jill quickly cut a hole through the chain-link fence, and Rod slipped through while the other two stood watch. He crept up to the building, and through a window that was cracked open he could hear the sonorous inhalations of a man snoring. They had half expected this, after Rod and Jill had been seen on the fence that night a couple weeks earlier. Gorham later noted that there was a student apartment in this facility, but it wasn't a watchperson. Rod was just relieved the person was asleep. His presence changed things some, but didn't stop the action entirely.

He moved to the mink barn, cut the hasp off the lock, and examined the mink inside. The breeding cards said they were a control group uninfected by the scrapie experiments. He wanted to simply open all the cages and unleash chaos, but the resulting mink battles would probably kill some animals, and the shrieking would wake the sleeping person, so he grabbed a transport box that could carry six separate mink and quickly filled it. He hefted it over the fence to Jill and Marie. He then replaced the lock on the door with one of his own and ran after the two women, who were already heading toward the pickup spot carrying the mink between them.

As they moved through the grass, they talked in whispers. It was already two forty-five A.M. on August 13, and the sky would lighten in a few hours. Their plan had been too ambitious. They had to choose between Gorham's offices in Bustad Hall and Gilbert's leg-trap lab. If they'd had six people and the kind of well-funded organization that the federal authorities attributed to them, they could have left several buildings in smoldering ruins and freed many more animals. During their planning, they'd talked about freeing the scores of other animals there, which included bighorn sheep, elk, and grizzlies. But they didn't. The action was limited to whatever Rod could do on his own with the remainder of the night. He decided to hit Gorham's offices, reluctantly abandoning the animals in Gilbert's leg-trap experiments.

"Unit one to base, do you read, over?" he said into his radio.

"Roger that, unit one, this is base, over," came back Joseph's voice immediately.

"You have a pickup at location A in eight minutes."

"Roger that, will pick up in eight minutes."

Rod handed off some of his unneeded gear to Jill and Marie, who would leave the campus immediately with Joseph and take the mink in a rental truck to a predetermined release point far outside of Pullman. They said their good-byes, and Rod was gone back to the coyote pens.

He took a can of spray paint from his pack and wrote, FREEDOM FOR FUR FARM PRISONERS—AMERICAN WILDLIFE . . . LOVE IT OR LEAVE IT ALONE, BRING BACK THE BISON, BRING BACK THE SWAN, and FRED GILBERT—YOUR [sic] NEXT! He also painted a crude coyote print in a circle, representing the never-ending circle of life. WSU police investigator Don Maupin would later note that he was impressed by this, saying, "They were good artists."

Rod was pouring sweat as he ran the mile to Bustad Hall, shedding layers and stuffing them in his pack as he went. Joseph would join him there as a lookout after dropping Jill and Marie at the truck. He ran past the bear laboratory and the pens that held bighorn sheep and elk, saying a silent prayer for them in the night. Within fifteen minutes, he stood, doubled over and panting, outside the building that held Gorham's offices. After he'd recovered, he walked to the glass door and gave it a jerk. The catch pulled free from the door frame and clattered to the floor. He stashed the pieces in his pockets and then pulled a ski mask over his face. Anyone encountering him at this point would definitely be freaked, dressed as he was in black cargo pants and boots, a black vest with a radio antenna protruding from it, gloves, and a full balaclava.

He took two steps at a time to the third floor, then radioed Joseph. "Roger, unit one, this is base on call and all clear." Rod swung the hallway door open, walked to rooms 337 and 339, and leaped up onto the file cabinets in the hallway. He popped up the ceiling tile, pushed his backpack into the crawl space, then hoisted himself in and replaced the ceiling tile behind him.

With his small flashlight in his mouth, he straddled the sprinkler pipe and moved to the hole in the cinder block wall. Pushing through, he was above the ceiling in Gorham's office. Lying on the sprinkler pipe, which was suspended from the cement ceiling above him, he moved out over the office and cut a hole in the drywall ceiling below him with a utility knife, then inserted a keyhole saw and made an opening big enough to fit through. He slowly poked his head into the hole like an upside-down gopher.

The glow from computers and other equipment illuminated the dark room just enough to make out more filing cabinets, a desk, bookshelves, and a brand-new computer still in the box. At the far end of the office was a tinted window looking out on the parking lot, and at the near end was a door to an adjoining office. The door to the hallway was directly below Rod.

He didn't see any motion detectors mounted in the corners of the room or an alarm wired to the door. With a length of parachute cord, he lowered his pack, which contained his tools and plastic bottles filled with hydrochloric acid. He then dropped to the floor in a crouch next to his bag.

He went straight to work, rifling through Gorham's desk, throwing documents to the floor, and searching for computer disks and photos or any other valuable information. It would have taken days for a thorough search, so he removed the acid from his pack and stuffed the bag full of computer disks and plastic sheets of slides. Within minutes, the floor was covered in paper documents. He started dumping entire desk drawers, file cabinets, and bookshelves onto the floor, standing on the pile as he turned out the contents of the entire office. He unboxed the new computer and smashed it to the floor, fully aware that he was making a lot of noise. He then moved into the adjoining office and pounded the expensive equipment, leaving a swirl of disemboweled electronics.

Finally, he spray-painted the walls with A.L.F.——WE ARE WATCHING and JOHN, THIS IS WHAT HAP——which is right where he ran out of paint.

He pulled on a small respirator and emptied the acid onto the research documents on the floor. Documents and plastic curled and melted, and noxious fumes rose quickly. He then found he couldn't open the hallway door because it opened inward and was blocked by the heap of papers, so he grabbed his pack and frantically scrambled back up through the hole in the ceiling, exiting the same way he had come in.

As he walked away, the offices looked normal from the outside, other than a few telltale papers from the pile that had pushed out under the door.

"They didn't do a hell of a lot," said Gorham in 2008, reached at his home in Washington. "They got into my office, they ripped up everything, the computers and all the equipment in the office, and they poured hydrochloric acid over everything. So I had to stay out of there for a while." Fingerprint powder, he said, is still on the hallway walls outside his office even now. They only took six mink. And the mice. "It wasn't really a big deal on the animals they took," he said.

The sky was beginning to lighten as Rod climbed into the Subaru with Joseph.

"How'd everything go?" Joseph asked as they drove casually back to Rik Scarce's house.

"Well, we couldn't get into Gilbert's lab, but we accomplished everything else we'd hoped to," Rod said, noticing that his voice quavered. The adrenaline had now turned to fatigue.

"How'd the pickup go?"

"Without a hitch," answered Joseph. The two women were already well on their way to the Clearwater River on the Nez Perce reservation in Idaho, to a spot they'd chosen for the release of the mink.

It was then, as the pounding of his heart subsided, that Rod noticed a stinging sensation along his legs and body where splashed acid had burned through his clothing. Not wanting to leave any evidence, he had gathered up the empty bottles and stuffed them in his bag, too. He urged Joseph to move a little faster, and when they got to the house, he immediately shed his clothes and jumped in the shower.

Joseph began throwing those and all the other clothes they had worn into plastic trash bags—pants, shoes, gloves, everything, as well as some of the tools they had used. Everything had to go, right down to their underwear.

At seven thirty-six that morning, August 13, Rod faxed an ALF press release to PETA from the Kinko's in Moscow, Idaho, ten miles from Pullman. At seven thirty-nine, he faxed that same release to the Associated Press office in Spokane. Jill and Marie were there with him, and the three of them actively composed the communiqué.

Two Kinko's employees noticed them. Since the employees had to handle the faxes, they also caught a glimpse of their communiqué. That would become an important break in this case.

The communiqué explained exactly why WSU had been targeted and ended with these words: "No industry or individual is safe from the rising tide of fur animal liberation. To abusers of native wildlife everywhere, beware. The ALF has just begun to fight."

They returned to Scarce's house to help Joseph scrub the place top to bottom. Scarce and his family were due back the next day, and he would certainly be suspicious once he heard about the attacks.

Joseph split for Portland sometime during the day and was gone from the scene.

Meanwhile, back at the campus, Washington State University police were all over Bustad Hall and were quickly joined by ATF and FBI agents out of Spokane. Caustic acid fumes were pouring out of Gorham's office, so they had to seal off the building and call in a hazmat team. Squad cars sailed out to check all of the animal facilities, quickly discovering the raids on Gorham's research unit and the coyote facility.

It turns out that Gorham wasn't in Pullman that day. He was on vacation. One of his colleagues called to tell him that, as Gorham put it, "someone had torn the hell out of my lab."

Gorham noted that the attack hardly affected his work. He had to clean up, but didn't lose any essential data. He thought this was true of most of his colleagues who'd been hit by the ALF as well: the attacks simply weren't effective. He read to me from a 1991 newspaper clipping he'd saved, saying he was proud of his quote in it: " 'It's safe to say there'll never be a vaccine for AIDS or a successful treatment of cancer or Alzheimer's disease without the use of experimental animals. I wonder if healthy ALF members would volunteer for those trials.' "

He did say, however, "About that time, fur wasn't becoming very popular." He said that people were throwing paint on people wearing furs and admitted that his university research did change some: after the attacks, he started using sheep for his scrapie studies. "I don't recall that Coronado had anything to do with that," he added.

The next morning, Rod picked up Scarce and his family and drove the long way around from the airport so he wouldn't have to drive past the WSU fur farm, which was still crawling with university police and FBI. He distracted the sociologist with questions about his trip as they walked past a newspaper box at the airport that announced the raid in screaming headlines. Much to his relief, the subject never came up. He dropped them at their house, and within a few hours Jill, Marie, and Rod were on their way back to Portland.

On the way, they swung down through Utah to check out some leads Jill had found in the library. The WSU coyotes had come from a big coyote facility at Utah State University in Millville. The National Wildlife Research Center facility there was conducting experiments they'd read all about in documents they'd unearthed at WSU.

They hiked into the hills behind USU and found the coyote kennels without too much trouble. They had climbed into an old hay shelter—a kind of metal pole-barn roof with no sides, which was stacked with hay bales—and set up their spotting scope on top of the bales. Rod was sketching the place while peering through the scope and saw the coyotes pacing back and forth in their runs. The three went back that night and heard them all howling, and made a solemn promise to come back for them.

They also passed by the Fur Breeders Agricultural Co-op in Sandy, Utah, just south of Salt Lake City, a key nutrition-study link that they had discovered from information gathered in their raids. Not only did the co-op supply feed to the many fur farms Rod and Jonathan had discovered in Coalville, Utah, during their Global Investigations stop there, but it turned out that the co-op conducted some of its own nutrition experiments with mink in cooperation with Idaho State University, which received a small grant from the MFRF.

On August 15, Rod sent out a second press release and a video on the WSU raid, which were received on August 16 by TV stations KHQ and KREM in Spokane. The release quoted a story from the June 19, 1991, issue of *Fur Rancher* magazine that was written by Gorham, noting his cooperation with Soviet fur animal researchers in solving disease issues. He's cited in the magazine as "one of the world's top authorities on fur medicine on fur farms."

The videotape ended with footage of one of the CAFF mink leaving a cage, entering a stream, and swimming away. The press release ended with a few lines that have echoed to this day, giving the entire campaign its name: "As long as one member of a native American wildlife species is held captive, ALF will continue Operation Bite Back until all hostages are freed."

THIRTEEN

Operation Bite Back

NOW IT HAD a name, Operation Bite Back.

And it also had a lead suspect, Rodney Coronado.

It didn't take long for the authorities to track the faxes to the Moscow Kinko's, and when local police went there to ask around, they got a very good description and a sketch of the man who had sent the faxes. The man was clearly Rod. They also got an Identi-Kit drawing of one of the women with him, but it just didn't look like anyone Rod had worked with. It could have been anyone.

Afterward, the Washington State University Police Department's Don Maupin went out to Moscow with his collection of photos. The Kinko's employees were quick to point out Rod. "That's the guy we saw," they said.

John Gorham told a reporter that he'd seen a fellow on TV talking about the attacks, a guy named Jim Perez, and thought he was a "dead ringer" for the Kinko's sketch.

Maupin's photo collection also had images of some others who were known associates of Rod's, including Lee Dessaux, Jonathan Paul, and some female activists. The ATF and the FBI had been churning through activist networks surrounding both Rod's personal life and CAFF, and slowly gathering photos. They knew there had been a couple of women with him at the Kinko's, or at least one, but these might not have been the same women Schuening and Maupin had talked about; several people, such as the Kinko's employees and some others in the WSU community, had gotten a look at the women who were with Rod and could not identify them.

Rod, however, was now the main focus of their investigation. He became a person of interest, wanted for questioning.

Two agents from the Spokane FBI office came down to poke around. One of them was Bob Houston, a blond, good-looking guy who was new to the bureau. His partner was a slower-moving fellow just about to retire. They were like Frick and Frack, and allegedly didn't add much to the investigation on the ground there. The WSU and Pullman officers teased them a bit, saying that the bureau's attitude was "Have you solved this case yet? If you have, we'll take the case. If not, call us when you do."

What they did do, however, was make connections between all the Operation Bite Back attacks. They began profiling the actions from Oregon State University, Edmonds, and WSU as a group, tracking entry methods used, incendiary types, spray-painting, communiqué syntax, and handwriting. That effort quickly expanded. Maupin said they formed an ad hoc task force, though it was never officially budgeted or recognized as one. The group would eventually include U.S. attorneys and assistant U.S. attorneys from five states; FBI and ATF offices in Portland, Spokane, and Seattle; Schuening and others from the Oregon State Police; the Mounties out of Vancouver, British Columbia, where Rod had skipped out on bail in 1987 and where they had their own serious problems with the ALF; and WSU and OSU campus police. Later, others started getting involved. They even had a couple antiterrorism agents out of the Los Angeles Police Department who started coming up for their meetings, as more and more animal rights protesters sprang up around Southern California.

The name on every investigator's lips was Rodney Coronado, but he was determined to throw them off by constantly moving around the country. After a few days in the Ashland area, Marie and Rod swung north again to Portland to pick up Jill.

The trio shoplifted supplies from a "corporate" natural food store in the city, then set off across eastern Oregon to Sandy, Utah. The target was the Fur Breeders Agricultural Co-op. If they were

successful there, they'd hit the Utah State University coyote facility, too.

After crossing the salt flats of Utah, they found themselves on
August 26 in an industrial area of the city of Sandy, cruising past the
co-op on a dusty paved road. It was a compound of scattered buildings that included a small mink farm next to an industrial canal. Big
rigs rumbled in and out of the place, picking up deliveries for around
the country. There were plenty of dark corners in which they could
hide.

After an initial pass, they decided to come back later that night
to scope out the place. Already, their methods were getting lax: they
were willing to forgo thorough surveillance to hit it as quickly as
possible and then move on to the next target. But they had long dis-
cussions in the car regarding this point. If they were going to use
fire, they had to be absolutely sure there were no people or animals
in harm's way, no way for it to spread, no disastrous conflagration.

Rod got a hotel room in Salt Lake City using one of his false
driver's licenses—he had acquired two of them, both from Iowa,
one issued to James Corrigan, DOB 7-16-53, and the other to Frank
Garcia, DOB 7-16-63. His photo was on each. They puttered until
after midnight preparing their nighttime gear.

In the early hours of August 27, Marie dropped Rod and Jill at
the freeway exit near the co-op, and the two of them walked along-
side the industrial canal behind the buildings. In the limited glow of
far-off streetlamps, they could see the dark shapes of mink swimming in the canal, which they had come to expect at every fur farm.
But Rod had to admit the action didn't look that good: the eight
short mink barns abutted the main office and the research building;
a fire in those buildings might put the mink at risk.

Jill stood watch as Rod tried to sneak into the feed-manufacturing
plant. Large diesel trucks stood idling at the loading dock. Rod
crawled on all fours with his small binoculars in his mouth to keep
them from swinging into anything and making a noise. He got close

enough to overhear two drivers, but gleaned little from their conversation. It was one thirty A.M., and they were just about to go out on deliveries.

There was one more building, removed from the others, but he couldn't determine its function. He found a ladder to the roof and crawled toward what looked like a skylight but was actually a vent locked with a flimsy latch. Prying the vent cover off with a screwdriver, he peered into the open three-by-three-foot hole. The light from an adjoining room did little to illuminate the contents of the space below him. Fully expecting motion detectors, Rod pulled a small rubber ball from his pocket and dropped it through the hole. The ball bounced around in the darkness, unanswered.

"Jill, I'm going into this building through the roof. Stay alert in case I trip some kind of silent alarm," Rod whispered into his radio.

He put on his small fanny pack and then dropped into the hatch legs first. He had to let himself fall the few feet to the floor, landing in a crouch.

The room was stacked with packing materials and other supplies related to the production of fur-animal feed. Rod was on the second floor, so he crept toward a wooden staircase and carefully descended to the first floor, where light bled into the space from a source far from the stairs. He could see the silhouettes of tractors and the specialized carts used to ferry mink food up and down the cages on a mink farm. It was all material used to care for mink, and a perfect target. Rod scanned the structure and realized the interior was entirely made of wood. With a southerly wind, a fire could potentially destroy the building without harming the mink, which were about one hundred yards away on the other end of the compound.

At exactly the moment Rod became aware of dog shit on the floor around him, he saw the outline of a large German shepherd. He held his breath. The dog sniffed the air but seemed relatively unconcerned and not on alert. It was either someone's pet or a piss-poor guard dog.

Either way, Rod slowly reversed his steps up the stairs without alerting the dog. He used a plastic five-gallon bucket as a step and pulled himself back onto the roof.

"Vehicle approaching your position," Jill said over the radio.

A car pulled up to the building while Rod crouched on the roof, and a man entered, then left again with the dog. When Rod reached Jill again near the canal, she told him the man had left the feed-manufacturing building at exactly two A.M., evidently at the end of a work shift, gotten his car, retrieved the dog, and driven away. Probably just keeping his pet there while he was at work.

During the car ride back to Salt Lake City, Jill and Marie said they wanted to call off the action. There were simply too many workers around, apparently in second and third shifts, and possibly other animals in the storage building Rod had entered. Rod, however, was ready to go. The women agreed to support him, but didn't want to participate. They'd drive him, but otherwise, he was on his own.

The next morning, Rod walked to a store and bought a pack of Virginia Slims 120s. He lit up in the hotel room bathroom and measured the amount of time the cigarette took to burn down to the butt without his drawing on it. About twelve minutes. He wouldn't have much time before it ignited the bottles of gas-oil mixture, barely enough time to get away. But Rod refused to turn back.

At one A.M. on August 28, they piled in the car, and Jill drove. Rod, dressed entirely in black, rode in the back.

"All right, I'll see you in a couple hours," he said as Jill used the emergency brake to slowly bring the car to a stop.

"Good luck," said Marie, and Rod slid out of the car with his heavy day pack slung over his shoulder and disappeared into the night.

He ran in a crouch to a fence, went up and over, and was on the roof of the storage building just after two A.M. Once again, there was still activity at the feed-manufacturing building, but as he lifted the roof vent, he found a deserted building. No people. No dog. No other animals. He used a length of parachute cord to lower his pack into the darkened room and then dropped in himself.

Moving quietly down the wooden staircase, he made a quick search of the building and immediately began gathering pieces of wood and cardboard boxes lying around the room and laying them in a pile beneath the stairs. Then he unshouldered his pack and removed all the elements of his now-well-proven fire starter: three two-liter soda bottles of gas and oil, two 7-ounce cans of Sterno, three 2⅝-ounce cans of Sterno, a 16-ounce can of Ross Rubber Cement, eleven sticks of wood-wax fire starter, and six paper match books. He assembled it all and looked at his watch. There were still forty-five minutes until pickup. So he waited, uncomfortably, next to the incriminating device he'd built under the stairs.

He took a can of red spray paint from his pack and sprayed in two-foot-high letters, FREE ALL FUR FARM PRISONERS and A.L.F., adding a circle with a bear paw inside it, with two feathers dangling from the circle's arc. He went to the second floor and looked out at the roofs of the mink barns across the way, wishing there was some way he could use the diversion of the fire to free the mink, but he knew that this was guilt talking and that it would end in disaster.

At three ten A.M., Rod pulled a cigarette from the pack and placed it between his lips, casually lighting it. Once it was burning, he pressed it into a book of matches so that when it burned down, it would set the matches aflame and then the whole makeshift incendiary. Then up and out the hatch. In less than three minutes, he was at the highway. At the pickup point, he figured he had five minutes before the bottles of petrol would go up.

He reached the shoulder of the highway exactly on time, but there was no Subaru in sight. The girls were supposed to go back to Salt Lake City and then return, so there would be no car hanging around to raise suspicions in the small town. After a few nervous minutes, during which time the fire should have started, Rod began to worry. He was just standing there, on the side of the highway, totally exposed. He felt he was covered in evidence, and he began to catalog it in his mind—cigarettes, Sterno, rubber cement, gas probably all over his clothes, remnants of wood and cardboard, mink supplies of other kinds stuck to his boots, no doubt. His fitful inventory was shattered by the wail of a siren, and he leaped back into the dark shadows as a police car shot past and kept on going down the empty highway. His heart beat wildly in his chest. After ten minutes, he felt everything had gone wrong. At about three thirty A.M., he walked calmly to a pay phone outside a nearby fast food restaurant, where workers still inside eyed him suspiciously in his black attire, and he tried to call Jill at the hotel room. When there was no answer, he called a cab.

A cab! For a getaway from an arson only a few hundred yards away. He had to cool out. Immediately after hanging up, he scrapped that plan and began to hitchhike, standing in the lights of the restaurant.

A guy in a small truck on his way to work at a Salt Lake City grocery store stopped and picked him up. He didn't seem bothered that Rod was dressed in what looked like black combat gear and was standing on the side of the road with a half-empty day pack in the dead of night. Just another young anarchist traveler. Rod tried not to let the guy get a full look at his face, but that was impossible. It was a long ride into Salt Lake City, and Rod was convinced that the next time he saw this guy would be as a federal witness.

The driver dropped him off in front of the supermarket where he worked, and Rod got on the pay phone there. Jill answered, and twenty interminable minutes later the Subaru wheeled into the parking lot.

"Holy shit, where have you guys been!?" Rod hissed as he leaped into the back. He was hot, and Jill was practically in tears as she explained that there was major highway construction all over Salt Lake City and that she and Marie had gotten hopelessly lost on their way out to Sandy. There was a highway diversion that wasn't in use during the day, because they were doing the construction at night, and even with a lot of stops for directions they hadn't been able to find the place.

Quickly, Rod cooled down and realized it didn't matter who was to blame; they had to get moving.

Later, he found out that the incendiary had not, in fact, gone off. Most interesting to ATF fire investigator John Comery, who examined the device, was not so much the construction of it but the extinguished cigarette butt, which had been in Rod's mouth and carried his DNA.

Rod had also narrowly avoided a potentially deadly screwup: the groundskeeper for the facility lived in a second-floor apartment in the storage building, hidden behind an open studded wall. There was a rag stuck in a hole in the drywall where the groundskeeper reached through to the light switch, which controlled the lights for the whole second floor.

It's not known whether the apartment was occupied on the nights Rod was in there.

The trio felt puny in retreat. Rod couldn't rest; he wanted to strike immediately and make up for the blunder. As they rolled across southern Idaho, he was running down a mental list of possible strikes. Jill and Marie were pretty disenchanted with the whole enterprise and were ready to step back for a little while. Rod understood and didn't try to change their minds. He could always recruit a new team. And he already had his eye on two or three places he wanted to hit before the snow fell and the next pelting season began. He'd go it alone if he had to.

FOURTEEN The Center of the Universe

AS SEPTEMBER 1991 broke and the long Indian summer began
in the Siskiyou Mountains, Rod bounced around the Applegate Valley. He had a little money from private benefactors, like the guy
who'd sent him fifteen hundred dollars for the OSU action, but it was
never enough to live on. Since returning from Utah, he had been living out of his car, near riverside campsites, stashing the Subaru in
dark keeps under the blue oaks and sycamores. He'd bathe in the
chilly waters of Humbug Creek, the Applegate River, or one of the
many tributaries that eventually spilled into the Rogue, then get on
his mountain bike. Occasionally, he'd come into Ashland to check
the CAFF P.O. box and drop in on Marie or one of the several locals
who had helped on the CAFF sanctuary. He was trying not to make
contact with any of his known associates. Most of them had asked
him to stay the hell away, after they had been visited by either the
Oregon State Police, the ATF, or the FBI. But Rod's admirable ability to live wild was trumped only by his need to be in company.

His reputation as a radical (but not yet as an arsonist) was known
in these parts, and he was welcomed by a lot of the back-to-the-
landers who'd settled the area in the 1960s and '70s. The mountains
all around Ashland were a sanctuary for intentional communities
and Vietnam vets who'd withdrawn to the tall trees, only to find
themselves battling their own government over the ongoing usage
of the cancer-causing herbicide Agent Orange. The chemical was used
to withering effect in the jungles of Vietnam, but during and after

the war the federal government also put it to use in Oregon preparing clear-cuts in the national forests and on Bureau of Land Management (BLM) properties. This began in the 1960s and continues today—but not in the Applegate. Back in those remote watersheds, armed veterans crept out of their recondite cabins in protest in 1979 and again in 1980 and occupied timber sales that were flagged for cutting. Suited up in their camo and loaded for bear, they prevented the government's aerial spraying, eventually putting an end to some of the planned cutting, too. The activists called themselves the Applegate Occupation Team, and there was at least one incident during these protests in which it was reported that someone— maybe one of the Occupation Team; they weren't identified—had shot at a helicopter. BLM rangers and special agents would thrash out into the woods, trying to chase these seasoned jungle fighters out of the trees. But it wasn't all war games, as housewives and retirees also joined the cause, invading local BLM offices on multiple occasions and chaining themselves to doors and desks. The mix of armed occupation and nonviolent direct action united the locals— well, as much as they wanted to be united, anyway.

The upshot was that fewer of the tall trees were cut down in the Applegate. Direct action works, if saving trees is your thing. And for the residents out there, it was. Siskiyou Earth First! and Kalmiopsis Earth First! were two active EF! branches in the area that formed after the Occupation Team disbanded, both focused on stopping the ongoing heavy expansion of federal timber sales, and they had plenty of recruits.

A man named Gently, one of Rod's old friends from Santa Cruz, came through the Applegate in October, and he and Rod biked down off the mountain to the Ruch Barter Fair. The Applegate Valley is known for its Mediterranean weather, keeping its sun even when neighboring Ashland and Medford are covered in winter fog, and this Indian summer was hot. The two riders splashed through the dappled shade of sycamores along the riverbanks, down out of the big ponderosa pines and Douglas firs and incense cedars into a narrow valley of old gray barns and orchards heavy with apples and pears, past roadside stands selling cider and honey, and into the tiny crossroads of Ruch.

It was the fourteenth annual Barter Fair, part county fair and part Woodstock, a gathering of more than five thousand who came to listen to music, trade for food and crafts and technology like solar panels, get stoned, go topless, and demonstrate by their presence that they were (mostly) against the Gulf War. Rod and Gently made their way to the acoustic stage for music and some vegan apple pie.

Strolling among the vendors, Rod ran into the woman who owned the cabin on the Elwha River in Washington that he and the other CAFFers had occupied during the rehab project. She introduced him to a local friend named Jeffree, who mentioned in conversation that he was seeking a caretaker for his own cabin on the Little Applegate River a few miles away. Rod immediately agreed to rent it, sight unseen, for fifty dollars a month, even paying in advance through the end of the year.

He retrieved the car and drove west along the Applegate River, then up Little Applegate Road until the pavement ran out. He continued on for a few miles down a rugged dirt fire road. Finally, he nosed his dusty Subaru off the road and killed the engine, listening to the water burble below him. The cabin sat across the Little Applegate River about twenty feet from the bank on the steep and shaded west-facing slope of a mountain, with a canopy of oak and sycamore and a mile of ponderosa pine above it. Jeffree had built a plank bridge across the icy river, which ran down through the deep, mossy hush of the gulch.

Rod stepped up onto the small wooden deck and pushed open the unlocked door. Inside sat a propane stove, a big Fisher woodstove, and a kitchen counter with a sink built into it. There was no running water, no electricity, no phone. But the loft above the kitchen was well made, with plexi windows looking out on the river.

An A-frame house with a grass yard stood a ways off across the creek, but he was secluded from the rest of the world. He was way off the grid. He was nowhere. It was perfect.

The property was owned by a woman named Cat, who had moved back to her family home in Texas. Cat had purchased the land from Chant Thomas and the Trillium community, a commune that lay just down the road, across the river.

Moving in next to Trillium was a major selling point for Rod, as he and Thomas already knew each other pretty well. Thomas had started Trillium in 1975 on the site of an old fish hatchery in the Little Applegate Valley and in 1988, after a breakup, had decamped to California for six months to get a degree from UC Santa Cruz. There, he had started Banana Slug Earth First! and met Rod. He had been impressed by Rod's organizing with the Hunt Saboteurs and had even intended to go out on one of the bighorn sheep sabs, but never made it.

Thomas is about twenty years older than Rod, and even in 1991 he radiated a kind of satisfaction that reflected the ultimate success of his communal experiment in the Little Applegate. He had been involved in major environmental battles in the valley, with a group called Threatened and Endangered Little Applegate Valley (TELAV), but he was neither a recluse nor a monkeywrencher like Rod. He was a peaceful resister, calling Trillium an "ecostery"—a twist on the word *monastery*. Everyone still called it Trillium, but he had transitioned it from a lifestyle experiment into a nonprofit learning institution called the Birch Creek Arts and Ecology Center. There, he and his staff offered accredited university courses in ecology in a program they called Dakubetede Environmental Education Programs (DEEP). The reference, of course, is to deep ecology, and the institute's interest is in applied conservation biology, a mix of science and Gaian theory regarding the interconnectedness of all life. The program in the gorgeous mountain hideaway is still thriving and well attended today.

After they reconnected, Thomas quickly grew close to Rod and became one of his few daily contacts during the eight months he lived there. They'd hang out in Trillium's ramshackle office building with a big crackling fire roaring in the woodstove, sitting on the old couches and smoking pipes, talking about Rod's new project: all through the fall and winter, he was writing up the CAFF rehab in a series of articles for the *Earth First! Journal* and other publications and editing the miles of Hi8 video footage they had gathered during that project and the Global Investigations work that had come before it.

The film editing was done in rented edit bays in Ashland, but up in the cabin Rod had only an old manual typewriter, a small stash of photocopies from the purloined MFRF papers, and a small but growing pile of books. He had a boom box hooked up to a car battery for music. The whole point was to not have a lot of visitors, so he rarely needed more than the minimal Goodwill furniture he'd collected in Medford, but he found himself in a constant state of privation. He would spend hours wishing that Marie would come over on a whim, which she did from time to time, or that Jill would come down from Portland.

Marie knew how to play the guitar, and would make tapes for Rod, and he was trying to learn how to play the mandolin. Together they got the *Rise Up Singing* songbook and tried to learn how to play the songs in it, and it was the first time in his life that Rod actually made music. He was in love with Marie but too committed to escape to make anything out of it that could last. Sometimes Jill would join them on her guitar, too, and that's when the cabin felt most alive, full of wood heat and singing.

Rod craved his sorties to the Trillium office. He used the phone and fax there when he had to, sending out CAFF press releases once in a while. But he never revealed to Thomas that he was behind the ALF strikes on OSU or anywhere else, and he never used his place for ALF work.

"Things like [arson], they're just not creative enough. They don't have enough élan," said Thomas disapprovingly. "The thing in Iceland, very creative, had a lot of élan to it. The Boston Tea Party did. Which is what I call spectacle activism."

Thomas knew very well what the permutations were. Not only did he teach about nonviolent direct action, but he'd also housed Mike Roselle, one of the founders of Earth First!, for a bit in the 1980s. In fact, one of the first uses of the term "Earth First!" was on a banner made at Trillium, a picture of which still hangs on a wall in Thomas's office.

"I learned all this in the antiwar movement in D.C., that you really strive for these theatrical displays—but you don't want to mix the two. You don't want to have monkeywrenching going on in the same action. We even raided a tree-spiking camp and left a nasty note and took their drills," he said.

Thomas said he didn't know that Rod was behind Operation Bite Back until our interview in 2007. He didn't know the activist had two personas, "like Superman and Clark Kent," as he put it.

"No, I knew the stuff was happening, but I thought that he was, like, you know, the uninvolved spokesman who got these anonymous communiqués and relayed what was going on."

As he wrote about rehabilitating the mink and the lynx, Rod felt the reawakening of the Native American in him. It had come before, but never this urgently. He had been feeling it since this project had begun, like the smell of desert rain a long ways off. His fight to save the animals was the same as the indigenous fight against the white man, the original inhabitants fighting off a genocidal invasion. The only difference was that the animals couldn't fight for themselves. Books on Indian history had begun to stack up in his cabin. During the previous year, he'd been reading about the guerrilla strategies of the Lakota war leaders Red Cloud, Sitting Bull, and Crazy Horse, and he turned to them for wisdom or at least perspective on his way forward. They weren't Yaqui, but he related to them as First Nations people. The tales fed his natural restlessness, and images of the Indian Wars in the Great Plains took over his mind. In mid-September 1991, he headed off to South Dakota, enervated and without a village.

Rod already saw a day when he'd need to fade even deeper into the green for a while. His story now was like an old Western: The army was out looking for him, one bad Indian, one Geronimo. One Crazy Horse. These are not names to throw around for effect. Rod considered them his mentors. He headed into Indian country to try to find some firmer spiritual ground.

During the ethnic cleansing of native peoples that had come in the wake of the U.S. Civil War, the Lakota had perfected their own brand of guerrilla warfare. Rod found inspiration in reading about how war chiefs like Red Cloud had defended their traditional hunting grounds against superior U.S. Army forces.

The most famous of these Lakota guerrilla attacks came to be known by whites as the Fetterman Massacre and by natives as the Battle of the Hundred Slain. The Lakota had been attacking trains delivering wood to Fort Phil Kearny in Wyoming. After one such attack in 1868, a small party including Crazy Horse taunted the soldiers who had defended the train, reportedly even wiggling their bare butts at them. A foolhardy captain named William Fetterman took the bait, leading eighty-one heavily armed troops over a ridge and down into a neighboring valley, where they were annihilated by one thousand to thirteen hundred warriors in the worst loss ever suffered, at that time, by the United States forces in the Indian Wars. It was a precursor to the destruction of Custer's Seventh Cavalry at the Battle of the Little Bighorn by some of the same tribes eight years later. The Treaty of Fort Laramie, signed by Red Cloud shortly after the Fetterman rout, granted the Lakota much of western South Dakota and defined huge tracts as "unceded" territory, protecting native hunting grounds. The so-called Powder River War, or Red Cloud's War, was the only Indian War lost by the

United States, and Red Cloud was the only leader to force the United States to sign a treaty in defeat.

Rod needed to touch some of that magic. On his way to South Dakota, he passed through Missoula, Montana, and there he stopped and saw a woman he'd met during the Global Investigations work, a woman who had made it clear that she'd like to get to know him better. She was an Earth First!er and a bicyclist, and he took some comfort there for a day or two. He drove into Rapid City, South Dakota, then traveled the dirt Forest Service roads through the Black Hills alone. The Lakota believe that their people sprang from these hills. They call them the Paha Sapa. Rod avoided tourist creations like Mount Rushmore and Flintstoneland and, shouldering his pack late on the sunny afternoon of September 23, climbed Harney Peak, the highest point in the Black Hills.

The Lakota call this the Center of the Universe, and Rod felt connected to the dirt under his feet when he arrived at the summit at dusk. He decided to sleep there on the dome of still-warm granite. He dozed a few hours, then awoke to the rising of a full moon and watched the entire peak light up as moonlight reflected off the million prisms of granite. The mountains came alive all around him, and he knew the spirit of the place. He felt humbled and awed. He cried and prayed for courage from the Creator and from the animal spirits. He asked the mountain lion for strength. He asked the hawk to guide his way. Rod realized he was no longer scared by what he had started with Operation Bite Back; rather, he looked out over this expanse and thought only of the elders who had stood on this exact spot before him, including Black Elk and war chiefs and native fighters through the millennia whose entire nations had faced extermination.

Who was he? A guy who had freed a few score mink and known a couple of lynx? He'd have to think like Crazy Horse and Red Cloud if the animal races were going to survive; he'd have to use the Indian worldview that he and the animals and the earth were united and were strong. The Creator needed nothing from him, but he needed everything from the Creator. The best he could do was to ask the Creator for pity.

He sat facing the west, watching the moon fall into pale blue and finally rest for a moment on the horizon as the sun burned through from the east. Daylight came on, and he could see around him tobacco offerings wrapped in cloth the color of the Four Directions tied by previous visitors to nearby trees. The Creator did not speak to Rod that morning, but it didn't have to; instead, the earth revealed herself to him as she had existed since the creation: alive, breathing, intelligent, a living being of which humans were only a tiny part. His people did not have dominion over the earth; they *were* the earth. On a high rock wall, he saw a beautiful white mountain goat. This was all the power and beauty he needed to believe in. The prayers left by all the others were a source of tremendous solace and connectedness. He came down off the mountain feeling part of the world.

In October, the police sketches of Rod and an unidentified woman from the Kinko's in Moscow, Idaho, were released to newswires and started turning up in papers and on TV all over the West. Almost immediately, death threats started coming in to the CAFF P.O. box and to the voice mail. Ordinary people made the connections between Rod, CAFF, and the WSU action. The threats started out as a trickle and quickly became a steady flow. Many people who had seen or read Rod defending the Bite Back actions reached the conclusion that he was either the guy doing the attacks himself or closely involved.

Violent undercurrents had been running through the movement all year. In February 1991, two animal rights activists published a mysterious document titled "A Declaration of War: Killing People to Save Animals and the Environment." It was attributed to an author named Screaming Wolf and had, as the publishers explain in their forward, appeared on a computer disk in their mailbox. The piece is positioned as a philosophical treatise on the goals of "liberators"—

allegedly a breakaway arm of the ALF that advocates killing people as the ultimate animal rights campaign. Screaming Wolf claims to be not a liberator himself, but a careful observer of them. The piece put law enforcement on high alert, but would have been more alarming if it hadn't been of such shady provenance. In terms of style and content, it reeks of a hit piece, propaganda written by a rabidly anti–animal rights evangelist.

No group of "liberators" ever surfaced in the United States, and the document would have been dismissed as lunatic ravings if it hadn't been written in exactly the pedantic, instruction-manual language beloved by law enforcement. They treated it as gospel. "Liberators believe in killing humans to save animals!" it screams, with lots of underlines and exclamation points, like a religious tract. Even if activists ignored it, the screed only deepened law enforcement fears that animal fanatics were out of their minds with zealous fervor and were out for blood. Coming on the heels of the 1990 U.K. car-bombings that many activists in Britain thought were the work of provocateurs, and the car-bombing of Judi Bari and Darryl Cherney in the United States, it contributed to an atmosphere that was growing increasingly poisonous.

Rod addressed the death threats aimed at him and CAFF in pieces he wrote for the *Earth First! Journal* and in other communications, but the FBI also picked up on them fast and began using them as a lever to work at Rod's parents, and in particular his mother.

In late October, FBI special agent John Zent visited the Coronados, telling Sunday how concerned he was about Rod. The Coronados received regular visits from Zent. Somebody, he said, might try to take a shot at her boy. Or Rod might hurt someone. The scent of blood was in the air, and the FBI was not above confusing the issue. Rod and his parents didn't like the implications: How would this go down? Would one of these angry people try to kill Rod? Or would the FBI ambush him and claim that a fur farmer or bounty hunter had taken him out?

Neither of these scenarios was far-fetched in the least. The violence visited on Bari and Cherney was only a year old at that point. Bari was still relearning how to walk.

Zent made it plain to Sunday: in order to help save her son's life, she had to turn him over to the FBI.

After she was car-bombed, Judi Bari lived with her young daughters in a couple of very remote cabins, hiding out in an attempt at security, and one of them was about fifteen minutes outside Willits, where she was surrounded by movement people. When I walked through the door in 1991, she was still relearning how to walk, and she said that if I reported that the house was messy, she'd never talk to me again, and she meant it. She had circles under her eyes like two purple bruises.

During Redwood Summer, she had tried to enforce a no-sabotage policy among the gathered tree huggers because she wanted to keep tensions low. She was not against monkeywrenching, per se, although she had renounced tree spiking because it endangered loggers and mill workers. Her argument was that sabotage wasn't the way to a mass movement.

"If you were to institute the Monkey Wrench Gang strategy on a large scale—if you went out in massive-enough numbers to make a dent in, say, the logging industry—all that would happen is that the industry would institute virtual fascism to keep you out of the way," she said in our interview that day.

Besides, she pointed out, sabotage wasn't nearly as threatening as organizing.

"Right before Redwood Summer, Louisiana-Pacific closed one of its mills and began layoffs that eventually left 190 people out of work," she said. "We got a coalition of loggers, mill workers, IWW members, and Earth First!ers to go to the Board of Supervisors and ask that the county use its power of eminent domain to seize all holdings and operate them in the public interest. That was a pretty radical thing, especially for workers to do. That's when the death-threat campaign against me started."

In November, Rod's cabin became a little icebox on the river, and he kept the stove stoked. Pelting season was approaching, and the writing seemed less urgent than reminding his opponents that the war was still a hot one. He and two of his previous accomplices, Tim and Joseph, attempted to burn two mink farms, one in Sweet Home, Oregon, and one near Olympia, Washington, but they were frustrated both times. Both of the farms had security, and at the Sweet Home farm a man, alerted to their presence, rushed outdoors brandishing a rifle. They were lucky to get away unseen.

The failed operations, however, drove Rod crazy. It felt like a bad-luck streak, and he refused to believe in bad luck. He made plans for another trip to Montana, this time on the attack.

Sometime before November 21, 1991, he wrote a fund-raising letter to an unknown benefactor asking for twelve hundred dollars so he could raid two Montana fur farms. He wrote, "Television stations in Seattle and Portland are having reports into the ALF and their recent fur campaign aired the week before Thanksgiving." He wanted to act directly on the heels of this publicity, and one of his targets was Gered Huggans's Rocky Mountain Fur Company in Hamilton, Montana. He'd been in the buildings, he noted in the letter, and they were all wood and no alarms.

On November 21, KGW TV in Portland aired an interview with Rod that was part of the series he had written about in the letter. He appeared under his own name as the founder of CAFF and as someone who'd once had ties to the ALF. Rod acknowledged that CAFF had broken the law by releasing the brood mink in Washington, and he said of his tactics, "I find no alternative but to escalate. I think we're going to be faced with a situation where we will have to get more aggressive, uh, simply because we're dealing with an industry that's doing everything within their financial power to survive. Until we obtain release of these animals, we will consider it a political struggle and deal with it as if they were human prisoners. If the situation comes where we have to increase our campaign, we have no, no, no apprehension of doing that. We have already broken a law. Why not do it again?"

In early December, Rod sat across from Jill and Joseph at a Portland bar, working on the ritualistic pints and fries. It wasn't the smartest place to be; they were paranoid and under intense scrutiny. Jill had recently been present at a friend's house when Agent Comery came to the door, but luckily for her that's as far as he got. The friend answered the door and politely delivered the response they'd been trained to give: "Get a warrant, I have nothing to say to you, good-bye."

They stayed in the bar late that night. Rod broke down everything he'd learned about mink operations in the Bitterroot Valley south of Missoula, hoping to convince his two trusted accomplices to take part in arsons in Montana. The valley was hard up against some of the largest roadless wilderness areas left in the Lower 48; small roads led into the massive Selway-Bitterroot Wilderness to the west and pockets of the Anaconda-Pintler to the east. This time of year, there was only one road running in and out, so it was risky. But the Huggans Rocky Mountain Fur Company was among the valley's most prominent farms, and ever since his personal tour Rod had considered it a prime target.

December was pelting time, which would mean hitting the farm when there might be twenty-four-hour activity. A successful arson would be very difficult to pull off, but it could also destroy that year's profits.

Rod also brought up the possibility that they might be met by violence. The Sweet Home farmer with the rifle had scared him, and he recalled that nearly everyone on the Huggans farm had been armed. Rifles had hung in the windows of every pickup, and some of the employees had worn sidearms.

"That possibility is so remote I don't want it to stop me," said Joseph.

Jill felt the same. Operation Bite Back was back on.

They rolled into an activist house in Missoula and found it full of old friends. The words "activist house" don't actually mean much in Missoula, as the entire town is full of environmental activists, green energy entrepreneurs, river runners, hunting guides, and all manner of well-educated outdoorspeople. Nobody asked too many questions about why they were there.

Rod took advantage of the time there to help with the editing and layout of the December 21 Yule issue of the *Earth First! Journal*, which would feature his photos and four-page article on the CAFF rehabilitation project, titled "Freedom for Fur Farm Prisoners." At that time, the journal was published out of the Ecology Center in Missoula, and much to Rod's delight, one of his old flames from Montana was in town to work on the issue. Rod and Jill were not an item, as they had once been, so editing the story gave them both an excuse to rekindle their romance.

At night, the Missoula crowd would let loose. The EF! scene there had always been notorious for the high volume of its partying, which sometimes ended in physical injury from pranks and rough-housing. But after a few days of this, Joseph pulled Rod aside and told him it was time to get on with their business, and the next morning the two of them disappeared into the Bitterroot.

The ground was covered with a thin layer of snow as the two men lay on the top of a small hill watching the Huggans outfit. A stake-bed truck stood outside the pelt-processing building, and men were unloading heavy dark-colored bags.

"Those must be raw pelts from other farms," Rod said from behind his binoculars.

"Uh-huh. I was looking at those guns the guys are wearing," Joseph said flatly.

The pelts the workers were unloading for further fleshing and processing were worth tens of thousands of dollars. The two had perfect timing; a fire in that processing building would do heavy economic damage to the farm.

At a military surplus store in Missoula, they found winter camouflage clothing and topographical maps of the entire Bitterroot Valley. Jill would drop them off with their mountain bikes near the farm, but the pickup was risky; it was a single stretch of two-lane blacktop, and she had nowhere to hang out. If Rod and Joseph missed the pickup or had to abort and escape on foot, they would have to hike north thirty miles along the Bitterroot River and back to Missoula. To the south was a spiral of Forest Service roads, often impassable in winter; the west and east offered only snow-covered trails through massive expanses of wilderness. Hiking out would leave footprints in the snow, possibly with dogs and agents on their tails.

Jill was getting anxious about the weather. A steady snow had begun to fall on the bright gold aspens of the Clark Fork River. It was time to strike.

They had to pretend to leave town so their Earth First! friends wouldn't know anything about the attack. It was safer for everyone that way. They said their good-byes and quietly moved to a remote motel on December 11.

Rod stopped in at the Buttery Grocery in Missoula that day to buy the components of the incendiaries. Later, he realized he'd left his wallet in the shopping basket at the store. It held his Washington State driver's license and his U.S. passport, but more important, hidden in the lining were his two fake Iowa driver's licenses.

He called the Buttery, and they told him the wallet had been turned over to the Missoula police. It was nerve-racking, but he bet heavily on the idea that the cops wouldn't put the impending arson together with that wallet and decided to pursue getting his documents back some time later, when his two friends were not at risk.

In the hotel room, he built his incendiaries, tucked them into their Tupperware containers, and rolled out a sleeping bag on the floor.

He awoke at one A.M. to see Jill making a cup of coffee on a camp stove and Joseph gazing at the snow falling outside the window with his hands in his pockets.

"Hey Rod, looks like a great night for a bike ride," he said.

"Yeah," Rod yawned. "That's just what I was thinking."

They put on their winter whites, strapped up their packs, and loaded into the warm Subaru, where Jill was cleaning her glasses. It was cold and still, the temperature in the low twenties. During the half-hour drive to the drop, they agreed that if Rod and Joseph missed the pickup, she'd return to the motel and register for another night. They drove through Hamilton on Highway 93 and about five miles farther south, the only car on the road. Just up over a rise, Jill swung the car onto a side road and killed the lights. They unloaded the bikes.

"Good luck. Don't get frostbite," Jill whispered.

The bikes were unwieldy with their heavy packs, but they finally mounted up and lumbered down the snow-covered road. They kept on the main road for about a mile, until they could see the low mink barns. They ditched the bikes on the shoulder and went through the barbed wire together.

The only sound was the crunching of the snow under their boots. Within minutes, though, they could hear and smell the mink. There was no guard fence, and as they approached, they saw several escaped mink running around under the bright yard lights.

Just forty yards from the pelt-processing building, Joseph took up watch and Rod went to work. He knew from his tour that the doors were alarmed, and he assumed the same about the windows, so he focused on the exhaust fans that drew air out of the pelt-drying room, which was now stacked with furs. He moved to a large fan spinning in a panel of sheet metal, took out a small pair of vice grips, and began removing the self-tapping screws that held the fan in place. The work made a fair amount of noise.

When Rod had enough screws removed, he cut the wires that powered the fan, and with a small shock the fan spun to a stop. Through the blades, he could now see stacks and stacks of furs. He began to bend the loose sheet metal downward far enough to allow him to slip in, but the bending was noisy and attracted the attention of one of the farm dogs, which came slowly trotting right up to him.

Rod froze and hoped he would lose interest, but in a few seconds the dog was growling, and then the growls turned to loud, full-throated barking. Rod waited, but the barking didn't stop, so he left the fan flapping and retreated to where Joseph was hiding, with the dog barking at him all the way.

"What do you think?" he asked Joseph.

"If someone comes to investigate, they're going to see that loose fan, and all they have to do is follow our tracks in the snow to know where we are," Joseph replied.

The dog continued barking frantically, and they both agreed that someone would eventually come out of the house, pulled from sleep, probably armed.

"Let's get out of here," Rod said at last.

They tried to ride away across the snowy road but kept crashing hard to the frozen asphalt, so they started ditching the most incriminating evidence from their packs, flinging bottles of fuel and the incendiaries into the woods to lighten the load. They rode north until they saw a single set of headlights in the dead of night, which caught them on the road with no time to hide. They prayed it was Jill. It was.

Driving toward Hamilton with the bikes on top, Rod jettisoned more items out the window and into the woods. As they drove through town, a lone police car tucked in close behind them, following at an uncomfortable distance, obviously running their license plate. This was bad news. They all held their breath, silent and scared. Any second, they'd see the lights pop and get pulled over. The edge of town seemed a continent away, but when they reached it, the cop turned abruptly into a side street and let them drive off unmolested. They all exhaled at once.

"Fuck, that was close!" Jill barked, visibly shaken.

Rod sat with tears in his eyes as they rolled back to the motel in Missoula. Jill attempted to comfort him, and Joseph began to rationalize their good decision to abort, but Rod would not be mollified. He was furious that he'd failed the mink on the Huggans Rocky Mountain Fur Company. First Utah, then Sweet Home, then Olympia, and now this. It took several hours for him to come back to himself and apologize to his friends for withdrawing the way he had. It wasn't their fault. He had to prepare better. He had to design actions that would not, could not, fail.

FIFTEEN Crazy Horse Retribution Society

ROD'S NEXT ACTION felt like a comeback. He had scouted dozens of fur farms in Washington and Oregon, and he kept notes on those prime for sabotage. The Malecky Mink Ranch in Yamhill, Oregon, was for sale late in 1991, and Rod decided it should never get a new owner. A 1995 presentencing report prepared by Ian Dingwall, a federal probation officer in Kalamazoo, Michigan, states,

> On December 21, 1991, the Western Wildlife Cell of the ALF placed a timed incendiary device in or near the fleshing room of the processing building of Malecky Mink Ranch in Yamhill, Oregon. The device functioned as designed, and at approximately 5:45 a.m., a passing motorist discovered the building engulfed in flames. The building contained the feed mixer, flesh processors, cooler, dryer room, freezer and workshop. The Malecky Mink Ranch had been for sale since 1989, and the last mink had been pelted in November 1990. Mr. Malecky had advertised the sale in the Fur Ranch magazine mentioned earlier in this report.
>
> According to reports, on December 21, 1991, Mr. Malecky was awakened by a telephone call from an individual who rented a trailer from him. The trailer was located 20 to 30 feet behind the processing plant. The renter told Mr. Malecky that the shop was on fire. As he was getting dressed, he heard a pounding on the front door. At the door was a young man who excitedly told him that he had seen the fire from the highway and had come up to tell

people. The fire destroyed the building completely. Afterwards investigators discovered a nine volt battery, a metal battery clip, a metal spring from a timer or clock, and the lock and hasp to the plant door next to a cigarette butt. The loss to the Malecky family was $120,000.00. Insurance paid Mr. Malecky $97,000.00.

Mr. Coronado called KGW television station in Salem, Oregon, according to reports. Mr. Coronado did not identify himself but stated he was a member of ALF, and they were claiming responsibility for the fire at the Malecky Mink Farm. On December 21, 1991, a press release from the Western Wildlife Cell of ALF sent to the Earth First Journal stated, "Western Wildlife Cell members of the Animal Liberation Front (ALF) raided Malecky Mink Ranch in Yamhill, Oregon, and set an incendiary device that destroyed the processing plant of this fur farm near Salem." It linked the raid to the June 10, 1991, OSU raid when it stated, "Malecky Mink Ranch was a recipient of information from Oregon State University's experimental fur farm."

Chant Thomas looked out his window on Christmas Day, 1991, and saw smoke from Rod's place down on the river. Chant was single then and had made a tradition of going on a medicine hike on the holidays when other Trillium members were gone. He went down to invite Rod and found him in the cabin, hunched over his typewriter.

"Hi Chant, come on in. I'm just doing some work."

"Well, I'm going to go for a hike to a real special place I'd like to show you, and I thought you might want to go," said Chant, peering up into the loft. "Since you've got no company here today. And since it's Christmas."

"Shit, is it Christmas?" Rod looked at him, incredulous. He had forgotten. He thought immediately of his parents and his brother and how much they'd like to have him there in Morgan Hill, how worried they must be. He couldn't call or send a package, afraid the

feds would trace it. And he was right; they would have. Agent Zent
and others were monitoring the family home pretty tightly.

The hike took them up out of the riparian zone into the big
trees, up on the ridgeline to where it narrowed to a knife's edge.
Out there on a stone outcropping was the old soul that Chant called
Sacred Tree. The tree was an ancient ponderosa pine, thousands of
years old, with limbs bigger than a man could put his arms around
that bent all the way back to the ground against a million days of
wind. They formed a kind of room underneath. It was the oldest
tree by far that Chant had ever found in the Eastern Siskiyous, and
the offerings and messages left there indicated that it had been a
point of pilgrimage since before any European had been on these
ridges. It took up the entire ridgetop, which was just fifty feet wide,
with serious drops of hundreds of feet on both sides, and it seemed a
kind of station, a broadcast point, a listening post where the lines
were clear straight to the Maker.

Trillium sometimes ran vision quests, or what were then known
as eco-psychology programs, helping people find a spiritual connection to the physical world, and few places held as much power as
Sacred Tree. Even before they ducked into the shelter under its
limbs, Rod was shaken by it.

"You can't [go] there without going, 'Wow,' and so I took Rod
up there, and he was like—as many people that go to this tree are—
he was impacted; he was impacted majorly," said Chant. "I mean, it
was probably half an hour before he could talk. When you're open to
this type of energy, you know . . . Soon, we started talking about
the tree and what it meant and all this."

The days that had visited the tree were significant, as it stood
bound there to the rock, part of the rock itself and drawing its nour-
ishment from under it since maybe before Christ walked. Its quiet but
not undramatic persistence was meaningful to Rod. In it, he saw the
indigenous nations looking out upon themselves from a high place,
sawn, clear-cut, corrupted, but maybe outliving all else in the end.

Chant showed Rod his own little variation on a Tibetan prayer wheel or the prayer flags that folks sometimes left to lay their entreaties on the mountain wind: he had hidden a simple screw-top jar at the tree in which he placed prayers written on slips of paper.

"Rod called it the grandmother tree. He told me later that it was one of the reasons he went back down to hang with his grandparents and get back into the tribal life down there," said Chant. "When he was on the run, I went to my little prayer jar, and here's a little note from Rod and, like, a little eagle claw or little feather or something. I know a lot of people are close to him around here, and he would just slip in and slip out. But he said that he kept coming back to this tree because it meant so much to him, even if he might have to travel hundreds of miles out of his way."

By mid-January 1992, Rod and Marie were inseparable. The other women in Rod's life had faded into the background during his months in the cabin. The two spent a lot of time together in the Applegate and then decided to go on the road. Not to work, but to visit, and to deepen their ties to each other. Rod wanted to take Marie out to the Mojave, to a special place he had visited during the desert bighorn sabs that was called Jackass Spring. The two of them hiked out there over the extended dirt two-tracks and enjoyed the tremendous emptiness of the place in winter, the smell of cold sage and dust, when the chill forced them to wear sweaters and hats in a landscape that suffered deadly heat in summer. They were alone out there, happy in the company of wild sheep hidden somewhere in those dry chaparral draws. Even while it was happening, Rod thought of it as one of the times he'd felt closest to a woman and one of his happiest trips, and he was grateful to Marie for her part in that.

On this same trip, Rod dropped in briefly on his parents in Morgan Hill and also visited his brother. It had been many months since he'd seen them, and he had to give them some kind of sign that he was OK. They were relieved to see him fairly glowing with good health and victory, his guerrilla heart bursting with the campaign of the last year, but it did little to salve their worry when his car disappeared again into the underground.

If federal agents were watching the Sea Shepherd Conservation Society during this time period, they must have been talented, because we never saw anyone. During the first three weeks of February, I sailed with Sea Shepherd as press on an anti–tuna seining campaign in and out of the Eastern Tropical Pacific. We bounced through all manner of yacht clubs and fuel stops from the Caribbean side of Panama through the canal and up the coast to Mexico and never encountered as much as a sleeping customs man. The *Sea Shepherd II*, the group's 190-foot side trawler, had come down from months of repairs in Key West, and Captain Paul Watson was raring to go. We'd dock with the yachties and sit in the bar while Watson ate a steak and entertained the natives with his inexhaustible repertoire of jokes. We could have been hauling an entire invasion force; no one ever checked. He really did know a hell of a lot of jokes.

Colón, Panama, just after the Americans arrested Noriega was one of the most nakedly homicidal places I'd ever visited. The bakery was guarded by two hired men with MP-5 submachine guns. A man with a broad Jamaican accent walked up to me on the street, stopping inches from my face, and announced, "My name is Smith. There are some men down the street who are going to cut you. I propose you turn around and go back the way you came." We mostly stayed on the boat.

Watson and I sat on the bridge of his command vessel, a ninety-foot Canadian Coast Guard patrol boat called the *Edward Abbey*. It was hot in Colón, and the green jungle night made the murderous town look beautiful. Watson was telling me that Sea Shepherd enjoyed the support of the Dalai Lama, precisely because it was nonviolent.

"Up on our foremast on the *Sea Shepherd II* is a little statue that was given to us by a Tibetan monk," he said. "And that statue is the image of Hayagrīva. Hayagrīva is the wrathful aspect of Buddhist compassion. Meaning that if you can't reach these people any other way, you go and scare the living shit out of them until they see what's going on. And that's what we do."

"I find it really funny that we're dismissed as a violent organization by groups like Greenpeace or other groups—as militant, violent terrorists or whatever," he continued. "We've never injured anybody. We've never sustained an injury. That's a better record than Greenpeace, who's had one death and numerous injuries. We've never had a criminal conviction. If we were a terrorist organization, we wouldn't be operating in and out of U.S. ports. If we were criminals, we'd be in jail."

Later, in the greasy little club there, a shirtless yachtie said over his drink, "What do you do when you find these tuna boats?"

"Ram them," said Watson without missing a beat. "Cut their nets. Enforce international law. Then tow 'em back to shore."

In the last days of January, Rod was on the road again in Montana, en route to South Dakota and eventually to Washington, D.C., to talk with some animal rights contacts there. This time, he was traveling with an Earth First!er named Deb Stout and a friend from Ashland named Kim Trimiew. Both of them had worked on the CAFF sanctuary, and had flings with Rod, each unbeknownst to the other.

Rod was rereading many of the books on Geronimo he'd read as a boy, including *Watch for Me on the Mountain* and David Roberts's *Once They Moved Like the Wind*, a history of the Apache resistance. He was looking for sustenance, for strategy, taking notes on the Apache war chief's guerrilla tactics during his most infamous strikes, like the attack at Nuri in Sonora. According to one of the books, Geronimo offered to sell a village of Apache women as slaves to the Mexican army at Nuri; when the women were presented, however, they produced rifles from under their skirts and wiped out the large—and heavily armed—garrison.

Rod was also hungry for books on the Yaqui, but he couldn't get his hands on many. Even though the Yaqui's militant history extended into the 1990s, with the uprising in Chiapas, there still was not much on them specifically. At least when compared with Plains tribes like the Lakota or the Northern Cheyenne. The radical American Indian Movement of the late 1960s and early '70s had been largely centered on those Plains tribes, and Rod felt as though he were being drawn inexorably to engage that living militant experience.

He read Mari Sandoz's *Crazy Horse: The Strange Man of the Oglalas* and biographies of Sitting Bull. As he traveled with Stout and Trimiew, he was reading Peter Matthiessen's *In the Spirit of Crazy Horse*, a recounting of a clash between federal agents and members of AIM on a farm close to Wounded Knee, South Dakota, on the Pine Ridge reservation, the site of an 1890 massacre of unarmed Indians by the U.S. Army. In 1973, around three hundred members of AIM occupied Wounded Knee after a dispute with their tribal leader, whom they saw as capitulating to the oppressive policies of the U.S. Department of the Interior's Bureau of Indian Affairs. A three-month shooting war followed. In the aftermath of that uprising, the FBI stepped up its infiltration and destruction of AIM as part of COINTELPRO, and many link that campaign to the 1975 gun battle that is the subject of Matthiessen's book, in which one AIM member and two federal agents were killed. AIM member Leonard Peltier was jailed for the latter two shootings but continues to proclaim his innocence.

Rod was familiar with the history of FBI counterterrorism programs, and he had long worked from the assumption that similar tactics would be brought to bear on persons like himself. But he was growing increasingly concerned that as he came under greater po-

litical and law enforcement pressure, he was not prepared spiritually. He could not find in the environmental movement the reflection
of how he experienced the wild as a Native American. As he grew
increasingly disturbed by the relative emptiness of the lifestyles that
typified this network, he began exploring native spiritual practice.

The three travelers were on their way to D.C. to find Rod and
Jonathan's Global Investigations video footage and to talk to mainstream campaigners who could support it in the press, but for Rod it
was also a scouting mission. He needed to rediscover what it meant
to live as an Indian and engage native traditions in his own way—to
travel what native activists called the Red Road.

On February 2, 1992, Rod visited the Little Bighorn Battlefield National Monument, near the town of Crow Agency, the seat of the
Crow reservation in Montana. The monument marks the site of the
most well-known battle in the Indian Wars of the late 1800s, in
which an estimated 949 lodges, or nine hundred to eighteen hundred Lakota, Northern Cheyenne, and Arapaho fighters, unified
under the Sun Dance alliance to meet General George Custer and
seven hundred soldiers of the Seventh Cavalry in open battle on the
rolling grasslands of eastern Montana. No withering guerrilla campaign, this was large-scale confrontation in which the Hunkpapa
band Lakota war chief Sitting Bull, along with Oglala commander
Crazy Horse and others, outmaneuvered and overwhelmed the U.S.
soldiers. The same native force had stunned Brigadier General
George Crook, the most notorious Indian fighter in the U.S. Army,
a week earlier at the Battle of the Rosebud on June 17, 1876. On
June 25, five out of seven regiments under Custer's command were
slaughtered, and Custer himself was killed as well as two of his
brothers and a brother-in-law. The bodies were stripped, mutilated,
and left in the sun in what the Indians referred to as the Battle of
Greasy Grass.

One of the items carried away by native fighters after the battle was the notebook of Lieutenant Donald McIntosh, a cavalryman killed in the fighting. McIntosh had carried the small black book inside his flannel shirt under his uniform, and it had a bullet hole through it. A kind of diary, the ninety-eight or so pages contain notes about supply purchases and loans to soldiers. Two years later, when Native Americans were being rounded up for forced marches to the reservations, a soldier took the diary from an Indian woman, and it became part of the permanent display of artifacts at the battle-field monument.

As Rod moved around the displays, he felt a growing rage. Most of the small museum was dedicated to the heroics of the cavalry and the tragedy of its defeat. The exhibit didn't mention anything about the Native Americans' successful attempt to stop genocidal expulsion from territories secured by treaty during Red Cloud's War. In a glass case hung some spiritual artifacts that Rod reasoned should belong to the Lakota, including a buckskin ghost shirt worn in battle, a medicine bag, and ceremonial pipes and rattles. He felt they were being desecrated. No Jewish Torah scroll would ever be displayed like that. No sacred Catholic relic.

Rod had never seen the cavalryman's journal before that day, but he decided it was a symbol he could use to send a message. He strolled around the place for a while, examining the glass-and-steel cases that held the displays, looking for surveillance cameras, then started loosening the bolts on the displays by hand. It was during regular business hours, and maintenance officials testified later that the bolts were hammered to prevent such tampering, but he got them off without tools and quietly stole the journal.

It's not clear whether Stout and Trimiew were aware that Rod had the notebook. He immediately mailed it to a friend in Oregon for safekeeping. The book was valued at $120,000 by the National Park Service, but Butterfield and Butterfield auction house, which had handled lots of artifacts from the Little Bighorn battle, found

that number "outlandish" and estimated the value at $10,000 to
$46,000.

In his haste, Rod left behind thirteen usable fingerprints. It was
one of the few bits of solid evidence he would leave at any crime
scene during the entirety of Bite Back. And that would make all the
difference.

A few days later, from a friend's house in Boulder, Colorado,
Rod sent out an unsigned press release taking credit for the theft of
the journal in the name of the Crazy Horse Retribution Society:

Crazy Horse Retribution Society accepts responsibility for stealing Lt. McIntosh's notebook from the battle monument. It was
done to draw attention to the continued genocide inflicted on Native American peoples and lands by the U.S. government. Custer's
defeat at the Battle of the Little Bighorn is described at the battlefield museum as a tragedy. The real tragedy is what leads native
people to such drastic actions. Rape, mutilations, poverty, religious persecution, and cultural assassination carried out by the
7th Cavalry continues to this day by other U.S. agents of repression on reservations across North America.

Misrepresentation of the struggle by Lakota, Cheyenne and
Arapahoe to maintain their ancient traditions by fighting imperi-
alist assimilation has forced native people today to take action.
The desecration of native religion by profane display of sacrad [sic]
objects in museums, and the destruction of sacred lands to mine
uranium and coal for bombs and T.V.s is not conducive with the
lessons given by the Great Spirit.

We demand equal representation at the battlefield in the
form of displays and exhibits approved by the American Indian
Movement. The explanation of the justified actions of Crazy
Horse and Sitting Bull to defend their home and people at the
Little Bighorn is necessary before the notebook can be returned.

Until the U.S. Government recognizes native sovereignty

and suspends exploitive attitudes, teachings and behavior against
the First Americans, we will rise up against the modern Custers
of U.S. society.

HOKA HEY

On February 9, the trio arrived in Midland, Michigan, at the parsonage of Reverend Dave Stout, pastor of Aldersgate United Methodist Church. Deb Stout had grown up near there, in Bad Axe, a
Brownie and a singer in the church choir. She had attended Adrian
College, which is affiliated with the United Methodist faith. The
Stouts were a family who talked together about all manner of convictions, and Deb's parents were well aware that she had followed
deep ecology down an activist road.

"Deborah has always been a thoughtful and reflective person
who, having determined what is right, has the courage and the
strength of character to do it," Reverend Stout wrote four years later
to an attorney in Spokane. "She has never conformed to collective
thinking or popular opinion for the sake of approval and belonging.
For example, when in her Middle School years, Deborah's class-
mates persecuted her African American friend, the only black girl in
the Bad Axe school system, Deborah steadfastly befriended and defended her, never wavering for a moment from her compassionate
conscience, fierce loyalty, and profound sense of justice."

Reverend Stout and his wife, Ruth, did not invite controversy
into their home, and Rod treated them respectfully; Rod's own parents often noted that their son had a terrific rapport with their adult
friends, and this was no different. He turned on the charm and made
himself welcome. All three of them stayed at the Stout house for a
week, until February 16, and engaged in nothing more questionable
than walks in the winter cold and deep kitchen-table conversations
over steaming mugs of coffee.

On the day they left the Stouts, however, Rod was behind the wheel and told the women, "I want to stop in East Lansing at MSU for a couple hours. There's some mink research information I want to check out."

It was, he said, related to the mink rehabilitation they'd done as part of CAFF. They didn't have to be part of it. Just drop him off on campus, and he'd meet them in a warm café later. They both agreed to wait for him. This was just a part of traveling with Rod.

In January, PETA had run a series of radio spots in western Michigan calling attention to the work of Dr. Richard Aulerich at Michigan State University. Local activists were concerned about the toxicity experiments he was carrying out on the school's mink farm. Michigan was awash in the legacy of the auto manufacturers, paper plants, and other heavy industry, which had left the state's rivers and streams loaded with PCBs, PBBs, dioxins, heavy metals, and other nightmares. The population of river otters, for instance, had been all but wiped out by these pollutants, and mink were in precipitous decline. Aulerich's research had already been used to set water-quality standards for PCBs. However, he had ongoing state and federal contracts to study these toxins as delivered in mink feed, and his own published records described how the mink died violently, suffering severe internal hemorrhaging and vomiting blood in the arguably useful Lethal Dose 50% (LD50) test.

Rod had also seen from his own reading that Aulerich received the second-highest number of MFRF grants. It wasn't all fur business, however. One breed of mink in particular sometimes produced deaf offspring as a result of crossbreeding, and Aulerich was investigating this problem; he was also hoping to use these studies as a model for inherited deafness in humans. The Fur Information Council of America pointed out that the MSU facility wasn't part of the fur industry, but was a "medical research facility."

The frustration for local environmental activists was that the heavy industries that had so polluted the state continued to dodge responsibility by paying for more and more studies in which more and more mink were killed. The Grand Calumet River, for instance, which feeds into the southern end of Lake Michigan, had once had an enormous concentration of paper mills on its banks. A 1990 study had already found a 100 percent mortality rate among animals fed sediments from that river. The activists felt that spending more time confirming that PCBs were toxic served no purpose. They wanted the river cleaned up.

It was the middle of the day when Rod got out of the car in front of Anthony Hall, where Aulerich kept his office. He entered the stone building and made a quick tour, taking note of the location of the office and possible ways into the building at night.

He rejoined Stout and Trimiew and then took the car by himself for another hour, looking for Aulerich's mink farm. This was more difficult to find. He drove southeast of the campus to MSU's research farms, which are spread over the rolling hills in vast cultivated fields and unmarked barns. He had learned that at least one of the buildings at the Poultry Research Center there was used for studies on mink, ferrets, and otters. After some driving back and forth over frozen February roads, he found it; there was no guard station, no fence, no security of any kind. He walked the circumference of the cinder block building that housed the feed-mixing equipment and the farm offices. Out back at the edge of the trees, there were five short mink barns inside a guard fence and two more rows of cages fenced in along the back wall of the building.

Rod immediately went up on the roof and found that he could loosen one of the metal panels by removing a few screws. The rest would take seconds to undo. Several hundred mink watched him from the cages below. From up there, he also heard the burbling chatter of turkeys and ducks in the adjoining buildings, and he quickly apologized under his frosty breath for passing over them on this action. Maybe next time.

*   *   *

Two days later, Coronado, Stout, and Trimieu were in D.C. to talk to Friends of Animals about getting copies of all the videotape that Rod and Jonathan had mailed to the organization during their work in Global Investigations. Other than the neck-breaking footage, almost none of it had seen the light of day, and Rod was desperate to put together a documentary film about what he'd found on fur farms across the country. He met with Betsy Swart at the Friends of Animals D.C. office, but did not end up leaving with any footage.

It was a setback, but, according to Friends of Animals, the footage hadn't had much impact, anyway. The activists claimed that not even the neck-breaking scenes had really jolted anyone who might have the power to change fur farm conditions. It had been compiled in a 1991 tape called *The Faces of Fur* and distributed by Friends of Animals. These people were in the halls of Congress regularly and had found that the neck-breaking footage had hardly fazed anyone there.

Rod was also pushing the CAFF rehab-and-release videos as a heartwarming, positive story, but the mainstream groups wouldn't touch it, in part because the animal releases were done illegally, but mostly because CAFF had fed its animals live food.

The three were staying with Sea Shepherd activist Ben White in Fairfax, Virginia, when Rod was told there was an anonymous message waiting for him in D.C., so he drove in. Some of the same people who had contacted him eighteen months earlier for the Silver Spring Monkeys investigation were curious about what he'd learned at Michigan State University. The message came with instructions, and he felt compelled to follow them.

Trimiew had family in Virginia, and Coronado and Stout left her there while they drove back to Michigan.

The story Rod would tell me after this action was the same one he would later tell the court: He got a message in D.C. that he needed to be in Michigan on February 26 so he could act as a press liaison for an ALF action; he didn't know what it was. He rented a hotel room on February 26 in Ann Arbor and then sent word to a contact in Bethesda, Maryland, via FedEx that he was in place. These were the explicit instructions from the contact in D.C. He allegedly didn't know who the Maryland contact was; he only knew the address. On that package, he used the name Leonard Robideau—a conflation of the names Leonard Peltier and Bob Robideau, Peltier's cousin and acquitted codefendant in the Wounded Knee skirmish. Then on February 28, a bunch of stuff from Aulerich's office was dropped off anonymously, and Rod took handwritten notes over the telephone from an anonymous caller so they could be written into a press release. He then FedExed the items and the notes to the Maryland address. Rod claimed he was "upset" to learn he had been made a part of an illegal action.

None of which was how it really happened. Except that bit about the address in Maryland; that was real. He didn't know the lady who lived there, and she might not have known much about what was being shipped to her, either. She was a volunteer for PETA, it turned out, and was regularly receiving all kinds of shipments and just holding them in her basement without ever opening them.

What really happened was that Rod returned to MSU and hit the place like a sledgehammer. On the night of February 27, he sat in a hotel room in Ann Arbor—an hour's drive from Lansing—and built his incendiaries. They were the timed variety, using a lightbulb filament to light match heads and Sterno. It's not certain whether Stout was with him at the hotel or not; he has always maintained that she was not part of this action. At any rate, he had other help: in interviews and written accounts, he has maintained that at least three people (his own accounts have varied) were involved in this action, which most likely means he recruited Michigan activists to help. This new group called itself the Great Lakes Unit of the ALF.

At about three A.M. on February 28, Rod was on the roof of the mink building at the Poultry Research Center in a cold light rain, twisting out the remaining sheet metal screws so he could yank up a few metal panels and drop into the lab. He immediately entered the small office and destroyed all the equipment he could find there, smashing what he could and rifling through experiment protocols, notebooks, slides, and computer disks. When he had tossed the unwanted files, feed, and equipment on the floor, he doused it all with bottles of hydrochloric acid, melting data logs, engine parts for food-mixing machinery, and gas chambers used to kill the creatures. He also poured acid into big floor-standing chest freezers. One of them was full of otter heads wrapped in tinfoil. Rod snatched one so he could document it later.

Out on the grounds, he moved quickly up and down the rows and grabbed only 2 of the 350 mink, placing them in transfer cases he found there. It was hard to leave the rest, but if he let them out they'd only fight each other. He removed all the breeding cards that kept track of experiments. There was one live otter there and some ferrets, too, and he wanted to take them, but he did not.

With his signature can of red spray paint he scrawled, AULERICH TORTURES MINK, MICHIGAN MINK MILITIA, FUR IS MURDER, A.L.F., and WE WILL BE BACK FOR THE OTTERS.

Acid steaming everywhere, he grabbed the two mink in cages, and fled. He crashed through the underbrush out to the edge of I-96, which runs behind the farm, and left the mink there for recovery later. He was picked up by a lookout and rolled back to campus in the cold predawn hours.

He opened a window in a basement room in Anthony Hall and squeezed through, quickly making his way to Aulerich's office in room 132. It had an old wooden door with louvered slats in it, and Rod broke a few of these out, reached through, and let himself in. Aulerich had been in this room for years, and it was fairly jammed with metal file cabinets and boxes of papers. Rod pulled all of these open and began tossing the papers out to make a pile in the cramped center of the room. There were so many files that he decided to just open the drawers and let them burn. He piled up papers, wooden coat hangers, and other fuel against Aulerich's wooden desk and set his incendiaries there and next to a bookcase.

While he was setting the incendiaries, a squad car with its lights flashing pulled up directly in front of the office window. He felt strangely calm as he went to the window of the darkened room and peeked out. He was confident that his accomplices on the outside would have warned him if he was in trouble. Somebody was getting a traffic ticket on the street. He didn't have time even to feel relief. He waited for the campus cops to drive away, then set the timers and exited the building the same way he'd come. On the way out through the basement room, which turned out to be a dairy research office, he pulled the computers and office equipment from the desk in there and smashed them on the floor for good measure.

"I wasn't concerned about the fire spreading because most of the combustible material was going to be inside. The building itself wasn't going to burn. The building itself was stone," said Rod. "A lot of mention was later made about two students escaping from the building, but I don't think they were ever at risk."

It was confirmed that two students were in the building at that time, but they were unharmed.

Aulerich's office, however, was totally gutted. A university photograph taken of Aulerich during the cleanup shows an unsmiling but avuncular-looking man in a flannel shirt standing in a pit of charred debris. All around him, the burned files and research materials stack up over his head, reduced to dusty black carbon and ruin.

The office contained thirty-two years' worth of raw data, and the MSU researcher acknowledged that a great deal of it could not be replaced. News reports afterward placed the damages at $1.3 million—about $125,000 in repairs and the rest in lost research. Aulerich never gave a press interview on the subject.

Stone structure or not, the fire did spread beyond what Rod had intended and destroyed the office next to Aulerich's, which belonged to Dr. Karen Chou. At the time, one of Chou's studies was utilizing bull sperm as a potential research model for toxicity and fertility studies that could replace experimentation on live animals.

Interviewed in 1994 and again in 2008, Chou said that this attack profoundly altered her life. Not only did she lose colleagues, who didn't want to become targets, but she had to warn her two young boys that they were not to discuss their mother's work with strangers. She was worried about them being kidnapped or harmed in any way. This, she said, was a huge disappointment.

"I'd like to teach my children to trust people unless proven otherwise, right? But it suddenly changed. Suddenly, I was saying, 'Don't talk to people if they ask you about what your mom does.' It's like, what am I teaching my children here?" said Chou.

Just after dawn on February 28, Rod was back at the hotel in Ann Arbor. He stuffed another FedEx box full of loot stolen from Aulerich's office, including documents, computer disks, and slides, plus a Hi8 videotape he'd shot of himself in a black ski mask inside the MSU mink facility removing a mink from its cage. He sent this second package, too, to the woman in Bethesda, putting the last name Robideau on the freight bill.

But when FedEx picked up the package at a drop box, it found that it had an invalid account number on it. Also, it bore a Toledo, Ohio, return address but a San Diego zip code. The package was opened by FedEx and then sent to the FBI.

The FBI quickly linked the package to the fire at MSU and began to search the hotels in the vicinity of the FedEx drop box Rod had used for both packages. Armed with photos, agents got a positive ID on Rod at a hotel about three hundred feet from the box.

Still, none of the evidence seized could prove that Rod had been anything but a courier, the ALF spokesman who had taken on the responsibility of delivering this material to PETA and the press. Which is exactly what he told reporters and law enforcement for years. It may be that he fed this same line to Deb Stout, who denied doing anything other than traveling with Coronado. More than two years later, she told a writer from the *Detroit Free Press* that she supported the action, saying, "I didn't hear that anyone got hurt . . . It's a campaign of economic sabotage, to make it economically difficult to do that kind of research."

The press release sent out by PETA after the MSU attack attributed the fire to the Great Lakes Unit of the ALF, saying, "Aulerich has helped fur farmers in America exploit and execute millions of animals with regard to neither their ecological importance or their psychological well-being. He has served as the fur-farm industry's problem solver."

By the time anyone was reading this, of course, Coronado and Stout were long gone. They headed back to Virginia to pick up Trimiew, dipping into the D.C. area just as a knot of FBI and ATF agents was descending on the home of the PETA volunteer in Bethesda to whom the FedEx packages had been addressed. In that house, investigators found the first package from Rod, which didn't help them much except to further confirm that he had been the courier. But the house was reportedly stacked with boxes of files, videotapes, and other incriminating evidence—especially concerning the Silver Spring Monkeys surveillance. In storage were elaborate plans to break into the Tulane primate facility in Covington, Louisiana; Rod's hand-drawn maps; lists of code names for Rod, PETA members, and other individuals; surveillance logs; and airline boarding passes. There were also keys, slim-jims (used for breaking into cars and buildings), two-way radios, and night-vision goggles. Some of this Louisiana stuff could be clearly traced to Rod, mostly by having his fingerprints all over it. He had assumed this stuff had been destroyed. Now the FBI knew for sure that Rod had been snooping around the Tulane facility in the swamp in early 1990. It just didn't know he'd been all over the inside of it night after night.

The woman who was storing all this stuff for PETA and others was an immigrant from Bolivia and very mild mannered. She cooperated with the agents, but later reportedly suffered what others described as a nervous breakdown.

Coronado, Stout, and Trimiew were unaware that any such raid was happening, nor did Rod know that the second package had been intercepted. They took their time winding back to Oregon, just three friends on a long road trip.

Federal agencies have not revealed how they knew who Stout was, where her parents lived, or that she, Coronado, and Trimiew had been there. This was part of a grand jury investigation, and a lot of it remains sealed.

But once they did have an ID on those three, big wheels started turning. Special Agent John Masengale from the ATF in Seattle and others had begun gathering intelligence on the CAFF sanctuary in 1991 after Rod started writing and talking about it in the press in conjunction with the ALF attacks. David Howitt, whose wife owned the sanctuary property, said that word got back to him that agents had been talking to people on the Port Angeles city council, veterinarians, inspectors from the Washington Department of Fish and Wildlife who might have been on the property, neighbors, and others around town. Now the feds went back to Port Angeles with photos. Stout and Trimiew were identified as having worked on the CAFF sanctuary. (Masengale died in the line of duty May 16, 1992, during an unrelated explosives investigation, but Don Maupin at Washington State University thought he had received intel on Stout and Trimiew from him.)

Working with the animals on the sanctuary was not a crime. Only releasing the animals was criminal. But it did make both of them known associates of Rod from a time a year before the MSU attack. Could these be the "two gals" Schuening and others had been talking about?

It was a theory that didn't pan out. Maupin put together collections of photos of Stout and Trimiew and immediately went back to his witnesses in the Kinko's and elsewhere around Moscow and Pullman. He and the FBI's Bob Houston thought they had a home run here—Houston, in particular, was dead sure these were the two women who had been with Rod at WSU, and said so in his meetings with other investigators. But no one recognized Stout or Trimiew from the photos. Maupin was very disappointed, but there was just no strong reaction to their images. They couldn't act on this information and had to keep looking.

When the FBI showed up at Aldersgate United Methodist Church, though, they came playing hardball. They assumed Deb Stout was involved in the Michigan State University attack, and they assumed Reverend Stout and his family knew all about it. But on this last count, it seems they were wrong.

The way they went about their investigation set much of Midland against them. It was March 1992, not long after the attacks, when two agents walked into the church office and told the church secretary and other staff that they knew the reverend was "harboring terrorist fugitives" and that they were accessories. The poor women had no idea what the agents were talking about.

Reverend Stout wasn't at the church at the time, but was home packing for a vacation when the agents confronted him. He also had to ask what the hell they were talking about. He had never heard about the MSU attack. None of them had. It hadn't been reported in their local paper. Stout was not a man to buck the system, but when he tried to cooperate and tell them what he knew—which was nothing—they immediately threatened to put him and the whole family in jail.

The parsonage phone was tapped. Agents invaded the Stouts' quiet suburban neighborhood. One morning, an agent stood for hours at the curb in front of his unmarked sedan pretending to read a map. When Ruth Stout approached the car, he drove off. The same type of car would sit in the church parking lot and follow her through town.

When the Stouts went to their summer cabin in Cedarville, on Lake Huron in Michigan's Upper Peninsula, agents followed them up there, too. In fact, they drove all the way up there, a five- or six-hour trip, just to knock on the door and hand Reverend Stout a federal subpoena to appear before a grand jury in Grand Rapids, Michigan.

John McCandless of the MSU campus police called Deb's brother Steve Stout at his job at Yageman's Appliance in Bad Axe a bunch of times that summer, as did the FBI, leaving messages with other employees. The object was to rattle him by making sure his co-workers and boss knew about the investigation.

One day in the second week of August, an agent from the ATF and Agent John Morrison from the FBI resident agency in Lansing were waiting for Steve's wife at the Kmart where she worked; the managers gave the men an office to question her. But she didn't know anything. One of them said to her, "I don't know what your financial situation is, but there is a thirty-five-thousand-dollar reward. If you sometime remember anything you forgot to tell us, please give us a call."

Later that same afternoon, they came to see Steve at work. He was filling out some customer service paperwork when he saw them come through the door. They asked him if he wanted to go out in the garage to talk.

"No, just do what you came here to do," he said.

They handed him a subpoena and said, "We'll see you at the grand jury."

Two of Steve's friends were also eventually subpoenaed.

In an interview with me at the time, Reverend Stout expressed his shock and disappointment. His feelings may have changed in the intervening years (the Stouts did not comment for this book), but in 1994 he said, "You don't suspect that [the FBI] carry on like this. I think the system has done this and turned them into junkyard dogs for special interests."

Special interests?

"Yeah. Fur industry. Lumber industry. Whoever has that segment of the government in their pocket, whether it's the ranchers or the loggers or the fur farmers."

SIXTEEN

They Came to Kill Me/ Helicopter Charlie

AROUND THE THIRD week in March 1992, Rod returned to his cabin in the Little Applegate. He was red-hot. Someone had sent him a copy of a federal affidavit used to get the search warrant for the home of the PETA volunteer in Bethesda. It was dated in March and was written by Special Agent Thomas Stieler from the District of Maryland FBI office. In it, Stieler interviewed Special Agent John Morrison of the FBI in Lansing, who described the MSU incident. Then he interviewed FBI special agent Bob Houston of the Spokane office, writing, "SA Houston stated that the ANIMAL LIBERA-TION FRONT (ALF), in particular, RODNEY ADAM CORO-NADO, date of birth July 3, 1966, was responsible for the destruction of animal research facilities at Washington State University (WSU) on August 12–13, 1991."

Stieler then goes on in the document to interview Special Agent John Comery of the ATF, who tells him how the incendiaries were similar at OSU and MSU.

This is the document Rod would show me at our first meeting in April in Venice Beach.

Rod read that document carefully, over and over, trying to measure what they really had on him. They might really know he had been at WSU, or they might know nothing except that he'd been at Rik Scarce's house and at the Kinko's. It is routine for law enforcement officers to exaggerate wildly on search warrant applications, since the burden of proof is nil. On a search warrant, it's basically up to the accused and the evidence to prove that the officer is wrong.

Of course, he didn't want to turn himself in. But he also wondered what the result would be if he didn't. Law enforcement agencies were in contact with all his friends, his family, and his fellow eco-radicals as well as environmental organizations he worked with; it was clear they were looking for him, but there was no arrest warrant and no indictment. Why weren't they making a paper trail? Instead, agents told his parents that they were really worried that Rod or someone else would be killed. Rod didn't read that as an expression of concern. He read it as a threat.

At the same time, more than one person had gotten back to Rod to tell him that cops had mentioned to them the thirty-five-thousand-dollar reward offered by the National Board of Fur Farm Organizations. That didn't sit right. If they were encouraging friends to rat him out for money, that would be one thing. But all this talk of someone killing Rod had him wondering if they were sending bounty hunters after him. Or perhaps individual cops who might have a bead on him could get one of their friends to do the job and split the reward. The combination of the reward money and the death threats worried him.

Fur Age editor Lisa Marcinek denied that the money was a bounty in an interview with me in 1995. And Teresa Platt, executive director of Fur Commission USA since 1998, said this was just a reward for information, no different than the offer backed by the Humane Society of the United States for information about some 2008 arsons by eco-radicals at the time of this writing. But at that time, Rod felt something different.

He retrieved the cavalryman's journal from a friend and spent a few days pondering it, mostly as a distraction, wondering how it might best serve the movement or even secure his own safety now. He had thought about burning it in his sweat lodge, as fuel in a native ritual cleansing. He knew that the contents of the book existed in transcripts, so it wouldn't really be lost to history. The book and its legacy of Indian-killing began to burn a hole through whatever shred of trust he had left that he'd be arrested cleanly. There in his cabin, he was more certain than ever that federal officers had no intention of arresting him. They were going to purposely ignore his message of decent treatment for native wildlife and instead focus on the force he used to destroy property, and they were going to meet that force with force.

Rod was isolated and paranoid. Ignoring the death threats, he decided, was just naive. The cabin was suddenly too remote. If bounty hunters found him there, no one would be around to witness the arrest and stop an assassination. He needed to hide in plain sight. He tore up the journal and burned it, page by page, in his woodstove.

From Chant Thomas's phone, he called the Sea Shepherd Conservation Society, which was then located in Santa Monica. They would put him to work there. He called Cat in Texas and told her he wasn't coming back, and to find another caretaker for the cabin.

On April Fools' Day, he left the cabin and drove to Eugene, Oregon, where he picked up a racy red sports car that was being donated to Sea Shepherd. The car had belonged to a trustafarian kid who had used it to follow the Dead. Rod was going to visit an EF! regional gathering in Northern California, but the location was remote, and he realized the little convertible didn't have the clearance to make those Forest Service roads, so he rolled on down to L.A.

Compared with the life Rod had been living in Oregon, working with Sea Shepherd was like going Hollywood. Captain Paul Watson had been in L.A. a long time and sold one of his books for a movie and had married former *Playboy* model Lisa Distefano. But from the group's office near the waterfront, he was directing assaults on tuna seiners in the Eastern Tropical Pacific, Japanese drift netters in the North Pacific, longline poachers off the Galápagos and Cocos islands, whalers in the Antarctic, and numerous other campaign targets.

Rod settled in among his old Sea Shepherd comrades and stayed almost two months, until the latter half of May. He lived on Watson's command boat, the *Edward Abbey*, which was anchored in Marina del

Rey. The other inhabitant of the *Abbey* was David Howitt. The group's larger vessel, the *Sea Shepherd II*, sat in the commercial harbor in San Pedro. The office was bustling with people and life, and Rod conducted several media interviews with me and other reporters about CAFF and Operation Bite Back. He worked around the office, answered the phones, and helped with campaigns. He was hidden in plain sight.

Howitt and Linda May were called before a grand jury during this time, and they went and answered questions honestly. Howitt related to Coronado, "Oh, you know, [the U.S. attorney and the FBI] told me that they think that your life is extremely threatened by people within the fur industry who want to get you."

While Rod was in Los Angeles, investigators raided the storage locker he had rented at Bear Creek Storage in Talent, Oregon. They found some items he'd moved from the cabin, including loads of fur-farming and research documents, camping gear, photos, and equipment left over from the CAFF sanctuary—and his beloved manual typewriter. They reversed out the keystrokes on the ribbon to reconstruct the fund-raising letter he'd typed, asking for twelve hundred dollars to hit the Huggans Rocky Mountain Fur Company in Montana and other farms. There were other notes and personal items in the unit. The letter read, in part, "The Huggans Rocky Mountain Fur Company is a building I have been in before. It is all wood, with no alarms and no close proximity to animals. The targeted building contains all the drying racks, and drums used in pelt processing. If we could cause substantial damage to that equipment, we would cause a serious disruption in the pelting season, and also push the Huggans family (third generation trappers) into a position closer to bankruptcy."

Beginning shortly after the MSU attack, agents also began backtracking records from Rod's telephone calling card, which placed him in the vicinity of every one of the Bite Back actions. That research also proved that he had been on the other end of several calls to the press in which he had identified himself as part of the ALF.

Whether it was from the storage unit or the phone records, federal agents now knew that Rod had stayed at the cabin on the Little Applegate.

And when they came, they came in full assault.

One morning in May 1992, Chant Thomas was getting ready for work. He had a construction company called Karma Builders that was tearing down and salvaging houses for materials, and business was good. He was standing by his truck in his driveway at about seven thirty in the morning, about to leave, when a well-dressed couple rolled up in a camper. They looked lost, so Thomas walked over.

"Can I help you?"

"Oh, we're looking for Rodney Coronado. Doesn't he live around here?"

Something about the way they asked gave Thomas a weird feeling. "Rodney? I've never heard of any Rodney Coronado up here," he said. "Maybe it's the Upper Applegate, which is an entirely other valley. So go up there and ask at this restaurant at McKee Bridge, and maybe they know who you're looking for up there."

He got in his truck and drove away. Unbeknownst to him, he probably drove right through an invasion force. Two miles down the mountain is a place off the road, a farm at the end of a long driveway that today is a nice organic outfit but in 1992 belonged to a crew of Applegate Occupation Team types, including a guy known as Helicopter Charlie. According to Thomas and other sources in the area, Charlie was a local guy, grew up in the area, went to Vietnam real young, and flew there as a helicopter pilot and mechanic. He made a living repairing helicopters, forest-fire spotting for the Forest Service, and doing other odd jobs, and he had several helicopters on the property.

Helicopter Charlie was just heading down the mountain himself that morning, not long behind Thomas, when he passed several vans full of what he called "ninja warriors" headed up the Little Applegate Road. The vans had government tags on them, and he brought his truck to a stop. He didn't like the look of them. "Why the heck do I need to go into town right away?" he asked himself and swung the truck around. He got back to his place and fired up a little one-man bubble helicopter, superlight and as maneuverable as a mosquito. He buzzed up over the treetops and headed up the river.

Right away, he saw one van full of agents in the parking lot at a public trailhead, then another one up the road, and a third set up at the mailboxes where the paved road ended. "Omigosh, they're busting somebody."

As Charlie was flying over this scene on the road, he saw a big helicopter (Thomas recounted that it was a huge Chinook, a tandem-rotor job, anyway, but that seems unlikely) come whopping over the hill from Medford, loaded with more ninja warriors. They could take and hold an entire community with this much firepower. Helicopter Charlie had spent a lot of time defending the Little Applegate, and he didn't take too well to this scene. The big chopper evidently landed at some point, but was airborne again not long after. What Charlie told Thomas a couple days later was that he started buzzing the big chopper, like a mockingbird fighting off a raven.

"He was buzzing it all over, he was under it, over it, he was flipping the guys off, he was laughing at them, you know," said Thomas. "He chased the helicopter back and saw them go over the mountain to Medford."

One of the residents of the Little Applegate looked a bit like Rod, at least in his coloring, with dark olive skin and black hair. When he moseyed down to the mailboxes at the end of the pavement, agents leaped out of the bushes and threw him to the ground. He stared up through a bristle brush of M-14s pointed at his face by men in ski masks and explained with some difficulty that there must be some mistake. Eventually, they realized they had the wrong guy and let him go. But he was pissed, and he stopped at Thomas's place later, saying, "I think your friend Rod is in some big trouble. I don't want him living around here anymore."

The agents had difficulty finding the exact cabin that Rod had been living in and first stopped at a different cabin across the stream. The masked invaders kicked in the door on the lady who was home there, and she started pleading for her life. When they asked about Rod, she pointed out his abode deep in the creekside shadows. The agents came creeping in through the woods, guns drawn. By coincidence, a potential new renter for the cabin was visiting at that moment, a guy from Williams just kicking around inside the rough-hewn place to see if he might want to take it for the summer, and when he walked outside black-clad guys in ski masks immediately put the cold zero of their gun barrels to his eye.

It was pretty clear from the state of the cabin, and the things this guy told them, that Rod was long gone. Only a single hawk feather hung in the room, a good-bye.

When Rod heard how they had come for him, in black jump-suits, with ski masks over their faces and guns drawn, he was more pessimistic than ever about his chances for survival. Why would federal agents disguise themselves? There was no warrant for his arrest. He had no known history of violence or resisting arrest. Flight, yes, but not violence. From his point of view, the whole thing reeked. In all likelihood, they simply would have arrested him. But he was convinced that if he had been home alone when the ninjas showed up, they would have killed him.

He slipped out of Los Angeles and disappeared. If they were coming to kill Rod Coronado, then Rod Coronado would cease to exist.

SEVENTEEN Indian Country

ROD BOUGHT HIMSELF a plane ticket to Rapid City, South Dakota, and by the time he landed, he had changed his name to Martin Rubio. Rubio was a family name on his mother's side, and it came easily to him. And Martin was another way to say "marten," a member of the weasel family like the mink. Through a friend, he'd found a cabin for rent on the Standing Rock Sioux reservation, no questions asked. He'd never met the owner before, but got off the plane in Rapid City, took a cab to a hotel, and the next day bought himself another used Subaru off a nearby lot.

He drove out to meet his new landlord, and a small group of people took him to a little rural cabin on the Standing Rock just west of the settlement of Wakpala, where he could live in anonymity. He was only a couple miles from the Missouri River and from the Sitting Bull monument, a strange and lonely statue on desolate bluffs high above the river. It was both exhausting and thrilling to start over from square one. No one knew him; no one knew what he did. He had nothing to account for here, but nothing to stand on, either. Martin Rubio would have to decide what he wanted to be.

He kept a lot of space between himself and reservation society. He didn't go barging in like Activist of the Year. Summer hit, and Rod found he relished a bit of time alone. He walked the grasslands, watching prairie dog towns and finding eagle feathers below the big sprawling nests. He liked to bake pies and listen to NPR while he did repairs on his cabin. When he needed company, he sometimes went down the road to visit his landlord, Pat McLaughlin, a Lakota who owned both the cabin and the parcel of land around it. McLaughlin always had stories to tell. Sometimes Rod would drink coffee with him, and he'd talk about fighting in WWII, house-to-house street fighting tossing grenades back and forth with the Nazis. Other times he'd tell about when he was kidnapped by the Bureau of Indian Affairs as a little boy and sent off to Indian school, where they cut his hair and beat him for speaking Lakota instead of English. Even as an old man, he told Rod, the experience still pained him.

Storytelling ran in McLaughlin's family. His brother, Robert, had taken the last name Sundance and had coauthored with Marc Gaede a powerful book about Indian life on skid row titled *Sundance, the Robert Sundance Story.*

This was Rod's first lengthy exposure to native culture. He slowed down enough to understand the hurt in his own people and exactly how it was related to the defense of wildlife and wilderness that had set him on his path. One day, he drove McLaughlin's son and granddaughter to see the girl's mother up in Grand Forks, North Dakota. They sat around the dining room table, and the conversation turned toward racism, and, one by one, they began sharing stories of their everyday life. Sitting in cafés in the Dakotas without ever getting served. Being followed around in supermarkets. The legacy of the Indian schools and similar assimilation programs. But they also talked from a deep knowledge of the land. They were still connected to the root of his own interest in the wild—and had been punished for it. Rod had been groping crazily, angrily, for a sense of belonging, and here it was in this living room.

He soon regretted stealing the cavalryman's journal; the theft had been big news, and he learned that some on the res were ashamed of that act, thinking it cast more poor light on Native Americans. He never admitted he had stolen it.

Meanwhile, the search for Rod continued. On June 29, 1992, I was in Santa Cruz to catch more interviews with Sea Shepherd, but while I was waiting to get ferried to the ships, they were raided. The *Sea Shepherd II* was just pulling up anchor during a heavy rainstorm, setting out on a campaign against Japanese drift netters in the North Pacific, when U.S. Customs and a Coast Guard boat ordered the crew to stop engines, barking out on the PA, "Prepare to be boarded." Paul Watson was also there with the smaller *Edward Abbey*. Both vessels were boarded in the lashing rain by ATF, FBI, and Customs agents, who combed them and asked Captains Watson and Jon Huntermer to produce passports for the whole crew. They never mentioned Rod's name, but they asked whether the captains had transferred any crew at sea.

"What's this about?" asked Watson.

"Just routine," said the officers. But it wasn't routine at all. The moment they made Vancouver Island, their next port of call after the drift netter campaign, they were hit again by the Mounties, U.S. Customs, and the FBI, who came on board with what Watson called "an army," including search dogs. But there was no Rod Coronado on those ships.

Watson moved the *Edward Abbey* down to Seattle and found out that some of his Seattle staff had been questioned by the FBI, so he called the bureau there directly and said, "Did you want to see me?"

No, they replied to him, they were just looking for Rod Coronado on "arson and terrorism" charges, according to Watson.

Watson wasn't the only one being hounded. The feds were shaking down the radical environmental movement. By June, a federal grand jury had been seated in Eugene to investigate the OSU arson, and another had been convened in Spokane related to the WSU attack. Soon there would be grand juries in Michigan, Louisiana, and Utah—nine of them, eventually, scattered over seven states. Agents were fanning out throughout the country to serve subpoenas and question known activists.

Sea Shepherd was turned inside out. Society member Myra Finkelstein was questioned in May, and member Renee Grandi got a visit in Whitefish, Montana, as did her boyfriend, Craig Anderson.

Their friends in Whitefish and at the health food store where Grandi worked were also questioned. Sue Rodriguez-Pastor was questioned, and David Howitt and Linda May both received subpoenas. Beth Fries and Peter Wallerstein would be questioned, and at least one other Sea Shepherd member (not named in the press) would be subpoenaed.

Rik Scarce and his wife, Petra Uhrig, were served subpoenas by the FBI on May 11 asking them to appear before the Spokane grand jury on June 9. Scarce was not a suspect, but acknowledged that Rod had stayed in their house. He was concerned about the nature of the grand jury proceeding, which is a troubling affair run by a U.S. prosecutor in which witnesses are not allowed to have an attorney present and can be compelled by a judge to answer any question or risk imprisonment. Scarce's questioning, in particular, was of keen interest to reporters: a former reporter himself, Scarce immediately began fighting his subpoena on the grounds that, as a matter of duty and academic privilege, he had to protect his sources as a research sociologist.

It was a fight he would lose, which was indicative of the aggressive nature of this questioning as it ramped up. Scarce would spend 159 days in jail in Spokane for refusing to answer some of the grand jury's questions, and he never did talk. He wrote about the experience of defending his academic honor in his book *Contempt of Court*, an analysis of the injustice of the grand jury system that earned him high marks in academia. He came out of it looking heroic, but it cost him half a year of his life.

That Spokane jail would be busy. Jonathan Paul was the first to land there, sent up for refusing to answer questions on Election Day, 1992, the day Bill Clinton became president. He would remain in jail for 158 days, but he never talked.

Oregon State Police investigators and federal agents knocked and cajoled and threatened their way through Rod's social network from Ashland to Medford and up and down the Applegate. Tom and Jessica were both subpoenaed. Portland was also crawling with notebook-wielding detectives. Earth First!ers at known locations like the Malka got repeat visits. Rod had touched a lot of lives in Oregon, but he was so secretive that most people honestly knew only as much about Operation Bite Back as anyone who read the papers: That Rod had made a commitment to being the press spokesman for the ALF. And that he had rehabbed some mink and cats on the CAFF project. Those who were questioned didn't have to lie; as far as they knew, this was pure harassment. And the harder they were pushed, the more they resisted.

Out in Michigan, the Stouts were being put to the test. Reverend Stout was subpoenaed twice to the Grand Rapids grand jury, where he answered truthfully until he began to feel that the prosecutors were lying about him being uncooperative, and then he began pleading the Fifth. His wife, Ruth, was subpoenaed twice to Grand Rapids and once to Spokane. Steve Stout was subpoenaed, and church staff and friends were questioned.

The U.S. attorney handling the case in Grand Rapids was hard on Ruth Stout, shouting at her and calling her a terrible mother. When she finally asked the prosecutor why he was being so hostile to her, he lost his cool and shouted her down. She exited the room shaken and very upset and then was flown to Spokane, where a different prosecutor asked her just a few questions and didn't even seem to know why she was there. The Stouts both thought it was strictly punitive.

On July 23, 1992, Deb Stout was startled by a loud pounding on her door in Bozeman, Montana. It was FBI special agent Michael Wright, who issued her two subpoenas: one to Grand Rapids, the other to Spokane. Michigan made some sense, considering it was known that Coronado had traveled there with Stout and Trimiew. Spokane, however, was another matter: the FBI's Bob Houston would routinely tell other law enforcement officers that he felt that Stout and Trimiew were the two women seen with Rod at WSU, as well. But there was no known evidence to link them to the attack. Rod later admitted only that they had worked with him on the

CAFF project. Deb would eventually be subpoenaed four times and asked to submit DNA evidence twice.

In a September 12 *Moscow-Pullman Daily News* piece by Ken Olsen, Stout summed up her response by saying, "This is clearly a political case and clearly the best tactic is not to cooperate."

Stout was fairly well known at that time in the Bozeman Earth First! community, where she wrote appeals on federal predator-control programs. She wrote a piece for the August 1, 1992, Lughnasadh issue of the *Earth First! Journal* titled "Low-Down on the Low Life: FBI Harassment of Activists Continues," which included these observations:

> We also need to think about the ways to support those who are being terrorized by the FBI. The bomb that blasted Judi and Darryl caught us by surprise; we never anticipated such a disgusting act of violence. People are sitting in jail in Arizona thanks to a low-life infiltrator. And now Rod Coronado . . . is living underground and completely separated from his support network. This isolation puts him in a dangerous and vulnerable position.
>
> This ain't no game, folks! They're playing hardball, and this topic needs to become more than a campfire chat.

Kim Trimiew was subpoenaed much later, not appearing before the Spokane grand jury until August 10, 1993, and her approach to the matter was different. She remained completely silent about the grand jury appearances, granting no interviews, writing no articles or books. She refused to answer questions and was jailed on October 5 for fifteen days but then released, pending her appeal on the question of how her testimony might be used under multiple jurisdictions.

Like Scarce, she would lose her appeal. On February 18, 1994— over two and a half years after Bite Back began—Stout and Trimiew were both sent to Spokane County Jail for contempt of court. Stout was released five months later, on July 18, 1994.

Trimiew, however, was kept in jail longer than any other witness in this investigation, serving 193 days before she was released on August 29, 1994. U.S. Attorney Frank Wilson and District Judge Fremming Nielsen expressed when Stout was released that they believed Trimiew would eventually talk, but she did not.

Federal investigators swarmed PETA, digging for more evidence that the organization was a major financer of the Bite Back arsons and attacks. It looked like they'd hit the jackpot with the evidence they'd pulled out of the volunteer's house in Maryland, but just like Friends of Animals, PETA wasn't financing arson. It was financing undercover investigations whose findings and images it could safely release to the media. It also paid for activists' legal defense as necessary; it had paid for Rod's legal expenses in the past and indicated that it would do so again.

Ten people associated with PETA were questioned or subpoenaed, including executive director Ingrid Newkirk and cofounder Alex Pacheco, both of whom were fingerprinted and submitted handwriting samples. Others included Amy Bertsch and the woman whose house was raided in Maryland. Some of them appeared before grand juries. The threat, reported in the press at the time, was that PETA would be hit with charges under the Racketeer Influenced and Corrupt Organizations (RICO) Act, which was designed to punish conspiracies related to organized crime. But the RICO threat would eventually melt away.

Two PETA employees appeared before the grand jury in Michigan, including Newkirk's assistant, Kym Boyman, who was *Bloom County* cartoonist Berkeley Breathed's sister-in-law. One of the organization's chief volunteers also had to appear in Louisiana. Having powerful lawyers didn't shield PETA employees from being contacted illegally by agents. Amy Bertsch was surprised outside her country home when two agents approached her out of the darkness as she emptied her trash, waving a subpoena at her—even though they knew those papers were supposed to go to her counsel. Same with Alex Pacheco: plainclothes officers tailed him in an unmarked car and then pulled him over with the flashers on and handed him a subpoena. Agents sat in the PETA parking lot. Often the organization's trash bins would disappear. PETA members responded by making sure they threw all their dog shit into those same bins.

The U.S. Department of Justice tried to force PETA to turn over its list of volunteers worldwide, but Newkirk refused, and the department eventually dropped it.

Even Emmy-winning reporter Andrea Austin from Portland TV station KGW received a subpoena, hand delivered by a pair of FBI agents, because of a news-special interview she had conducted with Rod in July 1991, just after the OSU attack. It was unusual to subpoena a reporter, but they were scratching at every lead they could get.

By the July 4, 1992, holiday weekend, Rod was going stir-crazy in the cabin and longed to see some familiar faces. Despite the dragnet attempting to sweep up all his contacts, he knew that many of his friends would be gathering that weekend for the annual Earth First! Round River Rendezvous, which was being held that year at a remote campground in Colorado. He threw his backpacking gear in the car and drove down.

He parked on a nowhere Forest Service road where he could hide his car and figured he was about ten miles away from the camp. From there, he hiked in and arrived in pitch darkness. He paid his twenty dollars at the registration table, but none of the night staff recognized him. He stashed his pack in the bush and crept up to the edge of the big fire ring, where scores of activists were sure to talk and sing late into the night. He saw many people he knew there, including a woman who had worked on the CAFF project. He waited until the crowd died down, resting in the dark forest. Finally, he crept forward into the light, hiding his face, and tapped her on the shoulder.

Without a word, she got up and found her gear, and together they made a discreet camp off in the woods under tall pines. When Rod wanted to speak to people in attendance, his new companion would go get them and escort them back to the camp, and often they'd all go to a nearby hot springs to soak.

One night was like the funeral scene in *Tom Sawyer*: Jonathan Paul, who didn't know Rod was at the Rendezvous, got up in front of the crowd and started filling them in on what was happening to Rod. He told them how Rod was being hunted by federal agents who had no warrant. He was worried for Rod's safety and wanted to warn everyone about the shakedown that was visiting the entire movement. "He is here!" someone shouted from the crowd. And sure enough, Rod was there, sitting in the back, keeping his head down. The comment kind of passed unacknowledged, as though everyone agreed, *Yes, he is here in spirit*. But Rod sank slowly into the bushes, wondering: who knew he was here, and why would they say so out loud?

That same night, a man came up to Rod and asked a couple of questions. He said Rod looked familiar, and he wanted to know his name. That was the final straw. Federal agents had been undercover within Earth First! for at least four years at that point, and every new face was a risk. He had to get out of there.

He drove the woman back to her place in Bozeman, but he didn't stay long. He felt eyes upon him in that activist town, and he fled to the relative safety of his cabin on the reservation.

ALF supporters in New Mexico had been in touch with Rod, and one woman in particular had kept up a steady contact and urged him to come to them. Rod called her Blanca, but that was not her real name. She was part of a collective there that had some land and, from what he understood, would put him up if he needed a place to lie low. Rod had spent a couple of months on the reservation and was restless. He had never met Blanca before, but she drove up from New Mexico. It was sometime in August.

Blanca was different than other women he had worked with; she was practicing native spirituality, and this was something Rod was keenly interested in. As his own situation became more and more precarious, he felt increasingly grounded in native prayer, pipe, and sweat lodge ceremonies that had been part of his life in the past but never an open line of communication between him and the Creator. In the early months of 1992, however, that line was crackling open. Blanca believed so strongly in the protections of this medicine that she was reckless, but that, too, was a way in which Rod wanted to believe. The logic was that if they were in the right, the Creator and the animal spirits would protect them. She wanted to be close to the action. Rod quickly grasped that she was open to anything, and after a day or so he began telling her about the U.S. Department of Agriculture coyote facility that he, Jill, and Marie had scouted at Utah State University in Millville.

The target at the university was Dr. Frederick Knowlton, a widely published expert on coyote population dynamics. By 1992, Knowlton had spent almost thirty years studying ways to slow coyote predation on sheep and other livestock among other issues, and he was not only an authority on coyote behavior but also a contributor to the work of the U.S. Department of Agriculture's Animal Damage Control program (the name was officially changed to Wildlife Services in the 1970s). That was reason enough to get on Rod's hit list. The program, often referred to as ADC, was one that had long raised the ire of the animal rights movement, which decried it as a legacy held over from frontier-day efforts to eradicate wolves, grizzly bears, coyotes, and other predators that took domestic sheep and cattle as fast food.

ADC's history was actually much more nuanced than that. It began in 1885 as an ornithological survey to help farmers identify birds that were "economically useful" so as to *not* kill them, and over the years it helped control outbreaks of rabies and populations of jackrabbits, prairie dogs, and the like. In 1915, it began paying bounties on coyotes and wolves to encourage "cooperative" interaction with farmers and hunters, thus encouraging citizens to do the eradicating, and this was so successful that the wolf was nearly driven into extinction in the Lower 48. When modern efforts to bring back the wolf began in the 1970s, images of ADC hunters shooting wolves from helicopters, airplanes, and snowmobiles—a practice that is ongoing today in Alaska and Canada—were burned into the minds of environmentalists. Many groups have lobbied hard for the end of aerial shooting, including members of Congress who threatened to cut the Department of Agriculture's funding. Some widely touted studies have also indicated that shooting coyotes actually increases their numbers by destroying breeding hierarchies and increasing opportunities for pups. In the early nineties, ADC contractors were shooting as many as thirty thousand coyotes a year from helicopters and planes, which was a ten- to fifteen-million-dollar program partly billed to taxpayers, and yet coyotes continued to kill sheep even as the ranching industry declined.

But aerial gunning isn't the only way coyotes are controlled. Today, a whole arsenal of government-approved techniques is in active use, including baited M-44 sodium cyanide charges that explode in their mouths, neck snares, cage traps, steel-jaw leghold traps, and even livestock protection collars put on sheep that are laced with a chemical called Compound 1080, which is lethal to coyotes but also to humans. Activists working with predator projects all over North America now try to influence Wildlife Services to use nonlethal means of controlling coyotes.

In a 2009 interview, Knowlton told me that when he worked on predator-prey interaction, he had worked primarily on nonlethal methods of controlling coyotes, from the livestock protection collar to guard animals like dogs and llamas. He was trying to stop the animal that was actually biting the sheep at the moment it was biting the sheep, so that more general approaches like aerial gunning didn't have to be used. But many in the livestock business were not convinced that outright killing could be avoided if their numbers were to be reduced.

"I have been involved in forty or fifty different studies of one sort or another. I'm not saying, at times, we weren't asked to do some things we didn't exactly like," he said.

Blanca was horrified, and it wasn't hard for Rod to back up his decision to hit Knowlton with documentation he had gathered. The doctor looked to be one of the USDA's top men for killing coyotes; he was all over the literature. The two reasoned that whatever experiments he was doing with the coyotes in Utah couldn't be good for those animals. Blanca immediately agreed to detour through his research facilities en route to New Mexico to see what might be possible.

In Millville, they hiked up close to the 120-acre Predator Research Facility in the low hills on the outskirts of town. From there, they could see the stretch of the dry Cache Valley, with the Bear River running between gentle mountain ranges north into Idaho. Together with Knowlton's office on the main campus of Utah State University in nearby Logan, the Millville facility was a field station of the National Wildlife Research Center, which still bills itself as the largest predator-research outfit in the world. Knowlton had worked for the center since it had begun in 1964, and created the Millville facility in 1973. The Millville layout featured a main building, a scattering of outlying chain-link pens that held groups of coyotes, and a kennel building that held another forty, positioned next to what they believed was a night watchman's house. Altogether, the place held as many as one hundred coyotes.

The pair then swung through the Logan campus to check out

Knowlton's office in the Natural Resources Building. From the rear of the building, they found his office on the ground floor, at the end of a long courtyard. Rod made sketches and notes of both locations, then the two of them slipped away. Blanca was eager to do some damage to Knowlton's work.

This wasn't an action they would undertake as a duo, however. Like the WSU hit, it was too spread out and needed coordination. So they went out in search of some recruits.

New Mexico was no longer the destination. Instead, they drove to Port Angeles to talk to David Howitt, who was then living in the harbor on his thirty-foot sailboat, the *Mirage*. Howitt had always been a friend to Rod and had hosted the CAFF sanctuary, but he would not be involved in Bite Back. They never even got a chance to ask him. Rod tried to hail David on a VHF radio but couldn't reach him, and he finally decided to go say hello to Linda May, who was living separately on the sanctuary property. Rod had a strong vibe that the boat and the property were being watched, so he had Blanca wait at the car as he hiked in quietly to see May. As he cut through an adjacent golf course, he spotted what looked like an unmarked police vehicle parked behind the Safeway supermarket and noted that the mustached man inside was peering intently at the road and woods that led to where May was. Rod thought that the radio call to Howitt might have tipped the authorities, because the man looked like a federal agent. He didn't see Rod crouched behind the trees, though, and Rod managed to sneak in a quick visit with May. Then he crept back out, gathered up Blanca, and immediately left town, feeling lucky to get off the Olympic Peninsula without a raft of cops on his tail.

They moved through Oregon, California, and Colorado, talking to activists along the way. None of Rod's regular contacts and associates could sign on to this action, but new activists made themselves known to the pair.

Some weeks after their tour through Utah, Rod and Blanca were back on the Standing Rock reservation. They arrived in the dark of night in her car, and Rod drove out to the Sitting Bull monument for a meeting he was anticipating with a mix of hope and dread. The parking lot was deserted, and he sat looking at the monument. The eight-foot-tall marker supported a stone bust of the Lakota chief on a remote bit of bluff looking out over the Missouri River. The lights of Mobridge, South Dakota, glowed on the other side. It was a forlorn place, down four miles of dirt road and with no buildings, and he didn't feel good about parking there. So he checked the place periodically through the night, catching some sleep in the car between visits. Finally, there was a truck. Jonathan's truck.

Rod's heart fell. After hugging his friend and his companion, a woman whom Rod knew, he said, "I thought you weren't going to bring the truck?"

"You don't have to worry. I had it scanned."

"Scanned?"

"Yeah, I had it electronically scanned for tracking devices. We didn't find anything on it."

That didn't do much to make Rod feel more secure. The feds knew all about that truck, and he didn't want that truck parked anywhere near him, so they agreed to take it across the river to Mobridge, off the reservation, and leave it there for the duration of the visit.

Jonathan and his friends spent a few days on the reservation, and Rod introduced them to his life there. They did a sweat lodge ceremony near his little cabin hideout that Jonathan found to be a profoundly moving experience.

"I wasn't going out to do an action with him. I was going out to meet with him, because I wanted to see him. We needed to talk," said Jonathan.

Jonathan was adamant that he would not be part of Operation Bite Back. But his own distance from the campaign did not make the time on the Standing Rock any more restful. Both men were gripped by powerful paranoia. At one point, they were certain they were being shadowed on the highway by an unmarked car, and both agreed that was the end of the visit. Jonathan and his companion went back to Eugene, where Jonathan was now living, without his having resolved some nagging old issues with Rod. It was just too dangerous for the two of them to be together.

"We felt like we were sitting on this reservation in this old cabin, waiting to be surrounded at any moment. For the first time in our lives, we were both kind of feeling like at any moment they were gonna storm us, and it was going down. So it was a pretty intense time," said Jonathan.

In the September 22, 1992, issue of the *Earth First! Journal*, Rod published a story under his real name that tied together the actions at OSU, the Northwest Fur Breeders Cooperative, WSU, Malecky Mink Ranch, and MSU as one ALF campaign called Operation Bite Back. He stated that he was in hiding, afraid for his life because of the bounty put out by the fur industry and the ski-masked raid carried out on his cabin, and that he'd carry on with his activism until he was killed.

Also in that issue of the journal, an unsigned story titled "Howlo-ween in UT" warned that USU's Predator Research Facility would be targeted on Halloween, saying, "There will be an action in Utah on Oct. 31 against Animal Damage Control's lethal control program. Site to be determined, but get your animal costumes ready, practice your howls and start thinking gorilla theater ideas."

Sometime around October 11, Rod was back in the Applegate hanging out with Marie at her place when he realized it was a full moon and he needed a hike to Sacred Tree. After Chant Thomas had shown him that place, the grandmother tree had become a regular destination for Rod. Marie, her brother, and Rod had been to visit some acquaintances in the nearby town of Williams and had scored some pot and magic mushrooms there. All three agreed they'd take the mushrooms and climb to the tree.

About thirty minutes after taking them, they were preparing to leave, and Rod made a trip to the outhouse. He was standing in there when he heard coyotes howling all around him. He remarked that the coyotes sounded like women, ululating and yowling, sometimes singing long sustained notes and then chattering like gals talking over coffee at a café table. He had heard coyotes all over the United States and Canada, but he noted that in this place, in this instance, they really seemed to take on voices.

Night had fallen when they started their walk down the road to the trailhead with the odd coyote yip as punctuation. The psilocybin was really coming on then, the old waves of joy starting to heave from the stomach to the heart and back down to bother the genitals, and the inky dark of the night was just taking on a color and form when the moon crested the mountain and poured sparkling cream light down through the trees. They turned up the trail with this mystic half-light showing the way, the three of them wide open to the creation, and they noticed that the coyote sounds were coming in closer. As they moved up the trail, they were soon accompanied on either side by what seemed like a pack of coyotes, yipping and barking, no more long howls now but the sound of a pack on the jog. Rod was wide-eyed then, head whipping back and forth to both sides of the trail, trying to see them. He felt it was a blessing, a visitation. But he couldn't see them; he only heard what he thought was the rustling of nimble feet in the oak leaves and the undergrowth.

The hike to the grandmother tree was only a mile, but Rod was moving more and more slowly. He and Marie stopped to peer through the trees, swearing they saw movement, and then suddenly Rod was seeing them, not coyotes but upright figures, running from tree to tree. Flesh-and-blood women running through the moonlight. He knew he was fully in the grips of a mushroom trip, but he also knew there actually were coyotes out there in the trees, and so he decided in that moment that they were taking advantage of his mind state to reveal themselves to him in a new way, as a community, as the Trickster.

"They know what we're doing," Rod whispered to Marie. "These animals are playing with us. They know we're in this other sensory zone."

He didn't get much farther than that. Rod couldn't go on. He was overwhelmed by the vision. The woods were full of figures and voices, and he started to get concerned. Were they trying to tell him something? Should he be trying to get to the tree, or should he stop and interact with them right here? His feet were suddenly rooted to the ground as if they were growing into the earth. He had to turn back. Marie's brother decided to push on to the tree by himself. Rod and Marie started back down the trail.

Rod felt like something was trying to break through to him, and suddenly it did, what he described as a "total awareness" that the coyotes knew who they were and about Rod's mission to save their kind.

"Oh my god, they know who we are," he said as he stood on the trail, slack jawed. "They know what we are doing, and they are behind us."

It got more intense. Soon, he felt the coyote women communicating that they were showing themselves as part of villages and families, community units that had been scattered by generations of war. They were the survivors of shooting and trapping and all manner of imprisonment, and they wanted Rod and Marie to see who they really were and why it mattered.

"We have to do this action," Rod announced out loud. "We have got to do this action at Utah State University."

"Ssshhh. Let's not talk about that right now, OK?" said Marie, who knew it would not be so unusual to run across other people on this trail.

Back at the cabin, Rod studied Marie and admired her good sense and her care for him, and as he looked, he saw her face slowly transform into that of a little bobcat, the eyes growing round and fuzzy ears protruding, and he thought it was the most beautiful thing he had ever seen. "She's an old soul," he said to himself. Her brother showed up, and they all realized how freaking high they were, and they talked and played music and enjoyed the ride until they drifted off to sleep.

Early the next morning, however, Rod got up before dawn and went back up the trail by himself. He wanted to be at the grandmother tree at sunrise. He bounded up the trail in the purple predawn and was sitting on the ground under the apron of ancient branches when the orange flash of dawn broke over the Siskiyous. Birds came in a small flock and landed in the branches around him, and he swore there, to the coyote nation, that he would proceed with the USU action and continue these actions, regardless of the consequences, until he could do no more.

In the predawn hours of October 24, during the dead black of the new moon, a group of seven saboteurs gathered in a canyon not far from the Predator Research Facility in Millville. Rod and Blanca handed out packets to the others containing maps and unfingerprinted money they could use to escape if they got scattered. Tools, radios, and police scanners were divided among them as they split into prearranged teams,

At this crew's earlier meetings, in remote Rocky Mountain camps, Blanca had passed a pipe, and they had smoked sacred tobacco together and prayed and talked about how the future of American wildlife was linked to that of Native Americans and warriors like themselves. But this time, they were all business, moving quickly and speaking in hushed voices. In the previous month, Rod had learned that Jonathan Paul had been called to the Spokane grand jury only days after his trip to the Standing Rock, and there was some indication that Jonathan might be jailed for contempt of court. Investigators were starting to zero in on people very close to Rod. All those gathered knew that this action was growing increasingly risky.

Rod and Blanca jumped on mountain bikes and rode to campus, then strolled arm in arm to Knowlton's office, where Blanca set up to watch the campus police station, which was right next door, and Rod proceeded to use suction cups and glazier's equipment to remove the entire window to the office. They had pretested the window for alarms by having a "student" run into it by accident weeks earlier. Inside, Rod gave Knowlton the same treatment Aulerich had received at Michigan State University: he quickly rifled through the desk for computer disks, key notebooks, and documents to steal, then heaped the remaining stuff into a pile and placed a quiet incendiary in the center. Then the two strolled back to their bikes and rode away.

At the same time, a separate team of ALFers jogged along in an Indian run down a mountain trail and into the Predator Research Facility. Their job was to cut the fences on all the coyote pens— except those in the large kennel building that stood next to the caretaker's house. They moved from pen to pen, snipping the wire, and as they did so, the coyotes sensed freedom and began digging feverishly under the fence right in front of them. These were hand-reared coyotes, born to the USDA and not wild, so they may have craved human contact. As soon as the fencing was held open for them, the animals dashed through and waited for their companions. In twos and threes, they went bounding off up into the hills.

When Rod arrived at the research facility, the others whispered how the coyotes had tried to help them, and Rod was moved to tears. They didn't know the coyotes were nearly as domesticated as pet dogs.

He had tested an unalarmed entry point to the research facility's main building, a bathroom window, but as he worked at removing it, he was making so much noise that they almost called off the action for fear of waking whoever was in the watchman's house. As if on cue, all of the coyotes still in the other unit began howling loudly, providing exactly the amount of cover needed to quickly get the window out. Incendiaries were planted, and they all ran back up the trail.

The incendiaries went off as planned, and the main building at the Predator Research Facility was soon ablaze. The fire in Knowlton's office, however, never really caught, and only a few papers were charred. By that time, Rod, Blanca, and the rest had been picked up by drivers and carted off to various locations. The fire at the research facility was fairly quickly doused by firefighters, but the documents piled on the floor were thoroughly soaked.

Knowlton told me that the mess at the research building in Millville looked bad, and fire marshals eventually came in with scoop shovels and slopped a six-foot-wide mound of papers into another office, but, amazingly, only a few pages of data were actually lost. Almost everything was recovered.

"Now, they were singed around the edges!" he chuckled, noting that one of the major studies in that pile of papers concerned the livestock protection collar. "They were wet and they had to be dried out. In spite of all that, we were able to recover it."

The Millville facility, however, was about one-third destroyed. Damages were set at more than $380,000. Eventually, a newer and bigger building was built of brick and steel. Twenty-seven pens had been opened and Knowlton said about fifty coyotes had the opportunity to flee but that only sixteen actually did. And none of those escaped. In fact, the reality was hardly the fairy-tale scene of emancipation that Rod and the ALFers had reported to one another and related in their press release.

Coyotes are territorial animals, Knowlton points out, adding, "When they got out, their first priority had to do with settling it with their neighbors. When I got there, we had animals running all over our facility. I couldn't understand why they had spray-painted the animals. But it turned out that what I thought was spray paint was blood. It was a big free-for-all."

All the animals were accounted for: fourteen returned alive, one dead, and one reported shot but not recovered. There was a big vet bill for patching them all up.

Knowlton said later that he didn't care what happened to Rod. He just wanted this kind of action to stop, because it wasn't effective in improving methodology used in science or in improving the lives of the animals.

When I asked whether ALF had achieved anything, he said, "It depends on their agenda. If it's to garner attention, they're probably reasonably effective for a short period of time. In terms of saving animals, no, they destroy animals. I came to the conclusion that—after knowing what happened in our situation—that they were abusing animals for their own purposes."

EIGHTEEN

The Animal Enterprise
Protection Act

LATE IN THE summer of 1992, federal authorities from all over the country began discussing what to do about Rodney Coronado. U.S. attorneys and assistant U.S. attorneys from all the districts that had seated grand juries on Bite Back gathered for meetings in Spokane, Seattle, and Portland to map out a strategy. They decided that Michigan had the best case—and possibly the only chance to put Rod behind bars. On the other attacks, there just wasn't enough evidence. If they could catch Rod—and that was still a question—the prosecutors agreed to accept a deal in which he would plead guilty in Michigan in return for not being prosecuted in other states.

The charge would be arson, plain and simple. But for many of those who were closely following Operation Bite Back, that just wasn't enough.

Arson crossed a line for many people—and, worse, it seemed to presage future attacks. Reports about the ALF in Britain were printed in all the fur and medical research journals, describing how animal fanatics advocated real terrorism against "vivisectionists" in the form of fires, car-bombings, and shootings. In Britain, the militant wing of the animal rights movement had launched an armed insurgency. The American biomedical research community, Ron Arnold's wise use movement, big agribusiness, university scientists, and others worried in the press that ALF tactics in the United States would escalate to murder.

A dozen states had already passed legislation to criminalize such attacks, but lobbyists from the biomedical research and agriculture industries, in particular, wanted federal protection. Congress awoke to the urgency of the situation and, on August 26, 1992, passed the Animal Enterprise Protection Act (AEPA). It wasn't a law the Department of Justice had wanted; the department believed it had enough laws to deal with eco-radicals and had actively fought it. But the AEPA did something that Arnold and others had long wanted by broadening the crime of terrorism to include property destruction. And Rod, as the prime suspect in the Michigan State University fire, was at the center of the discussion.

"We in the research community were feeling pretty frustrated with a number of incidents that had occurred, starting really with some stolen chimpanzees in Maryland, the fires at Michigan State; there were a number of physical attacks, doing damage to facilities throughout the country, and no apprehensions," said Frankie Trull, president of the Foundation for Biomedical Research, an advocacy group for the continued use of animals in medical science.

Trull had more than the business community on her side: much of the environmental movement agreed with her too. In public, at least, Rod's campaign was radioactive, and very few organizations or individuals wanted to be associated with it. The mainstream conservation groups argued against some of the provisions of the AEPA, but they largely lined up behind the idea of greatly increased penalties for eco-sabotage.

"Since this organization started in 1954, it has stood against violence," said John Balzar, senior vice president of communications at the Humane Society of the United States. "The very foundation of the work here is to protect animals from suffering and cruelty caused by human actions, and any tactic or strategy involving violence towards people undermines the core ethic."

By "violence," Balzar meant any destruction of persons or property, and he refused to get into parsing the differences. He added, "Tactics like that are ethically wrong, and they do fundamental damage to the credibility of the humane movement. It's abhorrent. It's a setback."

Even Friends of Animals' Priscilla Feral, who had supported Rod's research with Global Investigations, was dead set against Operation Bite Back, saying, "He took the approach that he was going to go in and burn these places, or wreck them. I strongly disagree with that. That's not the way forward. Plus, is it effective? They have insurance, and they replace the mink; they replace the cages."

The only well-known public organization that stood by Rod during this period was PETA; while it never openly endorsed arson, Ingrid Newkirk was happy to receive any seized tapes or data and was unapologetic about publicizing Rod's attacks—and remains so today. Many individual radicals supported him openly, as did the *Earth First! Journal*, but their support came without much cost. Almost everyone else turned their back on him, including the mentors who both said they continued to admire him, Paul Watson and Dave Foreman.

"I think it's poor strategy; I think it's poor targeting. I think anything to do with arson is beyond the pale," said Foreman. "The consequences are so great, the chances of harming people is so great, that it's just a bad choice."

"It's not just Rod; it's everybody in the ALF," Watson told me in 1992, and he's told me the same many times since then. "They're playing a game. They're young people, and they don't seem to really understand the seriousness of what they're involved in. I've had to battle this within Sea Shepherd for ten years, to keep people from crossing that line. We haven't had a criminal conviction, and I'm not about to start."

Watson clarified this in a 2009 interview: "I have no problem with property damage if the property is used for illegal or unjust purposes, i.e., the taking of life of sentient beings, but arson cannot be controlled and our movement cannot afford to kill someone even accidentally."

He also saw arson as a strategic mistake. Watson's position is the same today as it was during Bite Back: Sea Shepherd is not a criminal organization that goes after legally operating industries. It is, he says, "an interventionist group; we intervene in accordance with the United Nations World Charter for Nature that allows for intervention by nongovernmental organizations."

Burning down fur farms, then, was a failure on both counts.

Even Rod's buddy David Howitt eventually backed away. He continued to support direct action and still supports it now, but he drew the line at arson. Which makes sense since he, like Jonathan Paul, would go on to work as a fireman. In an interview for this book, Howitt said fire was just too dangerous.

Rod was completely on his own. Every cord had been cut. His actions jeopardized the entire movement.

The Animal Enterprise Protection Act created a new section in Title 18 of the federal code, titled "Animal Enterprise Terrorism." It was aimed at someone who would (a) travel across state lines or use the mail in "interstate or foreign commerce" and (b) cause, or conspire to cause, property damage to an animal enterprise. Someone like the Unabomber. Or Rodney Coronado.

The statute wasn't terribly impressive, however, in terms of the sentences it offered. For damages valued at less than ten thousand dollars, it was only six months in prison and a fine. If you killed someone, it was life—but that's often the sentence for murder, anyway. By comparison, the punishment for arson was five years, no matter how much damage you caused. So prosecutors weren't all that eager to use the AEPA. In fact, it went unused for years.

For Frankie Trull, however, it was a major victory. By 1992, she had already been battling to protect animal research for over a decade. She had, in 1979, started the National Association for Biomedical Research (NABR, pronounced "neighbor") to address regulatory and legislative issues regarding medical research. At that time, the ALF and other extremists didn't even exist—at least in the United States. The debate was then centered on how to treat lab animals more humanely, and NABR's scientist constituents wanted to amend the 1966 Animal Welfare Act so that the idea of "humane" didn't go too far. Trull started the nonprofit Foundation for Biomedical Research in 1981 to educate the public about the issue. She was incredibly successful at this. She engaged a long list of Nobel Prize winners and famous doctors, most notably the late Dr. Michael DeBakey, the most famous heart surgeon in the United States and credited with dozens of innovations, from developing the arterial bypass to helping create M.A.S.H. units during the Korean War. In 1995, Trull founded Policy Directions, a lobbying firm that works the pro–medical research agenda and other issues with Congress.

Trull's association members and industry clients began pushing for an AEPA-type law in earnest after the 1986 theft of four young chimpanzees from the SEMA Inc. biomedical laboratory in Rockville, Maryland. The chimps were to be used in AIDS and hepatitis research and were never returned to the lab. A group called True Friends released a video of the remaining chimps' living conditions in the lab, which drew outraged protests from famed primate researcher Jane Goodall, among other critics. Goodall was then allowed to tour the facility, which left her so horrified that she began dedicating her own time to addressing lab conditions everywhere. In the end, stealing the chimps helped lead to reform.

Bills had been introduced in Congress by the late Senator Howell Heflin (D-Alabama) and Representative Charles Stenholm (D-Texas) to increase the penalties for this kind of illegal action, but Rod's MSU attack provided just the push these bills needed to pass. For even though the bills had broad bipartisan support, Congress and the American public were wary of using the word *terrorism* to refer to property destruction. Up until that point, the word had only applied to attacks against people.

"I think that probably was the first time, because I know that it wasn't a slam dunk to pass the legislation," said Stenholm, now retired and a lobbyist with Olsson Frank Weeda, a D.C. law firm that works on animal issues among its many campaigns. "Anytime you bring up animals and humane treatment of animals, it tends to become very emotional. It's politically very difficult to deal with. But we spent a lot of time on that."

Even the fur publications were slow to use the word. A March 9, 1992, news item in *Fur Age* reported that Stenholm's HR 2407 had over 250 sponsors in Congress and was designed to turn "animal-rights vandalism" into a federal crime. The magazine called it vandalism, as did most people at the time.

Animal welfare groups, the American Civil Liberties Union, and the National Lawyers Guild pushed for amendments to these pieces of legislation in various committees, because they consistently went too far, stepping on civil rights and freedom of speech. None of the organizations, however, were against prosecuting arson.

Stenholm took on this issue after animal activists began a late-1980s campaign targeting Texas Tech University, his alma mater, to protest the use of cats in a study on sudden infant death syndrome (SIDS). The first attack caused seventy thousand dollars in damages, and the sabotage and threats continued for years.

"There was sabotage. I do remember basically threats saying, 'If you don't stop . . . ,' and there were some other break-ins. But they were getting out of hand. They were threatening the lives of the scientists. I received some threats myself, as a result of introducing the legislation," said Stenholm.

When his bill was presented before the House in 1992, Heflin submitted a written commentary that laid out what he believed was at stake. He described two June 1990 car-bombings in the U.K. that had been intended to hurt or kill a medical scientist and a veterinary officer—ironically, the bombings the movement attributed to provocateurs—then added,

The United States is not more than 2 years behind the U.K. in terms of terrorist activities being employed by a few extremists in the animal rights movement. We should learn from Britain's experience and do everything we can to stem the rising tide of illegal and increasingly violent acts being committed by animal rights extremists here in our country. The victims of the illegal acts of animal liberation supporters are not only research institutions and staff but all of us . . . The real price of the crime my legislation seeks to prevent is paid by all those who are waiting for cures and treatment for their afflictions. Human beings, of course, will pay the price, but so will all animal life, for animals as well as people benefit from this research.

The fact that these projected murders have never happened, not two years but sixteen years later, is not seen as evidence that the act was too heavy-handed.

"When we did both the Animal Enterprise Protection Act and the [2006] Animal Enterprise Terrorism Act, we talked to the British embassy at length. We should be very proud that we never allowed to happen here what happened in the U.K. But I'm not sure that our own community really appreciates that we really have fended off things that could have been worse," said Trull.

No one would be prosecuted under the AEPA for many years after it was passed—mostly because so few radicals were ever caught. But the "terrorism" designation was established, and it would quickly be reinforced by additional bills in 1996, the USA PATRIOT Act in 2001, and the Animal Enterprise Terrorism Act in 2006.

A note of weariness crept into Trull's voice as she talked about Rod and his colleagues. She'd been on the scene a long time and lamented the fact that she'd had to fight against the threat of physical violence for almost two decades.

"One of the fathers of animal rights—he was also a very thoughtful person, and we used to talk all the time—was [Animal Rights

International founder] Henry Spira. Henry said what made him so nervous about the activities that were going on that were really aggressive, where they were breaking into research facilities, is that the movement starts to develop a thug mentality," said Trull. "And thugs—these are his words—are attracted to participate because it gives them an excuse to do damage. And the real pure purpose of animal rights is lost in the whole activity of doing these illegal things."

"I think we all applaud anybody who wants to change public opinion. That's kind of what we're all about in this country. But this 'Either do it my way or I'm going to kill you' just doesn't play very well," Trull added.

Rod's status as a fugitive made him a folk hero to environmental radicals, but he saw that it might be working against everything he was trying to achieve. The federal government was tightening a snare around his whole world. Not only were federal agents hunting him with the intent to arrest or worse, but his actions were also forcing Congress to create new laws to punish him. He could stay underground forever, for a lifetime, but his true passion, his activist career, would be shut down; anytime he achieved even the slightest bit of success, he would risk being recognized and arrested. He looked for a way out.

In early December, I received at my P.O. box in San Francisco the following communiqué. It had been hand delivered and was dated December 1, 1992. This letter also ran in the December 10 issue of the *Earth First! Journal*, although they cleaned up some of the punctuation and misspellings that appear in this version.

Animal Liberation Front (ALF) spokesperson, Rod Coronado, who has been hiding due to threats against his life from the Federal Bureau of Investigation (FBI) and the fur industry, is willing

to surrender to federal authorities under the following conditions:

1) That all grizzly bears held hostage as experimental subjects by
Washington State University (WSU) be released to a wildlife rehabilitation center approved by People for the Ethical Treatment
of Animals (PETA 301-770-8969) and Earth First! (406-728--
8114), with the intent of returning the bears to their native homeland from which they were removed.

2) That WSU issue a public statement promising never to capture
or acquire more endangered species as research subjects or for
any other purposes.

3) That all tax-payer supported research being conducted on
mink, coyotes and otters by Washington State University, Oregon State University, Michigan State University and Utah State
University be suspended.

Although the Coalition Against Fur Farms (CAFF) and the
ALF do not approve of the incarceration of any native wildlife,
Rod Coronado believes that the hostage exchange of one species
for another is a reasonable alternative. If these three conditions
are agreed to, and met and negotiated through PETA and Earth
First! I, Rod Coronado, will turn myself in to federal authorities
in Montana at the tribal headquarters of the Blackfoot Nation. As
part of the agreement I, Rod Coronado, swear to cooperate fully
with Grand Jury Inquisitions into ALF activity that I am suspected in, relating to the defense of native wildlife and the environment. I swear to testify, and answer all questions relating to
my role as a spokesperson on behalf of the ALF, and as the Coordinator of the Coalition Against Fur Farms.

I, Rod Coronado, believe that my non-violent actions in

defense of the earth, are innocent acts to protect the ecological integrity of this country's natural heritage. This statement of conditions of surrender is in no way an admission of guilt to charges laid by the United States government, or any other law enforcement agency. It is my belief that with a fair trial, the citizens of this country will recognize that the real acts of terrorism committed on university campuses in the last eighteen months, are those carried out by Oregon State researcher—Ron Scott, Washington State researcher—John Gorham, Michigan State researcher—Richard Aulerich, and Utah State researcher, Frederick Knowlton.

Recent attempts by the FBI to portray me as a fugitive evading arrest are standard practices by the US government to convince the public that I am guilty and that I am a violent criminal—the first steps in justifying the assassination of Native American activists who choose to maintain their cultural and religious beliefs.

Through the example of US history, it is my understanding that if I was to continue my defense of Native American wildlife and lands, that I would be murdered by the FBI or people within the fur industry. The FBI, while questioning David Howitt in June 1992, acknowledged a threat against my life. In May 1992, when the FBI and the Bureau of Alcohol, Tobacco and Firearms (BATF) raided my mountain home in southern Oregon, the presence of automatic weaponry in my attempted arrest is a testament of the US governments' willingness to use deadly force to squash my representation of Native American wildlife, and those who defend them.

In over ten years of non-violent resistance to the destruction of native wildlife and lands, I have never caused an injury or loss of life to any living being. Through my obligation as a citizen of the earth, I have only ever targeted the implements of life's destruction, i.e. whaling ships in Iceland. I have never, nor will I ever carry or use firearms or explosives in my defense of my earth mother. My religious beliefs recognize the sanctity of all life and would never allow me to justify a violent act that would result in the loss of life. It is only because of the FBI's record of violence against Native Americans such as Anna Mae Aquash, Leonard Peltier, Tina Trudell, Pedro Bisonette and other American Indian Movement (415-552-1992) activists that I avoid contact with the US government by living a life in hiding.

In the Spirit of Crazy Horse,

Rod Coronado
Coordinator, Coalition Against Fur Farms
Spokesperson, Animal Liberation Front

NINETEEN

The Native Underground

CHRISTMAS IN 1992, for Rod and Blanca, meant connecting with ritual Native American celebrations of the winter solstice. They had to stay hidden, but that didn't mean Rod couldn't continue his spiritual inquiry. He was living in a cabin just off the Zuni pueblo, in the northwest corner of New Mexico, and though he and Blanca were engaged in what Rod called an "unhealthy" relationship, they continued to spend a lot of time together as lovers and fugitives. She was beginning to ask for more commitment to the relationship, but Rod, as was his usual habit, was already digging deeper and deeper into his new campaign: finding his native roots.

In December, he attended the Shalako ceremonies held by the Zuni, a series of dances and dramas enacted at the winter solstice and the most important Zuni ritual of the year.

This was not just a matter of interest for Rod. Intense fear and love were driving him deep into his own native forms of worship. He had begun to plan his movements around specific ceremonies and could not be dissuaded of their significance.

The Shalako is a blessing of the houses and a plea for rain and good crops in the stark mesa lands inhabited by the Zuni. The visitations Rod saw on the day of the ceremonies came in three waves. First, the Mudheads arrived, clown-type characters with mud-daubed faces that appear in the village to announce the arrival of the Shalako dancers. Then, the Council of the Gods arrived and stopped before each of the homes where the Shalako would reside and shook their bags of deer bones at each one. The homes were carefully prepared, often at great personal expense to the families who owned them. Two of the gods entered a preselected home and were dusted with sacred cornmeal, then a banquet was served.

When the Shalako appeared, they materialized out of a gathering dusk on an open field. The six great masks were much taller than an ordinary man and very heavy, but each was operated by one dancer who not only carried the mask in great swooping descents, the motions of an attacking eagle, but also opened and shut the popping eyes and clacked the beak. Feathers spread out around the masks like the petals on a sunflower. The dancers inside were hidden by blankets that made up the bodies of the costumes. They came on with great pomp, clacking and gesturing, dancers taking pride in keeping their steps despite the unwieldy burden.

The six entered the houses prepared for them, and at midnight more dancing commenced. This went on for long hours, and the gods finally left their houses around noon the next day. The entire village followed them out of town and back across the field. As they left, well fed and feted, they took prayers with them for rain. In dusty country, one of God's main jobs is to bring drink.

The Shalako are not private ceremonies like those of many tribes, but have a certain touristy element to them. Rod lined up with the others in a fenced-in area for spectators and was still profoundly moved. These were the rituals that bonded human beings to the earth, not to deities whose mission seemed to be denial of the earth and pursuit of some future life after death. These were rituals about loving the rain and the coyote and the mink nation, and Rod drew strength from them.

In 1992 and 1993, my reporting on Rod led me to other Native American environmental battles. The radicalism I occasionally found there had a certain clear-eyed righteousness that explained a lot about why Rod felt good in that company. In May 1993, I was north of Kamloops, British Columbia, on the Chu Chua reservation reporting on a dispute concerning the Shuswap tribe and their life's blood, the Thompson River. The Thompson is a northern tributary of the mighty Fraser, which loops west to the Pacific, and a businessman in Vancouver had proposed taking off a certain amount of the cold, moose-washed water of the Fraser and piping it to Southern California, which was experiencing another drought. How much water could one man-size pipe take out of the Fraser? Enough, some preliminary studies showed, to heavily impact the already-threatened salmon and steelhead runs. The very idea of it hurt the Shuswap who ate out of the river.

One early morning, I sat on the bed of a Shuswap fellow named Joe Jules, and he showed me the hell game. It was played like dice, rolling two chunks of antler, and he said they called it the bone game or sometimes the hell game because they played just for the hell of it. Our breakfast was wienies, mac 'n' cheese, and fresh liver from a deer he'd killed the night before. His little boy was in a camo jumpsuit, and his little girl watched me as she ate, and his wife, Cookie, cooked and poured coffee. Another guy sat close by, a guy with old tattoos of an eagle on one forearm and the grim reaper on the other who carried a .30-06 with the stock wrapped in camo tape and who didn't have a name he wanted to use. He called himself Jules's bodyguard. "Just say I'm a Shuswap warrior," he said. He sat grinning at me, just grinning like I was about the sorriest thing he'd ever seen because I didn't already understand how this water thing was gonna go. He let Jules tell it, and he just looked straight through me.

We'd talked a lot about the river, who governed what and who was going to have last say over what. These particular guys had already been in an armed scrap with the Mounties, and that's where this ruction over selling the water was headed, too, if it had to.

Without preamble, Jules picked up a drum and began tapping it, then began to sing. His voice filled the little house and immediately jumped up to that high coyote note that fills the world when Indians sing. He tried out a couple of tunes, then said he had one that was a prayer for the river and the salmon and the floodwater that decides to return every spring, and he laid into it, and the others began to whine like they couldn't help themselves, and they all jumped in, the bodyguard and Cookie and the kids, singing with Dad.

There were a lot of Jules among the local Indian bands around this time, and some of them were chiefs and councillors. The drum throbbed like the breast drumming of a grouse I'd listened to for hours the night before on a friend's farm. It was probably true that the Shuswap had some legal claim to the water, and sending it to the States by pipelines and tankers had been a subject that just wouldn't die with the crown in Ottawa, but Jules had found a way to let me feel another logic. It was right there in the song: It was not that the Shuswap controlled the fish or the river. It was that they *were* the fish and the river both, and the deer hung in the garage and the sweat lodge submerged in floodwater at the end of the road. They were it, and it was them. I couldn't help thinking that this talk we were having was really about the terms of Canada's surrender. The Shuswap would outlast them all.

I also couldn't help thinking about Rod, who was somewhere on this same road.

When the song ended, the drum's final notes rang in the metal rack above the stove where the family dried their salmon, and the bodyguard started to chuckle. It was a low, throaty chortle that put me right down in my chair like two hands pushing down on my shoulders and was one I'll never forget. You don't forget being face-to-face with your own irrelevance.

"The drums still scare the shit out of white people," the bodyguard said.

Jules lay back on the bed. "They think they're all war songs," he added.

"Yeah, listen to them crazy Injuns on the warpath again."

Then the bodyguard smiled that smile and said, "But if that

woulda been a war song, buddy, you woulda been the first to know."

Around this same time, in the spring of 1993, Rod attended a conference in Rapid City, South Dakota, called "Warriors with Wisdom," put on by the American Indian Higher Education Consortium, which addresses federal policies on education. He was traveling with some Native American ecologists, stitching together a new life for himself. He had begun volunteering for an initiative called the Intertribal Bison Cooperative (ITBC), and when its first office opened in Rapid City in May 1993, Rod moved there too.

This was a relatively new organization, founded in 1990 by tribes throughout the West to reestablish American buffalo herds on their traditional grazing lands. The ITBC had begun with elements from nineteen tribes, but even by the time Rod worked with them there were many more, and by the time of this writing in 2009 there were fifty-seven affiliated tribes with herds totaling fifteen thousand head.

"Martin" operated pretty freely in Rapid City. The only way to start a new life was to embrace his new identity wholeheartedly. Going after any more fur industry targets was just too risky, especially after the December 12, 1992, edition of the news program *60 Minutes* had aired the neck-breaking footage he had shot at Bruce Campbell's farm. Anyone in the fur-farming industry who hadn't known that onetime fur farmer Jim Perez was really an ALFer—and my conversations revealed there had been some— knew they'd been duped after that news buzzed through the industry. This led to heightened security and renewed calls for more federal enforcement.

Rod's new South Dakota contacts, however, had no idea who he was. His boss at the ITBC let the mysteriously intense young activist house-sit for him. Later, Rod rented a house in Rapid City through a family he knew on the Standing Rock reservation.

In his new work, Rod befriended many activists in Lakota circles, especially among the traditionalists who were practicing ritual medicine, governance, and religion. There was one particular man, a Cheyenne River Sioux tribal member named Jim Griffin, who became a friend. Coronado found that Griffin was deeply interested in tribal participation in Dave Foreman's new Wildlands Project, which proposed establishing and expanding green corridors to connect all remnant wilderness left in North America. Through Griffin, Coronado met a number of tribal leaders, including Alex White Plume, a future president of the Oglala Sioux tribe who came to some fame for growing industrial hemp on the reservation, which is illegal, and defending his right to do so on the grounds that it was a fiber crop.

That summer, Coronado, Griffin, and another tribal activist named Rocky Afraid of Hawk drove to an international bison meeting in La Crosse, Wisconsin, and Coronado tried to forward a grant proposal, but it got a cold reception from all the ITBC members. He was puzzled by this, because he had otherwise been accepted by the group, but when he asked Griffin privately, he was told that many native people they worked with figured he was an FBI agent. He had just showed up one day, always seemed to have money, and never talked about his past. After this talk with Griffin, which happened in June, Coronado figured it was time to move on.

First, though, he spent a few days at White Plume's family sun dance.

Among the Lakota, June is the season of the sun dance, one of the most iconic native ceremonies still practiced in the Americas, an intensely physical prayer regimen in which traditional medicines are used to achieve deep intoxication or trance and dancers endure severe treatment as living sacrifices to support their prayers. One has to be dedicated to pray like this: Traditional accounts report that the sun dance begins with four days of dancing around a central pole, during which time the participants gaze into the sun and dance to exhaustion. Medicine men then step forward, pierce the chest skin of each dancer with a length of bone, and use that bone to tether the dancer to the pole with a rawhide lead. In order to make his sacrifice, the dancer must release himself by pulling back against the tether to rip the bone through his skin. Another variation is to be pierced through the back and have rawhides fixed to heavy bison skulls, which the dancer drags through rocks and bushes, trying to catch the skulls and tear the piercings free.

These practices are protected, and it's not clear if they continue in this manner today. But I saw the scars on the chest of a teenage Lakota dancer around 1998, and they were not small.

Though visitors are sometimes allowed to attend, most of these ceremonies take place in jealously guarded privacy. The concealed locations are not only a defense against New Age interlopers but also a vestige of these rituals' having been practiced in secret for over a century after they were outlawed by whites. Only in 1978, with the passage of the American Indian Religious Freedom Act, did Indians have the right to practice them freely.

At the White Plume ceremony, Rod was only an observer, but with his friend Albert White Hat, it was different. He was invited by White Hat to be a fire keeper for the sweat lodge and support a young dancer in White Hat's Hollow Horn Bear Sun Dance in the town of St. Francis, on the Rosebud reservation. Rod had been a fire keeper at one of White Hat's sweat lodge ceremonies, so he had some idea of what it involved, but the sun dance role was a job he took on with some hesitation. It was intimidating, and he didn't want to come off as a dilettante or a tourist, so he took instruction from a couple of native men who had come from Wisconsin. Gradually, his position became more established as the ceremony kept on and he kept on tending the fires, tirelessly, quietly.

Rod was increasingly humbled by the physical toll exacted upon the dancers, who endured even torrential rainstorms. All the dancers were required to have a good sweat at the end of the day, and he made sure the lodge was ready. Sometimes whole families would come, and he would stand ready at the lodge flap and listen to their songs and pray with them. As the days passed, families began asking for him specifically, which was a great honor.

Finally, he was asked to support his dancer directly, and as he entered for the first time the arbor where the dancers were making their physical prayer, it hit him as if he had passed through a wall of flame. Inside that circle, he said, he felt a "free-flowing energy storm of beautiful power that reached deep inside you to your deepest senses." It was a power he had never felt, but had intuited. He had known it was there and could be tapped in his campaigns for the wild. He found it living and in full flower in this ceremony.

"I knew all along that the sun dance for the Plains people was one of the most intense ceremonies of their ceremonial cycle," Rod said. "And I was overwhelmed. I thought it was beautiful. There was a lot of strength there. They wanted me to pledge to dance the following year, being very open and inviting.

"Something told me, 'This is not right. I'm not a Lakota or a Cheyenne. I've got my own culture. And my own culture I don't know anything about.'

"As the intensity of the season got stronger, I was feeling more and more lost. And on the final day of the sun dance, when I was in the arbors supporting a Yaqui brother who was dancing the sun dance, I told myself, 'I gotta go to Arizona. I gotta find my elders who are alive, and I have to learn my culture.'

"So the day the sun dance ended, I went home, packed up all my stuff into my car, and drove twenty-six hours to Tucson."

TWENTY   Among the Yaqui

PEOPLE ON THE Pascua Yaqui reservation said that Martin Rubio came among them like an angel. He was a young man, fit and motivated to work. He had no addictions, no drinking problem, no domestic complications, no old scores to settle. No past. Rubio was a name they knew and trusted. He was politically, environmentally, and spiritually awake. He was an answer to a prayer.

At least to Don Anselmo Valencia, vice chairman of the Pascua Yaqui. Even then a man of advanced years, Valencia was not just the tribal president of the pueblo but also a practitioner of native Yaqui ritual medicine. In late July or early August of 1993, Coronado was first introduced to Valencia on the thousand-acre reservation about ten miles southwest of Tucson and began volunteering there.

By November, he was working full-time on the res with Valencia and the Yoemen Tekia Foundation, a traditionalist cultural and spiritual society that seeks to preserve Yaqui language and culture ("Yoeme" is another indigenous name for the Yaqui).

Valencia took him under his wing. "Martin came to my husband," said Kathy Valencia, Anselmo's wife. "He said that he was Yaqui and that he wanted to learn his culture."

The reservation, like so many in the United States, was plagued by endemic poverty and all that it brings—alcoholism, drug issues, domestic violence, gangs. The Pascua Yaqui youth could see few prospects from the vantage point of the reservation, whose social life centered partly on a pair of convenience stores near each other on the main drag, on opposite sides of the reservation border. The off-reservation property had its windows stacked to the ceiling with cases of beer, partly as a protection against random shootings. The one on the res didn't sell beer, so its windows were clear. Reservation kids embraced the gangland identities that they saw in gangster rap videos on MTV, dividing the res into Crips and Bloods.

For decades, Valencia had been trying to supplant these tempting forms of cultural validation with traditional Yaqui culture. With Coronado, that program went into high gear. Together they formed the Yoeme Nation Youth Junta, making a special Monday-night kids-only program on the res and engaging the children in native celebrations like deer dances as well as special programs on Yaqui history, spirituality, and artwork. Oftentimes, elders with special skills or stories would come and talk to them. Rod would take the kids camping. The point was to instill pride and awareness of their heritage and give them something to hang on to other than a blue or red hankie.

The connection between Rod and the Pascua Yaqui was strong, but his legal situation was becoming increasingly precarious, and he still struggled with intense paranoia. Even before he'd arrived on the res, his legal status had changed significantly. On July 16, 1993, the Western District of Michigan had finally issued a federal warrant for the arrest of Rodney Adam Coronado, indicting him on charges of "Maliciously Destroying / Damaging Property by Fire or Explosive Materials." It was official at last, and posters went up in post offices and federal facilities all across the country—including Tucson. Those posters noted that "Coronado has been in possession of firearms" and "should be considered armed and dangerous." The source of that bit of dangerous information—misinformation, apparently—is unknown.

Occasionally, Rod would simply take to the roads. For a period in August and September, he rented a house in Olympia, Washington, and tried hiding there. David Howitt had moved back to the Olympic Peninsula, and they would visit from time to time. ALF fugitive David Barbarash, who was on the run for having stolen twenty-three dogs from a lab at the University of Alberta, turned up at Rod's house one time with one of the women Rod had worked with on Bite Back. The two of them were evidently dating, and he was pleased the two of them had found each other.

But the pull of the Yaqui was strong, and he went back there.

Living near the University of Arizona campus in Tucson—once even in a disused milk truck parked in a friend's backyard—Rod networked with the local chapter of the Student Environmental Action Coalition (SEAC) and brought the Yaqui and student scenes together when he could. At that time, the university and other backers, including the Vatican, were building the first in a series of large telescope projects atop nearby Mount Graham, a 10,700-foot peak, and this had become a major campaign focus for local mainstream environmental groups and Earth First!ers alike. The mountain was a sacred and fiercely defended site among the Apache, and Rod looped in the kids on the Pascua Yaqui reservation to give them a way to safely express their feelings about the violation. In early 1994, he drove a bunch of them to a big protest action called SEAC-topia, which took place on Mount Graham. Those campaigns continue today.

On the reservation, adults and children alike took up sacred running, a form of prayer, often with a targeted purpose such as the regularly scheduled Sobriety Runs. Rod would work these, handing out water.

The physical environment was hot, dusty, and challenging, with wild weather that could be suffocating one hour and then slashing cold rain and hail the next, driven down by frozen winds off the Santa Catalina and Tucson mountains. The rows of houses were in disrepair and seemed to hunker among the cactus. As he came to know the children and teens individually, he spent more and more time among them, trying to fill in for missing parents and lost meanings. He also had a couple of girlfriends with whom he grew very close.

Operation Bite Back was quickly becoming a distant memory. Rod engaged in no animal actions in either 1993 or 1994. He wasn't any less militant; the object of his militancy was just transformed.

On October 12, 1993, Rod met Raul Cancio, the head of the Yaqui Coyote dancers, at a sunrise ceremony on the pueblo led by Valencia. The Coyotes were one of four dance societies that performed all-night ritual dances in the complex seasonal cycle of Yaqui religious ceremonies, and Rod accepted an invitation to volunteer with their group and learn the dances. Months later, the two of them talked excitedly about news from the Río Yaqui that indigenous fighters in Mexico were taking up arms as part of the Zapatista uprising. This was their heritage, and the Yaqui were anxious to support the Oaxacan resistance.

Valencia had Coronado working on big projects all over the pueblo. The most renowned and important Yaqui festival happens at Lent, and its mix of symbols reflects the influence of post-1500s Catholic traditions on indigenous summer solstice celebrations. Valencia put Coronado to work building a new church altar to be ready for Lent. Kathy Valencia would make him white-bread sandwiches, and Anselmo would deliver them, eating together with Rod and sharing tales of Yaqui history. On the Saturday preceding Palm Sunday, the Yaqui pascola and deer dancers performed. The first time Rod was a part of this event as a volunteer for a society was Easter 1994.

According to Rod's own description of these dances, Yaqui prophesy foretold the coming of the Spanish and the tribe's transformation into a warrior society. Part of that transformation required the Yaqui to give up vegetarianism and start hunting their "little brother" the deer. The founding myth says that the pueblo held a big fiesta to honor the deer, and at that ceremony a real deer came and showed them all how to do the deer dance. Three deer singers call the deer from the Yo Ania, or "enchanted world," and play a water drum that represents the heartbeat of the animal. Two raspers imitate the sound of dancing hooves. The dancer acting the deer plays it coy, as a deer would be, then shows everyone his dance of gratitude. The accompanying pascola dancers are like the jesters of the ceremony, sometimes called the "old men of the fiesta," joking with the crowd and handing out treats like cigarettes or water. Rod was thrilled to be part of the Coyote society and play a role in this timeless drama.

He cleaned and repaired all the ceremonial objects and grounds, then volunteered for kitchen patrol.

During the festival, the ceremonial captain of the Coyotes, Cancio's superior, personally asked Coronado to assist the aged *moro* of the dancers and musicians. This meant leading the dancers into the ceremony and providing for all their needs. At times, Valencia would come over and sit near Coronado and quietly explain to him what each movement and song meant.

This didn't go unnoticed, and Rod admitted to himself that this must have raised suspicions among the others. He was a man who had come out of nowhere, with no past, and now he was deep in Valencia's confidence. While seated at a big table eating with the participants in the dances, Rod realized that a prayer had been granted: his family had been returned to him in the form of the Pascua Yaqui. He was overwhelmed with gratitude and decided that evening, in the flickering shadows of the fire and the close fellowship of the feasting, that he had to reveal his true identity to Valencia.

When the ceremony ended the next morning, Valencia drove Coronado and some of the dancers home in his old pickup truck. Coronado nervously mentioned that he had to talk to Valencia. The old man gave no hint of surprise. They drove to a quiet place and parked, sitting in the cab and gazing past the deer antlers fixed to the hood of the truck as day bloomed over the open desert.

Rod said cautiously, "Anselmo, my real name is not Martin Rubio. Rubio is my mother's name. I am a fugitive from the authorities. But I didn't come out here to hide. I came here to learn what I could of my own culture before whatever is going to happen to me really does happen."

After a silence, Valencia said calmly, "You must be Rodney Cor-onado, then."

Coronado never discovered how he knew. But Valencia admitted that he had known since the first day they had met; the elder had decided it wasn't his place to ask about the assumed name, and he had been confident that one day his pupil would want to tell.

"I know it's hard to believe, but don't worry about it," Valencia said to him. "I may be an old man, but I still have some power that I draw from all these plants and animals around here. I can protect you here, but not when you go out into the cities."

Coronado started weeping and his teacher comforted him. "I'll do some ceremonies for you," Valencia added. "As long as you haven't killed anybody, everything will be OK."

After their talk, the Easter ceremonies took on an entirely new significance. As the players re-enacted the resurrection of Christ, Rod felt renewed too. He had new life in his connection with this man, a man who took understandings Rod had previously shared with fellow warriors and with animals and made them part of a hu-man community.

Rod moved a small cot and a writing desk into a crowded little A-frame shed in the Valencias' backyard. Their four-room reserva-tion house bustled with the energy of Kathy Valencia and their teen-age daughter, Heather, who were a foil to quiet, stoic Anselmo, a man of few words. Two tiny sika deer from Japan strolled the dirt yard looking for any scrap of green to pluck, as did two pairs of honking geese, ducks, and a constantly twittering flock of songbirds that fluttered from ocotillo to smoke tree to the eaves of the house. Birdcages were stacked around the backyard, filled with golden pheasants and banded white doves churring and fluttering. A dingo dog investigated any strangers who came to the fence. The two TVs were almost always blasting some nonsense inside the house, but evenings they'd all sit out on the patio—sometimes in winter coats with the desert's cold season upon them—enjoying the wild array of succulent plants Kathy tended there and talking about life.

Rod was home.

In the dusty, dull wind roar of the res, the warrior society Rod had hunted for all his life just walked up and tapped him.

"Martin embodies the reasons behind the Coyote Society," said Joe Cancio, leader of the Coyotes, interviewed in 1994. "The Coyote Society and the bow elders were entrusted to keep the pueblo protected from outside forces, from influences—alcohol—and they were the society that doled out the punishment. They usually try to work with that offense and find out what the problems were. And Martin has that heart. That good heart—you take with him right away. The reason that I would like to see him back here is 'cause the kids here need role models."

Part of Valencia's vision included deepening the tribe's connections to the ancestral homeland on the Río Yaqui in Mexico, and he began to include Coronado in that work. He became Valencia's driver on the long trips to the tribe's traditional lands, a couple hundred miles due south in Mexico. Valencia was engaged there in helping to govern the restless tribe; the Yaqui are a guerrilla society with a proud heritage of militancy, and they seemed to be forever squabbling over internal matters as well as fighting a long-running battle over mineral and water rights with the Mexican government. Rod sat in on tribal governance sessions and saw ancient tribal power exercised in a strange modern context.

On one of these trips, he also visited the grave of one of his great-grandmothers. He told her that he was back home and had dedicated his life to the pueblo.

Later, when Rod was facing prosecution for Operation Bite Back, he wrote the following letter describing his native spiritual discovery, which was included in his presentencing report:

What I have been taught and what I believe is that all life is sacred. Everything on this earth is a creation of god and should be cherished and appreciated. My earlier beliefs addressed the specific sacredness of animal life, but what I attempt to live is a life where the circle of respect and reverence is extended to all of god's creation. I may use the term god, but I also say Creator and in my prayers and native language the term is Achai Ta 'aa which means Father Sun. I believe in Jesus Christ and yet I believe and practice pre-christian and catholic ways. I feel that my beliefs have become clearer ever since I moved back to a Yaqui community. My beliefs as a traditional Yaqui may have only come to surface in the last three years, but it has been such a revelation as to permanently change every way I live, much to my relief that most everything I believe in has been reaffirmed as I learn more and more of my traditions and culture.

The belief that rocks, air, water and animals are all sacred does not mean I do not believe in their use or consumption. Appreciation is a strong belief of mine, and I believe in acknowledging appreciation for all the blessings we are given each day. I pray everyday and give thanks for the sun to have shone, and for air, water, food, family. Since my return to my heritage and homeland I have also made a vow or what might be called a religious promise in return for my blessings and good fortune in my homecoming. Many Yaquis make vows or commitments to traditional religious societies in our culture. My promise is to the Wiiko Yau uura which means bow leaders. They were and are the oldest of our ceremonial societies and their foundation was at the instruction of prophesies spoken through a talking tree. It is our responsibility to protect the homelands, the people and the culture. Our society was originally a warrior society formed to fight the Spanish conquistadors in the 1500's. I am one of very few members who is taught my responsibilities by our nation's spiritual leader, Anselmo Valencia. Most members associate their involvement with the dancing and the ceremonial rituals. Though I share their appreciation, I consider the greater responsibility to be our civil obligation to the people.

I believe I had to go on a long journey to discover who I am, and now that I have I must make amends for my behavior in the past that may have broken the law or hurt others. I believe the best way to do this is to live here amongst my people and I feel obliged to resolve all my legal matters so I may return to their service as soon as possible. I cannot say that I was dragged into the wrong crowd or a criminal element. I was fully aware of what the consequences of my actions might be. But, my community has given me the strength to pay the price for my criminal behavior. Though ideological differences still exist between the indigenous perspective and what might be called the dominant worldview, I still acknowledge that I stepped over the line of acceptable behavior in a free society. I do now honestly feel that I have discovered a much more effective way of influencing positive change in our society, and it is within legal bounds.

Rod's full commitment to his native identity would lead to some breaks with the radical movement, most notably with Sea Shepherd. Watson and Coronado would have a falling out when Rod supported the traditional whaling of the Makah people of Washington State, which Watson opposed.

Even with that break, however, Watson's strong opinion of Coronado was undiminished. In a 2009 interview, he said, "Rod Coronado was one of the most courageous, dedicated and passionate activists in the Animal Liberation Movement. He was one of my very best crew members when he served with Sea Shepherd from 1986 to 1993. But he saw a different path to take and he did so and I applaud him for decisions and for his victories. I am a strong advocate of loyalties and whatever path Rod had chosen to take was a path that I was honor bound to respect. I defended him against his critics on every occasion."

* * *

On the morning of September 25, 1994, Rod was alone in the Valencias' kitchen and washing dishes when he heard a knock on the door. He wiped his hands and opened the front door to find a white woman there, a tribal cop. She was a bit excited and talking fast, but she explained that someone had brought an injured hawk to the fire station, and she knew the Valencias were good with animals, and maybe he could lend a hand. Rod was cautious, but he wanted to be helpful, so he jumped in a squad car with her and rode to the reservation fire station.

At the station, the big doors were rolled down, an unusual occurrence that caused Rod a moment's hesitation. But then, if the hawk was loose in the station, maybe they had to keep the doors down to keep it from injuring itself.

He had been working openly on the reservation for over a year, even though Wanted posters were up all over the West with his picture on them and his real name and all his aliases. All of them except "Martin Rubio"—still, it would have been easy for anyone to spot him from his photo with his big ears and his leaky smile. The posters were available in every post office and lots of federal offices, including the Immigration and Naturalization Service offices, which were frequented by many from the tribe.

They jumped out of the car, and the officer let him go through the door first. She seemed nervous about the big raptor.

"Yeah, it's right in the door there. You can't miss it," she said.

He stepped through the door and was immediately thrown down on the cool cement floor. Agents piled on and pinned him down, calling him by his real name, Rodney Coronado. Rod had always vowed to resist arrest when it came, and he tried to struggle, but he was physically overpowered and finally handcuffed. A couple of beefy agents jerked him to his feet, and someone began reading him his Miranda Rights.

After a few moments, they led him outside to a waiting car, and as they hit the blinding desert sunlight, Rod broke free. He tried to sprint off through the reservation, but, wearing handcuffs, he only made it a few yards before he was tackled again and shoved, coated in reservation dust, into a squad car.

In a later interview, he admitted he had tried to flee. "Yeah, I tried to take one last jog around the pueblo," he joked.

The entire Pascua Yaqui reservation was stunned to find out that the man it knew as Martin Rubio, who was operating at the very inner sanctum of its religious and cultural life, was really someone else—someone the government was calling a terrorist. Stunned, but not convinced. There probably couldn't be a population in the United States less impressed by claims made by the U.S. government. Very soon, within days, the Yaqui began organizing to help Rod fight a no-bail provision, writing scores of character letters on his behalf, finding attorneys, fund-raising. As far as they were concerned, he had earned it. The file of letters written on Rod's behalf would become a dossier about one hundred documents thick and include impassioned testimony from supporters in all parts of his life, from people who knew him while he was growing up in San Jose to local administrators who worked with the Yaqui to neighbors near Scotts Valley. They all said the same thing: Rod was utterly committed to nonviolence.

I went to see Valencia only a few days after Rod was captured, and we had dinner and talked about the state of the Yaqui. I was in his house for several hours, and, despite my questions, never once did he mention Martin Rubio or Rodney Coronado.

Rod was hauled back to Michigan, where a grand jury handed down a five-count indictment before U.S. District Judge Richard Enslen in Kalamazoo. This was a big deal for the Department of Justice: it was pointed out by U.S. Attorney Michael Dettmer that until the prosecution of Rodney Coronado, "no known member of the ALF has ever been convicted of a felony."

The basic charge was arson, but he was also charged under the Hobbs Act, an old racketeering law that prohibits robbery or extortion to interrupt interstate commerce; other charges included various explosives-related crimes, committing a federal crime of violence, and transporting stolen goods. Just before Christmas, 1994, he was released on a $650,000 bond. His parents mortgaged their home to post it, and when I spoke to them, they reiterated how proud they were that he had been working with kids on the reservation. They were convinced of his transformation into a peaceful Native American activist and were willing to back it up with their life's savings.

He went straight back to live with the Valencias. While Rod had been held in Michigan, Don Anselmo had survived a life-threatening bout of pneumonia and was in poor health. The kids in the Youth Junta needed explanations about how Martin Rubio was really some other guy with a big history, and time was suddenly short for a twenty-eight-year-old man.

For all the mayhem Rod had set in motion, federal prosecutors acknowledged in court documents that they didn't have any evidence that made him the perpetrator of Bite Back crimes. What they had was conspiracy. They had evidence that he had handled the two FedEx packages of documents and videotape sent from Ann Arbor to PETA; they knew what hotel he'd stayed at in Ann Arbor and about his visit with the Stouts; and they had phone records that proved he'd been in the vicinity of every Bite Back attack and had been the anonymous ALFer talking to the press. They had his published articles explaining why he was underground and setting the terms of his surrender. They had his typewriter ribbon transcript, which indicated that he might have been planning an attack that had (as far as they knew) never occurred. They had a lot, in fact, that supported his public claim that he was just the messenger, even if he'd endeavored to be more than that.

The big prize, though, was thirteen of Rod's fingerprints all over that Plexiglas case at the Little Bighorn Battlefield monument. In his storage space in Talent, investigators had found a newspaper article about the stolen cavalryman's journal, and that helped them match him to the crime. The journal was government property, and Rod could have faced a long stretch for that—more than for the arson charges. Prosecutor Dettmer compared it to having burned the *Mona Lisa*.

The government used the journal as a lever, and on March 3, 1995, Rod pleaded guilty to one count of arson at MSU in exchange for getting the robbery charges dropped. By previous agreement with other jurisdictions, now including Utah, this would also satisfy for all of the other Bite Back crimes. It made him responsible for at least $2.5 million in damages.

In the conclusion to his presentencing memo, Dettmer calls Coronado a "terrorist" and notes that "since the defendant's indictment and arrest, the firebombings and massive property damage that were a hallmark of 'Operation Bite Back' have ceased. However, the intimidation and fear that these crimes were designed to inflict continues to this day."

"Nowhere is this continued intimidation more evident," he continues, "than in the events that have transpired since the defendant's guilty plea. In several instances, the defendant has appeared in the media to exhort others to take his place as a 'hero to the animal and environmental movement.' In contrast, the victims of the defendant's crimes remain so afraid of the defendant and others like him that they would not speak to the Court's own presentence investigator unless he guaranteed their anonymity."

The presentencing documents that Dettmer cites are fascinating, in that they do illustrate how much the fur industry came to fear ALF attention. Twenty-six Bite Back victims were identified, and eighteen agreed to be interviewed anonymously; their key comments were condensed into eight pages. They admit to feeling they were "surveilled" and living in an "environment of distrust," ordering phone taps because of harassing calls, and changing their behaviors, like not standing "in front of the office door while opening it" because of fear of a bomb.

For example: "*Victim No. 4*: This victim felt that ALF was watching them, and there was no place to hide. This individual's spouse became very terrified and worried, especially about their children. Every time a car passes the house, they feel one of their children may be kidnapped."

Another "pulled a rifle out of the closet, reassembled it and bought ammunition." Yet another describes Rod's crimes as "terrorist" acts "as despicable as rape." Several interviewees say that his sentence should be life or 25 percent of all his life wages, and that PETA and Friends of Animals should also pay. One victim says, "Life in prison with hard work was an appropriate sentence."

Rod was sentenced to fifty-seven months and spent more than four years in a medium-security federal prison in Tucson, only a few miles from the reservation. As part of his plea, he was privately deposed by U.S. attorneys and admitted his role in all of the Bite Back crimes. He never mentioned accomplices or anything that could be used against anyone else. This information was sealed and has never been released, but it did alleviate the need for continued exhaustive federal investigation into his role in these crimes. In return, he would not be prosecuted for them.

After Rod's arrest, eco-radical attacks dropped off for a number of months. However, in the summer of 1996, acts of environmentally motivated sabotage exploded—just the beginning, as it turned out, of a very steep rise in attacks that continues today. Several of the 1996 attacks were fur related and identified in communiqués as part of Operation Bite Back II. There were attacks at Latzig Mink Farm in Howard Lake, Minnesota; a mink farm outside Salt Lake City; and a mink farm in Hinsdale, Massachusetts, and a furrier's home was spray-painted with YOU CAN'T HIDE in Onondaga, New York. Other attacks in Minnesota, Massachusetts, and Utah came in the fall. Perhaps most worrisome to animal industries was an ALF hit on Rus Dun Egg Farm in Fayette County, Tennessee, where radicals burned one truck, planted incendiaries in three others, and sabotaged the warehouse air-conditioning units. The use of arson was spreading. Soon there would be an activist zine called *Bite Back* and a Web site by the same name. The legend was only growing.

In fact, the tactics were getting more and more radical. The fall of 1996 saw the first U.S. appearance of the Earth Liberation Front, which took property destruction to new heights.

The summer had been a hot one for forest activists defending a stretch of old-growth timber that was being sold off for logging along Warner Creek in Oregon's Willamette National Forest, southeast of Eugene, and a few of the people out there were Rod's friends from the Earth First! community in southern Oregon. One hardcore punk rocker named Jacob Ferguson—whom Rod had never met—was out there keeping loggers and Forest Service agents (lovingly referred to as "Freddies") out of the trees and was looking for ways to escalate the fight. All summer long, scores of activists had dug trenches through a square-mile area of the forest, put in barricades, and chained themselves to barrels of cement as they occupied the timber sale, a stand of trees which they saw as a key piece of a Cascade Range bioregion they called Cascadia. Ferguson and others, though, were looking to go on the offensive. He had heard tales about the emergence of the Earth Liberation Front in England, and he liked the sound of it.

As the ALF had done with animal rights issues, using illegal action to expose or destroy animal industries, so the ELF approached environmental issues like clear-cutting, road building, and urban sprawl. The Earth Liberation Front would undertake actions that Earth First!, with its public journal and regional offices, could not claim without risking prosecution.

When the Forest Service canceled the Warner Creek timber sale at summer's end and handed Cascadia a victory, Ferguson was ready to step it up. In October 1996, he and his new girlfriend, Josephine "Sunshine" Overaker, attempted to destroy a ranger station outside tiny Detroit, Oregon, on the Santiam River, northeast of Eugene. They failed to ignite a jug of gasoline that they had hoped would burn the place down, but they did torch one of the Freddies' pickup trucks and spray-paint EARTH LIBERATION FRONT on a nearby shed.

Two days later, Ferguson, Overaker, and another accomplice, Kevin "the Dog" Tubbs, hit a different ranger station in Oakridge, on the Willamette Highway en route to Warner Creek. This time, they left the place in cinders. The Earth Liberation Front was firmly established in the United States, and the torch had passed from Rodney Coronado.

TWENTY-ONE Terrorism

ROD WAS RELEASED from prison in 1999 and laid low for a number of years, confining his activism to working as an editor on the *Earth First! Journal*. Eventually, after he was off probation, he started working on a campaign to stop a mountain lion hunt in Sabino Canyon, a popular hiking destination in Tucson, and in the course of protest he dismantled a mountain lion trap. He was arrested in the act, and since it was a government lion trap and a second offense for Rod, he was charged with a felony. He spent eight more months in Federal Correctional Institution Tucson and was released in spring 2007. Fortunately for Rod, prosecutors couldn't give him a terrorism sentence under the Animal Enterprise Protection Act, because there was no interstate element. Unfortunately, the local U.S. attorneys were even more determined to find ways to put him away for terrorism in the future. They were pissed. Assistant U.S. Attorney Wallace Kleindienst even went so far as to call Rod "a danger to the community."

"I know he wasn't tried here for being a violent anarchist," he told reporters after the verdict. "This trial wasn't about Rod Coronado being a terrorist, but he is one."

The authorities were desperate to snuff out this eco-terrorism thing, but the more they talked about it, the bolder the acts seemed to become. In 2001, the ELF and the ALF took credit for acts of vandalism and property destruction all over the country, including a wave of fires in new suburban housing developments. It was becoming an epidemic, spread by scores of disaffected newbies, and law enforcement officials were under enormous pressure to end it. So, they started to pay more attention to what movement heroes like Rod said in public. If they couldn't charge them with acting like terrorists, they'd try to get them for talking like terrorists.

On August 1, 2003, Rod addressed a group at the Center, a popular LGBT (lesbian, gay, bisexual, and transgendered) community center in the Hillcrest section of San Diego. The event was open to the public and was sponsored by a vegan advocacy group called Compassion for Farm Animals. Rod had flown in to participate in a series of events the group was calling "Revolution Summer."

Compassion for Farm Animals was hardly the stuff of violent overthrow: its mission was to advocate veganism. One of the group's founders, David Agranoff, was a twenty-nine-year-old horror fiction writer and taught kids with autism. He and his wife constituted about half of the group's membership. They barely made up a carpool, let alone a terrorist cell.

"Mostly what we did was pass out dairy-free ice cream in Balboa Park, maintain our Web site, and do community potluck dinners. That was our terrorism," Agranoff chuckled.

Coronado's exact schedule that day was never in dispute; federal investigators determined early on that he was telling the truth about his whereabouts. He rose in the predawn darkness at the offices of the *Earth First! Journal* in Tucson, where he was crashing, and boarded an early plane to San Diego. He was met at the airport by Agranoff, and together they went back to his apartment so Coronado could catch a nap.

Before Rod's plane arrived in San Diego, however, a huge fire was set at an unfinished 206-unit La Jolla condominium complex, which caused fifty million dollars in damages. The building had been the site of protest over expansion into a sensitive coastal canyon area. Four hundred people had to be evacuated. A banner hung at the site read, IF YOU BUILD IT—WE WILL BURN IT. THE E.L.F.S ARE MAD.

Agranoff and Coronado later claimed they didn't hear about the fire until that night, when a group of reporters, assembled in front of the Hillcrest center, started asking questions about the blaze. There, Rod said he had "no goddamn idea" who was behind the attack but did seem to go out of his way to lend his support. "I would rather see an apartment complex burn to the ground than developers making money off the environment," he told one newspaper. Rod was never a suspect in the fire.

"Anybody who did that arson knew that the last thing they should be doing was hanging out where I was," said Rod. "Because they knew that the feds were going to be all over my shit."

Rod assumed that federal agents regularly attended his talks, and in this case he assumed half-right. In the wake of this big fire, they were all over him. FBI case agent David DeFusco said that while agents did not attend the speech, members of the bureau's counter-terrorism task force did—which included local sheriff's deputies and police officers. A detective from the San Diego Sheriff's Department was outside taking down license plate numbers while an undercover San Diego Police Department detective named Joseph Lehr sat in the audience in plain clothes, taking notes.

Rod doesn't change his talks for the sake of undercover officers present and makes that a policy. He hadn't committed any arson since the Millville, Utah, fire in October 1992, almost eleven years earlier, but his radical past was part of the standard speech he had been delivering on the lecture circuit for years, and he gave a version of that same speech that night in San Diego.

"I'm not going to sanitize my speeches for fear of throwing them a bone," he said of law enforcement. "Let them listen. I was pretty known for a standard lecture about animal and earth liberation, deep ecology, and then contexting it within my own personal experiences, with my own Native American heritage."

Agranoff said that about one hundred people were at the San Diego talk, and he was thrilled. "Usually, we'd get about fifteen people. We'd publicized the hell out of this," he said. It was a public event, and he didn't know most of the attendees. After the talk, Coronado fielded a question from Agranoff's wife, Cari Anne Shaw, a person both Coronado and Agranoff are confident even the FBI would acknowledge was not an ALFer or ELFer. Her question, according to a tape recording that surfaced during the trial related to this speech, was "How did you build an incendiary device?"

Rod didn't miss a beat. He'd answered this before. Trying to recall his wording, he said later, "I was like, 'Oh, well, I did this: I made a crude incendiary device'—and I walked over to a table where we had the food set up, grabbed an apple juice jug, saying, 'a device like this.'" He then went on to briefly describe the pieces of his kitchen-timer incendiaries in light detail. "And then you create a circuit, and that ignites underneath this [the jug] and—boom! Just like that."

No known person ever made an incendiary from the description Rod gave that night. The feds waited two and a half years to make sure, but no crime was forthcoming that could help define this as an act of incitement.

Not that Rod was pulling any punches. After his brief description, he added, "You can still use, you know, the tactics we engage in."

Detective Lehr, however, gave prosecutors even more to work with. He didn't write down Shaw's question the way she'd said it. He wrote down, "How do I make a bomb for an action?"

The words "for an action" seemed to imply intent, which would mean Rod's response would be intended for use in an action. The wheels started spinning.

On February 22, 2006, Rod was at his part-time job in Tucson working for a major dealer in fossils, handling shipments of trilobites, ammonites, prehistoric sharks' teeth, and the like. He had been working for the guy on and off for years, helping in particular with the big Tucson and Denver fossil and mineral shows. He was living near the University of Arizona with his new fiancée, a woman with no connection to his past, and her three-year-old daughter. Suddenly, a couple of SUVs full of FBI agents pulled up in front of the metal warehouse building. He could see them through the glass, tinted against the searing desert sun, and watched them pour through the swinging doors.

"Is this about the San Diego thing?" he asked them.

Rod and I sat in the Epic Cafe, a couches-and-coffee university haunt in Tucson, as a cold squall kicked dust up against the windows. It was March 2006, only a few weeks after he'd been arrested.

The 1997 statute they'd uncorked for this had only been used twice before, and only once successfully, which might explain why they waited so long to use it on Rod. It was short and direct and carried a five-year maximum sentence. The entirety of 18 USC § 842(p) (2)(A), which was introduced by Senator Dianne Feinstein (D-California) and cosponsored by Senator Joseph Biden (D-Delaware), reads, "It shall be unlawful for any person to teach or demonstrate the making or use of an explosive, a destructive device, or a weapon of mass destruction, or to distribute by any means information pertaining to, in whole or in part, the manufacture or use of an explosive, destructive device, or weapon of mass destruction, with the intent that the teaching, demonstration, or information be used for, or in furtherance of, an activity that constitutes a federal crime of violence."

The vague question of "intent" worried Rod, but he quickly had more serious cause for concern. According to Rod's attorney, Gerald Singleton, federal prosecutors had informed him that they could try to have Rod sentenced under new federal terrorism sentencing guidelines made available by the 2001 USA PATRIOT Act, which allowed a judge to add as many as twenty years to any sentence at his or her discretion. Singleton and the San Diego U.S. attorney had calculated that Rod could be looking at eighteen years.

Of course, you can download bomb-making instructions from

the Internet, and it'll be quicker and more precise than attending a speech. As of the writing of this book, it took only a few clicks to find instructions for incendiary devices, thermite, pipe bombs, fertilizer bombs—no end of goodies. Lots of these how-tos are produced by authoritative sources like the U.S. Army. *The Anarchist Cookbook*, which is full of such recipes, and other much more detailed titles are available and popular on Amazon. You can also buy instructions in pamphlet form at many gun shows. That's because the knowledge is not illegal—using it, or *intending* to use it, is. So they needed to get Rod on intent.

At the Epic, he looked tired, and he'd started to go gray. I hadn't seen him face-to-face for about a decade, and the threat of imprisonment clearly weighed on him. He was almost forty years old, but his eyes still shone, and his intellect seemed, as always, to flicker around the room.

The Epic was within walking distance of his house, and he generally met people there. His fiancée's little girl slid off his lap to flirt shamelessly with a trio of grandmothers. Rod's own five-year-old son by a Native American woman of Anishinabe heritage, who he'd met at the University of Arizona after getting out of prison the first time, was coming to town in a few days to see the deer dances at the Lenten *pahko*, or celebration, on the Pascua Yaqui reservation. The two children had become his focus, and he and his fiancée were planning a wedding. The squall outside turned into a deluge and fell hard on us like a rock slide broken straight off the Santa Catalinas.

"I was naive. I told myself, 'This is cool. I'm just going to do some Earth First! organizing and still be a spokesperson.' I thought that would be sustainable, legally," he said. "I didn't think that would end up costing years of my life in prison."

"I was from a different generation, where we believed there was a hard-line difference between eco-terrorism and civil disobedience," he added. "I hadn't really taken into account how this government's new antiterrorism legislation would be applied to radical environmentalists and animal rights activists. I know that they considered us a threat and had been working to get us labeled as a number-one domestic priority."

At that, they had succeeded. FBI press spokespeople had told me as early as 1999 that ALF activists were a "top priority," but now agents routinely told the press that the ELF and the ALF were the number-one targets, even after 9/11. On May 18, 2005, John Lewis, the deputy assistant director of the FBI's Counterterrorism Division, testified before the Senate Committee on Environment and Public Works, saying, "One of today's most serious domestic terrorism threats comes from special interest extremist movements"; he named the ALF, the ELF, and Stop Huntingdon Animal Cruelty (SHAC).

At that same Senate committee hearing, however, Lewis also cautioned that "distinctions between constitutionally protected advocacy and violent, criminal activity are extremely important to realize," adding, "Law enforcement only becomes involved when volatile talk turns into criminal activity."

It's hard to tell now whether Lewis meant that the government would go after activists when they flipped from talk to action, or that the government had simply redefined one as the other. Because Rod's talk did not turn into any "violent, criminal activity." But they would send him to prison anyway.

He saw me looking at the omelet on his plate that day and admitted he wasn't even a strict vegan anymore. It was an interesting moment: I could see him wrestling with the ideology that had defined his life only months before. He seemed worn down. He was worried about the condemnation that would come from his own movement as he tried to retire from direct action and speaking out in support of direct action. He was pleading for them to let him go.

"I really do believe that the movement has to afford me a little bit of personal respect to take care of myself, and to accept that I'm no longer going to be the person they've seen me be for the last twenty years," he said.

In September 2006, from his prison cell (on the mountain lion–trap charge) in Florence, Arizona, he released an open letter to the movement publicly renouncing direct action.

Dear Friends and Supporters,
Some of you know me only by my lectures, writings, actions and statements, some as a father or personal friend. To say the least, these last couple of years have been truly life-changing. I've been arrested twice by the FBI, chased by a helicopter, indicted for serious charges, charged w/less serious crimes and it seems almost constantly accused of being a terrorist though my actions my entire life have never caused a single physical injury let alone death. That's not to say I haven't done things I regret. I have. But this open letter is meant instead to be a statement of facts in regard to what I now believe. It is part response to questions raised by past supporters who have always heard me unequivocally support illegal direction actions taken on behalf of the Earth and animals.

I believe there comes a time in everyone's life when we have to honestly ask ourselves why we are here, doing whatever it is we do on this beautiful planet. These last two plus years have surely been such a time for me. All my life I have endeavored to protect the earth and her non-human children we call animals. I still do and always will believe in respecting life be it human or non-human and this planet we all call home. A large part of my personal and spiritual evolution has been in the last nearly five years since I became a parent of a beautiful human child. As a warrior I used to think that having children was an impediment to any struggle for peace and justice. Never could I have been more wrong. I believe our creator chose me to be a parent of my son because I was a warrior. A man who believed that peace for the Earth and animals could only come through aggressive and sometimes destructive actions.

Raising a child requires a parent to practice the very principles you seek to teach your children. Indeed such is the case with all living beings. I always believed I was fighting to create a better world for all future generations, yet to preserve what I wanted to protect, I chose to engage sometimes in the destruction of property used to destroy life. I still see the rationale for what I've done, only no longer do I personally choose to represent the cause of peace and compassion in that way.

As a parent, I have been forced to realize that violence is everywhere in our society and as a parent I believe in not raising children to accept violence as a necessary evil. I believe in teaching and living peace with the hope that only through example do our children have a chance of escaping a violent future. In my years past I have argued that economic sabotage was an appropriate tactic for our time. Like all strategists I have also been forced to recognize that times have changed and it is now my belief that the movements to protect earth and animals have achieved enough with this strategy to now consider an approach that does not compromise objectives, but increases the likelihood of real social change. Let our opposition who believe in violence carry the burden for its justification, but let those who believe in peace and love practice a way of life that our society sorely needs now more than ever.

A society built around violence cannot stand the test of time. But a life built around the tenets of mutual respect, compassion, peace and harmony can be our only way out of this nightmare. What is won through violence must be protected with violence and I don't want to teach my children that. As long as governments and corporations sanction physical violence any who attempt to stop them with violence will be labeled terrorists.

There is little we can do to change that in light of the media's role and influence over the public's perception. That is only I believe in their ability to label the cause of peace and justice as such.

Many people have bravely given their lives and freedom to forward the cause of animals and nature, now let us continue that march in ways that do not allow the opposition to excuse us as terrorists. I believe in promoting the rights of animals and a safe environment through the demonstration of a way of life based on creating sustainability rather than fighting within a system that respects only force and violence. We are fortunate to live in a society that allows nonviolent options. Systems of war and violence shall crumble and we should free ourselves from the rubble while there's still time.

There is no shortage of good works in order to build the society I believe in, only a shortage of those willing to make a life-long commitment towards creating peace. We know where the dominant society has left us. With less rights and privilege than corporate charters and profit margins. It is now time, I believe, to fend for ourselves and create the democracy denied to us. Time for us to become active in educating our children, in growing and providing healthy food to all, medicine and care giving to those who need it, not just those who can afford it. This is how I believe we create a better world, not through any acts of violence but with great demonstrations of love for each other and all life around us.

I condemn no one forced into a life of self defense through violence, I only pray for another way forward to a lasting peace. There is still time. Time for a government by the people for the people . . . and earth. But not without the patience and perseverance to build peaceful alternatives rather than short-term strategies that offer too little in the way of long-term change. My position is just the voice of one man on a journey solely his own. I speak for no greater movement though I hope the desires of many. Struggle for me has become a very personal battle. Not only against a legal system intent on imprisoning me but equally important is my personal struggle to be a better human being. To my children, my partner, my community and myself. Because if

I can't accomplish peace in my own life, how is it that I can hope to accomplish it on any larger standard?

What our world needs now is a whole lot more love and a lot less violence. Nothing in this world will change overnight. But if we live peace and teach our children well, they might still inherit a world better than ours. Maybe I'm just getting old, or finally thinking about the legacy I will leave behind, but I still have much to live and give and I want to find the commonality between people who want only a safe and happy life for their children. Don't ask me how to burn down a building. Ask me how to grow watermelons or how to explain nature to a child. That is what I want to grow old doing. Please afford me this. I have fought my battles and continue to fight for mine and my family's freedom. I only want to not be remembered as a man of destruction but a human believer in peace and love for all. May the creator bless and protect us all with the sacred gift of life that is ours to do with as we shall.

The 2001 PATRIOT Act finally roped eco-radicals squarely into the sweep of terror legislation by defining eco-terrorism as "the use or threatened use of violence of a criminal nature against innocent victims or property by environmentally-oriented, subnational group for environmental-political reasons, or aimed at an audience beyond the target, often of a symbolic nature." This language greatly expanded the definition of domestic terrorism and would become incredibly important in a surge of high-profile arrests and prosecutions that would sweep the movement around the same time as Rod's speech trial.

And in 2006, Congress approved the Animal Enterprise Terrorism Act (AETA), which was written specifically by industry lobbyists like the Foundation for Biomedical Research's Frankie Trull to expand the definition of terrorism conspiracy. The first use of the act resulted in the convictions of activists who had posted the home addresses of research executives on a Web site. When persons unknown used the addresses to harass the executives, the new law made the Web site owners eligible for those twenty-year sentencing enhancements.

Original drafts of the AETA went even further, and mainstream groups stepped in when they felt that certain language was meant to curtail protected speech and protest.

"The Animal Enterprise Terrorism Act in 2006 contained language that was viewed not just by us but by the [National] Lawyers Guild and others as potentially infringing on lawful activities. Like protest. Or boycotts," said John Balzar of the Humane Society of the United States. "It used words like 'economic disruption,' and one of the tactics that we use and that civil rights groups use and other groups have used with their heads held high in American history are things like economic boycotts. So when we ask our members to send Ben and Jerry a letter saying, 'I'm not going to eat Ben & Jerry's ice cream until you stop using eggs from hens held in cages,' we wanted to preserve the right to do that."

"But we made clear every step of the way that we supported the chief aim, which was to increase penalties for acts against people and property," he added.

Those penalties might get stiffer still, if only because eco-radicals—and specifically animal rights extremists—have increasingly employed true violence and terror. The ALF and the ELF now have a lot to answer for.

The principled movement has always been able to tout its nonviolent record in the United States, where radicals like Rod have assiduously avoided endangering human life directly. In the last few years, however, activists of all types have favored hitting their targets at their home, rather than at their place of work. And increasingly, they have put them at risk—or even attempted to kill them. It is now impossible to avoid calling some of this action terrorism.

As ever, the situation is more aggravated in Britain. By the turn of the millennium, the group Stop Huntingdon Animal Cruelty was on an outright terror campaign in the U.K., attacking all individuals and institutions that supported research company Huntingdon Life Sciences (HLS) in any way—not only employees of the company, but those of all the companies with which Huntingdon did business. In February 2001, for example, an HLS managing director was attacked in the U.K. by three men wielding pick axe handles. They were out for blood.

In the United States, SHAC first appeared in spring 2001, going after HLS and investors like Morgan Stanley Dean Witter and a bank called Stephens Inc. in Little Rock, Arkansas. But very quickly it progressed to protests outside the homes of HLS executives and paint-bombing and smashing lights at the home of Warren Stephens, the president of the investment bank. Similar attacks visited the homes of executives from Marsh Insurance, which insured parts of HLS. Then it escalated. In 2003, SHAC USA, as one splinter was then calling itself, attacked the Bay Area homes of executives with HLS-affiliated biotech company Chiron Corporation—in one case, leaving bloody toys strewn on the lawn of an executive and smearing cat shit on the entrances to the house, and in another, stenciling PUPPY KILLER on a woman's car in etching acid. Another entity, called Revolutionary Cells-Animal Liberation Brigade, followed that up with two bombings at Chiron headquarters in Emeryville, California.

Surveillance camera footage suggests that a twenty-seven-year-old San Rafael, California, activist named Daniel Andreas San Diego planted the two bombs at Chiron—one set to go off an hour after the first, when firemen and investigators would be present. The second bomb was spotted by a night watchman, and no one was hurt. A third bomb attributed to San Diego that did go off at the Shaklee Corporation was wrapped in nails. The only rationale for a bomb wrapped in nails is a desire to kill or injure people. As of this writing, San Diego was still at large.

The ALF and the ELF also started favoring home-assault tactics, spray-painting slogans on homes, breaking in and stealing personal credit information, and putting tombstones in people's yards. The idea spread to all kinds of groups.

In Southern California, Los Angeles Animal Services (LAAS) was under fire to create no-kill animal shelters, and protesters picketed the homes of key executives and harassed their wives and children at all hours of the night. On Halloween night, 2005, a fake bomb was left at the home of LAAS head veterinarian Dr. Cassandra Smith.

This communiqué was posted on the Web site Bite Back:

The night was quiet as we drove down to Cassandra Smiths [sic] residence [deleted] Chino Hills. we quickly exited the car and left a ficticious [sic] package bomb on her doorstep. after much mayhem, Smith found out the "trick or treat" was a dud. Cassandra, while our explosive was a trick this time, our promise to strip you of everything is the truth. you are an uncaring puppy killer. the package contains two old road flares with wires going to a rape alarm, a watch and an antennae [sic]. Smith was told we would deactivate the bomb if a public resignation was released.

See you soon, alf

By the time of the Cassandra Smith incident, the ALF and the ELF seemed on the verge of bloodshed, and the subject returned to the attention of 60 Minutes. A November 13, 2005, segment titled "Burning Rage" focused on whether or not the ALF and other animal rights organizations were "violent," and it starred none other than Rod Coronado. This was before his letter renouncing direct action.

The late Ed Bradley asked Rod if he went around recruiting "impressionable" people, saying in the narration, "Coronado says he knew nothing about the [La Jolla] condo complex fire, yet he has traveled around the country and encourages people to do this sort of thing."

"Encourage through explanation and demonstration of my own actions," Coronado told Bradley. "I've showed them how I set fires. I showed them how the ELF and the ALF, what their mode of operation is."

"I'm asking for people courageous enough to take those risks for what they believe in," he added.

A self-avowed ALF cell leader also appeared on the show, masked, and said he thought it was "abysmal" that the FBI was targeting them, since, unlike neo-Nazi groups, the ALF had never hurt anyone.

It would, however, if Dr. Jerry Vlasak had his way. On that same *60 Minutes* program, L.A. trauma surgeon Vlasak, a spokesman for the Animal Liberation Front Press Office in L.A., came right out in support of murder. Vlasak was already infamous for making a statement in Britain about killing researchers, saying, "I don't think you'd have to kill, assassinate, too many. I think for five lives, ten lives, fifteen human lives, we might save a million, two million, ten million nonhuman lives." This quote had gotten Vlasak banned from the U.K. He'd reaffirmed the statement for Senator James Inhofe (R-Oklahoma) when he'd appeared before the Senate Committee on the Environment and Public Works in October 2005. Vlasak had explained that he wasn't the one who'd be doing the killing, of course, since he was a surgeon and had taken the Hippocratic oath. But he kept right on during the *60 Minutes* segment: when Rod said he thought that arson could be a nonviolent tactic, Vlasak disagreed, saying it was obviously a way to hurt people—and that was OK.

"I think people who torture innocent beings should be stopped,"

Vlasak told Bradley. "And if they won't stop when you ask them nicely, they won't stop when you demonstrate to them what they're doing is wrong, then they should be stopped using whatever means necessary."

Coronado disagreed with Vlasak then, as he does now. "I have always believed that if animal rights activists started justifying violence to supposedly *prevent* violence, we would lose our moral high ground and join the ranks of so many others on both sides of the law who also kill and maim in order to supposedly fight for peace," he wrote me in 2008. "Targeting property was our modus operandi. Targeting people? Never."

Others in Vlasak's hometown were eager to stop wasting their time with property damage and kill their way to victory. On June 30, 2006, ALFers left a burning Molotov cocktail at the Bel-Air home of Lynn Fairbanks, a UCLA researcher who used vervet monkeys in her lab studies. Actually, they didn't firebomb her home; they mistakenly placed their bomb on the porch of one of her seventy-year-old neighbors instead. The accompanying communiqué, posted July 12 on the Animal Liberation Front Press Office Web site, didn't mention any intention to scare her, as the one addressed to Cassandra Smith had. It seems clear the device simply didn't go off right. There were two subsequent incendiary attacks on UCLA researchers, and those didn't go right either. So they got lucky.

They won't always be so lucky, the logic goes. The attacks continued to escalate all over the country; as I was finishing this writing, a UC Santa Cruz researcher was firebombed, and he and his wife and two small children had to escape from their second floor by means of an emergency ladder as smoke filled their house. A second firebomb totaled a researcher's personal car but resulted in no injuries.

Rod was in prison at the time and immediately wrote to me, saying, "When I heard about it in here on the news I was disgusted that anyone claiming to be opposed to violence would so stupidly endanger human life. What was done there was just plain cowardly. I condemn it."

Vlasak's comment on the fire, picked up by the Associated Press, only suggested there'd be more to come: "It's regrettable that certain scientists are willing to put their families at risk by choosing to do wasteful animal experiments," he said.

TWENTY-TWO   The Green Scare

Active Evil is better than Passive Good

—William Blake

BY 2006, SO many of Rod's colleagues in nonviolent guerrilla action were being prosecuted for terrorism that the radical community began calling it the Green Scare—after the anticommunist Red
Scare of the 1950s. The 2001 PATRIOT Act and the new 2006 Animal Enterprise Terrorism Act gave federal authorities the tools to
prosecute grand, sweeping conspiracies and hammer even the most
marginal characters with huge sentences. The lookouts. The girlfriends. Using these tools, the FBI and the ATF launched a new initiative and called it Operation Backfire in what seemed like a nod to
Rod. The targets weren't innocent people; they were arsonists like
him, committed to "maximum destruction." But they were also
deeply committed to never hurting a living thing. One of them was
Jonathan Paul. So far, only people who espouse nonviolence like
Jonathan and Rod have been threatened with the new terrorism sentences. Which leads to some troubling questions about the new definition of domestic terrorism.

Operation Backfire was directly aimed at the ELF, which was
leaving a trail of destruction across the country, and particularly at
an ELFer who called himself Avalon. But the ramifications of this
federal operation changed the legal landscape, not only for Rod and
his speech trial, but for all activists utilizing direct action today.

Avalon's real name was Bill Rodgers, and he was an Arizona
Earth First!er who had helped launch the Earth Liberation Front in

the United States. He became the target of intense interest after he masterminded the destruction of the brand-new Two Elk Lodge at Vail ski resort in Colorado in 1998. Radical environmentalists had a history of fighting ski areas—the 1988 FBI infiltration of Earth First! in Arizona was initiated after attacks on the Arizona Snowbowl, near Flagstaff—and the Vail company that had built this lodge had done so under protests from local environmentalists, who worried because it opened up one thousand acres of new back-bowl terrain in what was believed to be endangered lynx habitat.

According to accomplices, Avalon set eight different fires at Vail and burned the new lodge to the ground, costing the resort twelve million dollars in damages in what was the most expensive eco-radical act of arson in U.S. history at that time. The fires made the front pages across the country: this wasn't some obscure testing lab or bloody slaughterhouse; it was Vail. That helped the Earth Liberation Front become the new code word under which unaffiliated and unknown activists took up arsons against tract housing, condos, and other new construction all over the country. It opened a new front in the netwar, and this time the target was sprawl—especially into previously wild or ecologically sensitive terrain.

And it would have been the perfect crime, too, if it hadn't been for one of Avalon's future accomplices, Jacob Ferguson. By all newspaper accounts, and a well-researched story by Vanessa Grigoriadis in *Rolling Stone*, Ferguson, Kevin Tubbs, Josephine Overaker, and a cast of other characters went on a spree that stretched from 1996 to 2001, starting with the previously mentioned attempt to burn the ranger station in Detroit, Oregon. The loosely affiliated crew burned Forest Service properties, a whole dealership's worth of SUVs in Eugene, a corral for wild horses, and the offices of Superior Lumber in Glendale, Oregon. They downed an interstate electrical transmission line and committed at least fourteen other acts—plus who knows what else. The circle grew to include more than a score of people, some involved in actions the others didn't even know about.

Ferguson described himself as the "muscle" for many of these actions. He was also a chaotic street punk with a pentagram tattooed on his head who had a rap sheet just like his father, a thief and check kiter who had spent a good deal of Ferguson's childhood in prison. Ferguson had long dabbled in heroin and speed, but his life slowly imploded under the pressure of his underground life as an ELFer, and when his heroin habit spun out of control, the feds found their opening.

In the spring of 2003, undercover agents who believed Ferguson was connected to the Eugene SUV fires tailed him while he was copping drugs and cut him a deal: Wear a wire to implicate his friends, and he could get the fifty thousand dollars in reward money offered for help in solving the Vail fire. Or, go to prison on drug and other charges. Worried about his young son growing up with a dad in prison just like he had, he took the deal.

Up until that point, prosecutors admitted they had a cold case. They had nothing. Other than Rod, only a handful of ALFers or ELFers or any other kind of eco-radical had ever been nabbed in the United States. In early 2002, the Department of Justice got a flow of new antiterrorism money and apparently had few other domestic terrorists to catch in the wake of 9/11. The department began reassigning agents to the Eugene case, and it grew and grew. Still, the only real breakthrough came when Ferguson began wearing a wire.

Operation Backfire arrests began on December 7, 2005, based on Ferguson's secret recordings, and eventually fourteen people would be indicted. Many were charged with conspiracies that could link them to a federal destructive-device charge that carried a mandatory thirty-year sentence and life for a second conviction—and then there were the terrorism add-ons. It would likely have been difficult for the feds to get convictions and lengthy sentences on these crimes, as it always had been before, but the laws had been so significantly changed that the arson conspiracy that had gotten Rod five years, for instance, was suddenly punishable, in many cases, by multiple life terms. The possible sentences were so long they were a terrible joke: two indictees, Nathan Block and Joyanna Zacher, were reportedly looking at life plus 1,115 years for minor roles in two noninjury arsons, and the others faced similar absurdities.

This grisly situation unleashed something that had never happened in the eco-radical movement before: a massive snitch fest that sent cold shivers through the entire community. In an effort to cut deals and diminish their sentences, lovers rolled on lovers, brothers and sisters in the movement burned one another, and a whole economy was unleashed in which information was the currency.

Avalon took it the hardest. When prosecutors at his second hearing began talking about him being the "mastermind" of the Vail fire, he knew he'd been betrayed. On December 22, he committed suicide in his prison cell by suffocating himself with a plastic bag.

As the tight-knit web of confidences unraveled in wild squealing, indictments and superseding indictments emerged steadily from the tatters. The resulting sixty-five-count indictment related to twenty incidents of arson and destruction in Oregon, Washington, Wyoming, Colorado, and California. The trials took place in Eugene and in Tacoma, Washington. Defendants Rebecca Rubin, Joseph Dibee, and Sunshine Overaker were never apprehended and are believed to have fled the country. At least a half dozen other people not named in the indictments escaped prosecution by supplying information.

Three more ELFers were nabbed in Auburn, California, in early 2006 and charged with conspiring to build a bomb on the testimony of an FBI plant named "Anna," who was paid sixty-five thousand dollars to infiltrate their cell and occasionally had sex with its leader Eric McDavid. His two associates traded testimony for freedom. McDavid never actually used the bomb, thankfully, but he was sentenced to more than nineteen years in prison anyway. The Department of Justice, it seemed, had found a way to crack the radical movement at last: introduce either drugs or sex to loosen tongues and soften allegiances, and then threaten people with sentences so hideous they coerced testimony.

Only four of the Eugene defendants refused to talk, and one of them was Jonathan Paul.

Jonathan didn't know most of the people on that indictment; he'd only worked with a few of them and only on one action: in 1997, he'd helped burn down the Caval West horse slaughterhouse in Redmond, Oregon.

"It was a Belgian business that was slaughtering up to five hundred horses a week to export to Europe and Japan," he said. It was taking private horses, but Paul and others claimed that many of the horses were wild, "adopted" for $125 from the U.S. Bureau of Land Management and then sold for a quick profit. The company denied such charges in the press. "But it was the only place that never rebuilt, too. They were completely shut down," Jonathan noted.

Only two plants still process horse meat in the United States. Both are in Texas, and both sell primarily overseas.

Like his sister Caroline, Jonathan had become a firefighter, and rose to lieutenant at a firehouse in Williams, in the Applegate Valley. His wife, Tami, worked at the same firehouse, in charge of emergency medical technicians. From that vantage point, Jonathan regretted his role in the arson.

"Arson is a tactic that you shouldn't take lightly. I never did. It wasn't something I liked doing, or being a part of. Unfortunately, for this situation, it was the best way to do it. And I never did it again after that, mostly because of my concern about people getting hurt. I wouldn't do that kind of tactic again, in my life."

"I'm not a firebug," he added. "I'm not someone who's fascinated with that tactic. I didn't become a fireman because of that. Being a fireman is just another way I can help people."

Jonathan got fifty-one months on a noncooperation plea deal. The pleas arranged by the others eliminated most of the outlandish life-plus-infinity sentences, but were still significant, ranging from three to thirteen years.

Most alarming to the environmental and animal rights movements as a whole, however, were the sweeping rulings issued by U.S. District

Judge Ann Aiken in Eugene on the use of the federal terrorism sentencing enhancements.

"The use of the terrorism enhancement for crimes involving property damage alone is unprecedented. It has never occurred in the history of the United States," said Lauren Regan, an attorney with the
Civil Liberties Defense Center in Eugene who worked on the Oregon
Green Scare cases. "Every other case where the terrorist enhancement
was sought or implemented by a court involved the death of a human
being in a serious way. Like the USS *Cole* bombing. Like trying to poison drinking water, or blowing up a federal building with humans inside it, flying planes into a building. This is a *huge* leap."

None of the fourteen defendants were charged with terrorism.
But the discretionary enhancements meant that many of them got
"terrorist" sentences anyway. Besides giving the judge the discretion
to add twenty years to any sentence, terrorism sentences would
affect security designations in prison—they might get greatly re-
stricted access to visits, media, and parole, for instance—as well as
future employment, finances, and travel outside the United States.
"Terrorists" might be on the no-fly list for life. Garden-variety arsonists would not be.

Attorneys for the Eugene defendants filed multiple challenges to
the enhancements (and some of these are still ongoing in the U.S.
Court of Appeals for the Ninth District). But Judge Aiken came back
with a memorandum including the following key rulings:

- Use of the enhancements does not require conviction on a federal
  crime of terrorism, so long as the offense was "intended to pro-
  mote" such a crime.

This ruling is seen as greatly expanding the definition of what
can be punished as terrorism. With one brief set of paragraphs, life
changed for many people in the radical community and otherwise.
Clearly, lobbyists for big industry simply need to expand this idea of

"promotion" or the scope of "a federal crime of terrorism" to stop legal protest dead in its tracks.

- Anyone involved in the conspiracy, no matter how minor the role (such as lookout, girlfriend, etc.), can be eligible for the enhancement.

- Use of the enhancements does not require a substantial risk of injury to humans. That was the old definition of terrorism and is now obsolete.

In the wake of this memorandum, Aiken went right ahead and used the enhancements, applying them to four of the twenty incidents and to seven of the defendants. Jonathan Paul was not one of them. Aiken only applied the enhancements to those whose acts could be seen as influencing the government, and Caval West, it was decided, had no connection to the government.

"The definition basically says, if you burn a house down for greed, that's just arson. But if you burn down that same exact house with a political purpose, particularly one that is meant to draw attention to a government injustice, then the government can turn around and punish you in an extraordinary way by utilizing this terrorist enhancement," said Regan.

The Aiken rulings hung over Coronado's speech trial like a cold fog. If he were to lose the argument over intent, it was easy to see how U.S. District Judge Jeffrey Miller in San Diego would be under pressure to recognize his actions as promoting a crime of terrorism and put him away for decades.

However, other Green Scare cases were also worrying the environmental movement—and one, in particular, was muddying the First Amendment arguments that Rod would use in his trial.

Across the country in New Jersey, six members of Stop Huntingdon Animal Cruelty were the first (and so far, only) activists to be
convicted under the 2006 Animal Enterprise Terrorism Act. The
SHAC members had sent harassing faxes to Huntingdon Life Sciences executives, but the crime that concerned most observers was
that they had built a Web site. On that Web site, they had posted the
home addresses of HLS executives, and those executives were subsequently harassed, and a pipe bomb was even left at one of their
homes. The catch was that these acts were committed by persons
unknown who were never identified and also never linked in any
way to the Web site. Still, the SHAC 6 were convicted as part of a
conspiracy under the new allowances of the AETA.

"The truth is, if you carry this forward, this logic, almost any
group that does activist activities, particularly using the Internet,
is in terrible shape," said attorney Andy Erba, who represented
SHAC and is appealing the decision in the Third Circuit. "The
government took the position that the various postings on the
Web site . . . incited people to take action. But, absent the proof
of imminent action, you really can't just prosecute ideas. It's un-
constitutional."

The gist of Erba's upcoming appeal is that there has to be some
connection between the speech and the act in order for it to be incitement. It was never proved that the vandals who attacked the
Huntingdon execs had ever even seen the Web site.

Rod's case involved a similar twist: no one ever built incendiaries as a result of his speech. Under the 1969 case *Brandenburg v. Ohio*,
the classic test of illegal speech, incitement requires (a) intent and
(b) imminent action—usually connection to a substantive crime.

Judge Miller himself indicated during Coronado's September
2007 trial that the Feinstein statute being used in the case was confusing on this point, and that the jurors would have to determine
this meaning on their own. They struggled with it, and then hung
eleven to one in favor of acquittal. They deadlocked on whether or

not Rod could have believed that his incendiary-making instructions would result in an imminent action.

It also didn't sit well that the undercover cop had tilted Cari Anne Shaw's question just a little in order to imply intent. This was only proved definitively by the last-minute submission of an audiotape from the Hillcrest speech, and it definitely soured the government's case.

From the start, Rod's crew of notable attorneys had made this a case about words, positioning it as a warp of the First Amendment. The idea that no subsequent crime was needed to prove imminence was a significant change in the law.

San Francisco civil rights attorney Ben Rosenfeld wrote in a widely published essay on Coronado's case, "Make no mistake. This is a pure free speech case. Measured against any historic test of free speech, Coronado's behavior—that is to say, his speech—was alarmingly innocuous and *uncriminal*" [emphasis in the original].

"This statute could have very, very wide-reaching implications," said Coronado attorney Gerald Singleton of the Feinstein law. "It would basically chill a broad variety of speech. Pretty much anything to do with environmentalism, animal rights, a lot of the militia movements. Whether or not you agree with these movements, the whole point is what [Noam] Chomsky and [Supreme Court Justice Oliver Wendell] Holmes always said: if you believe in free speech, then you believe in the freedom of speech that you hate."

U.S. attorneys couldn't nail Rod under the Feinstein law— "demonstrating how to make a destructive device with the intent that someone would commit arson" was the actual charge—but they could just keep prosecuting him into oblivion.

As Rod himself admitted, the Hillcrest talk was his "standard" speech that he'd given many times. Video footage of a January 2003 speech at American University, in Washington, D.C., showed him very much in the same fiery mode. Rod said that prosecutors threat-ened to repeat the San Diego charge for the D.C. speech, and to pursue another charge in Arizona.

"They told me they were just going to keep coming with these charges—I mean, this was my standard speech. But I just wanted to end this once and for all. I need to get my family together and not worry about this year after year. So I took a plea of a year and a day," Rod told me in a phone interview after the decision. The FBI case agent acknowledged that there were other potential charges, but denied that Rod had been "threatened" with them.

He surrendered to federal custody on May 9, 2008, and was held in a medium-security prison in El Reno, Oklahoma.

In published commentary on the case, San Diego–based Teresa Platt, executive director of the industry advocacy group Fur Com-mission USA, made a provocative point when she wrote, "All this has to make me wonder. If Coronado had given his speech the day *before* the ELF $50 million arson in San Diego, would he have been found guilty even if it was not proven that his demonstration of the device was directly related to that particular arson? In other words, one day later, would that arson have been 'imminent' enough to convict?"

This is an excellent question. Singleton said no, they'd still have to prove that the person heard Rod's speech and that it was directly related to the crime. But that's not how the Animal Enterprise Ter-rorism Act was applied in the SHAC case. Erba said, "The world is changed after 9/11, and people just take a totally different view of activities that, in the sixties, as terrible as they were, people thought were de minimis." So we're in a gray area even talking about it. The lawyers tell me I'm OK writing about it in a book. But I guess we'll find out soon enough.

In October 2007, a small party was swinging at Jonathan Paul's house high up in the mountains fifteen miles above Ashland, Oregon.

It was the weekend before Jonathan was to report to federal prison, and as we sat at his kitchen table, a small parade of people came by, a couple of them firemen, who had volunteered to help take care of stuff while he was gone: cut wood, plow the driveway, keep up the twelve-foot wooden fence he'd put around the beautiful solar-powered home because the feds were constantly taking pictures of him.

We got a good laugh looking at the Web site of Stephen Colbert of the late-night comedy show *The Colbert Report*, who had done a hilarious spoof of Jonathan's trial. The page on Colbert's "Truthiness" wiki site began with the statement "Mahmoud Ahmedi-Jonathan Paul-nejad is a terrorist."

The talk kept swinging back to the Green Scare prosecutions and who the snitches were and whether or not these outlandish sentences were going to just rub out direct action altogether. I asked, wouldn't it just be too risky?

Jonathan jumped in. "I don't think it's gonna stop these things," he said flatly. He made it abundantly clear that his own engagement in radical action was long over, but there was always someone new. "We just read about another action done against a researcher in UCLA—flooding their house with a hose. But I think it will, hopefully, teach people in the future that if they choose to participate in this kind of thing, that they think hard about what they're doing and consider their tactics, like, 'Is this tactic the right tactic to get this done?'"

Then he added, "But I don't think it'll ever stop because the other side won't stop."

Rod Coronado in front of his home in Tucson in 2006, after federal agents arrested him for making a speech in San Diego. (Len Irish)

ACKNOWLEDGMENTS

Rereading transcripts of Rod's 1995 prosecution in Michigan, I saw that many of my own early stories on this case had been entered into the court record along with those of other reporters to whom I am indebted. I have been working on this book for eighteen years, and there are so many who helped bring those stories along that it feels like a movement history unto itself.

First, I must acknowledge the work of Rod Coronado, whose tolerance for endless interview, willingness to share his own writing and open his archives, and faith in the press made this story trackable over the years. Ray and Sunday Coronado and Ray III were a big help with early stories, and Cynthia Coronado-Brown contributed significantly to the book. Also, in interviews years ago, Deb Stout and her family, as well as members of the Pascua Yaqui, especially Kathy Valencia, were especially illuminating. Rod's wife, whom I promised not to mention by name, was a tremendous help while I conducted research, especially because Rod was in prison during the writing of this book.

Much of the information in these pages first appeared, in different form, in magazine and newspaper stories. I am forever grateful for the steady hand and good sense of Legs McNeil, Bob Keating, and Drew Hopkins, then at *Spin*, who set me on this path, and to Kit Rachlis at the *LA Weekly*; Alex Heard and Will Dana at *Outside*; Sid Holt for my favorite story, "The Tracks of the Coyote," in *Rolling Stone*; Peter Moore, Chris Napolitano, Lee Froehlich, and Chip Rowe at *Playboy*; Andrew O'Hehir at the *SF Weekly*; Mark Blackwell and Randy Bookasta at *Raygun*; Steve Appleford and Natalie Nichols at *Los Angeles CityBeat*; and Karen Pickett, Jim Flynn, and many others in the editorial collective at the *Earth First! Journal*. Thanks to the legions of caring and unsung editors, fact-checkers, and attorneys who kept me from embarrassment and ruin.

I owe a debt of gratitude to a coterie of fine reporters, including Rik Scarce for his book *Eco-Warriors*; Ken Olsen for scores if not hundreds of published news articles about Rod, Operation Bite Back, and eco-radicals in general, most of them in the *Moscow-Pullman Daily News*; Mike Geniella; Vanessa Grigoriadis; tireless purveyors of North Coast news Nicholas Wilson of the *Albion Monitor* and Bruce Anderson and Alex Cockburn of the *Anderson Valley Advocate*; and Sarah Ferguson and Bill Weinberg, who first introduced me to the *Earth First! Journal*.

Speaking of which, none of this could have happened without the many tree huggers who've let me pitch tents next to their fires, attend their strategy meetings, and drink martinis on their bus and keep it on the record. They are so numerous I'm almost certain to leave some out, but they include Paul Watson, David Howitt, Suniva Bronson, the late Jon Huntermer, and the rest of the crew of the *Sea Shepherd II*; Dave Foreman, Mike Roselle, and Karen Pickett; Ramon, Catfish, Packer, the late Cindy Strand, and anyone else who dares to call themselves the Ancient Forest Bus Brigade; Sarah Seed, Lauri di Routh, and the rest of the Seeds of Peace; the late Judi Bari, Darryl Cherney, Alicia Littletree, Betty and Gary Ball, Lauren Regan at the CLDC, Jonathan Paul, Lee Dessaux, David Solnit, Stephanie Fraser and the survivors of American Peace Test, the late Corbin Harney for my first sweat, Phil Knight, John Sellers, Twilly Cannon, Pam Davis, Sergeant Sphincter, Syd Haskell, the Dann sisters, Mark Davis, Marc Baker, Peg Millett, Ilse Asplund, Ingrid Newkirk, Sheila O'Donnell, and all the others who ever shared a pot of gruel and a cup of cowboy coffee.

A tip of the hat to all of the members of the Blue Ribbon Coalition, the Sahara Club, yellow ribbon timber families, mill owners, cowboys, Freddies, county sheriffs, outfitters, Wise Use conventioneers, sagebrush rebels, People Firsters, fur farmers, and spokesmen for the DOE, BLM, USDA, and NFS, as well as federal marshals and FBI agents who gave me rides, quotes, and a chance to tell their side. Special thanks to Teresa Platt of the Fur Commission USA, for outstanding help with context and documents, and deep gratitude to Ron Arnold, for intellectual rigor and positively straight shooting.

Big thanks to photographers Michael Schumann, Max Aguilera-Hellweg, Len Irish, and especially Melodie McDaniel for love and friendship.

For belief in this book, thanks to Karen Rinaldi, editor Kathy Belden, Miles Doyle, and Sloan Harris at ICM. For editorial assistance, salaams to Ana La'O, Cat Manabat, Alicia Lozano, and T. J. Kosinski.

Love and thanks to my family in Michigan, Bruce Kuipers and Diane Hamilton, Brett and Joel Kuipers, and Tom and Nancy Wilson, and eternal gratitude to Anne Lehman, whom I dragged through the wilderness and who lived much of this book. Special thanks to Meg Cranston and Spenser Kuipers for enduring the years of living it all over again.

INDEX

A NOTE ON THE AUTHOR

Dean Kuipers is an editor at the *Los Angeles Times*. He has been an editor at *Los Angeles CityBeat* and *Spin* and a longtime writer on the radical environmental movement. He is the author of *Burning Rainbow Farm*, *I Am a Bullet*, and other books. He lives in Los Angeles.

ML

6/09